It Happened in Brooklyn

BOOKS BY MYRNA KATZ FROMMER
AND HARVEY FROMMER

THE SPORTS DATE BOOK

SPORTS GENES

BASKETBALL MY WAY
(with Nancy Lieberman)

THE GAMES OF THE XXIIIRD OLYMPIAD:
OFFICIAL COMMEMORATIVE BOOK
(editors and principal authors)

IT HAPPENED IN THE CATSKILLS

IT HAPPENED IN BROOKLYN

GROWING UP JEWISH IN AMERICA

MYRNA KATZ FROMMER AND HARVEY FROMMER

It Happened in Brooklyn

AN ORAL HISTORY

OF GROWING UP IN THE BOROUGH IN THE

1940s, 1950s, AND 1960s

The University of Wisconsin Press

The University of Wisconsin Press
1930 Monroe Street
Madison, Wisconsin 53711

www.wisc.edu/wisconsinpress/
3 Henrietta Street
London WC2E 8LU, England

First published in the United States in 1993 by Harcourt Brace & Company

Library of Congress Cataloging-in-Publication Data
It happened in Brooklyn : an oral history of growing up in the borough in the 1940s,
1950s, and 1960s / Myrna Katz Frommer and Harvey Frommer.
p. cm.
Originally published: New York : Harcourt Brace, 1993.
Includes index.
ISBN 0-299-20614-9 (pbk. : alk. paper)
1. Interviews—New York (State)—New York. 2. Brooklyn (New York, N.Y.)—Social life
and customs—20th century. 3. New York (N.Y.)—Social life and customs—20th century.
4. Brooklyn (New York, N.Y.)—Biography. 5. New York (N.Y.)—Biography. I. Frommer, Harvey.
F129.B7 F76   2004
974.7'23043—dc22   2004054618

FOR JENNIFER, OUR DAUGHTER,
THE ONLY ONE OF OUR CHILDREN TO HAVE
BEEN BORN IN BROOKLYN

Contents

PART ONE

WHEN WE WERE A COUPLE OF KIDS

A tidy neighborhood life of courtyard, schoolyard, and sidewalk play, of stickball and stoopball and double-dutch jump rope; exploring the borough by bike, train, and foot; pastoral pastimes at Prospect Park; Saturday afternoons at the movies; Broadway on the other side of the bridge; baseball bliss in Dodger Blue at Ebbets Field.

Perfect penmanship and Permanent Records; patriotic assemblies in red, white, and blue; sparrows and robins; teachers tender and tyrannical; IQ exams and Open School Nights; nuns in the classroom and on the volleyball court; the pleasures and terrors of elementary school.

PART TWO

LIVING TOGETHER

the shorefront from swanky Manhattan Beach to swampy Canarsie; watching the boats come into the harbor along the bustling docks.

PART THREE
THE DAYS OF OUR GLORY

(and the crinolines went swish, swish, swish); staking out at Bay 2; making out at Plum Beach; standing in line for the rock 'n' roll shows; fighting for turf with zip guns and knives; battling on the basketball court; and moving up to Brooklyn College—all you needed was the grades.

Introduction

We are speaking here of a time as well as a place: the three decades at mid-century, bracketed by two wars. If you lived it, your address said Brooklyn, New York—but you really came from Bensonhurst, Brownsville, Bay Ridge, Borough Park, Brooklyn Heights, Prospect Heights, Manhattan Beach, or Midwood if your family was rich; Williamsburg or Red Hook if it was poor.

Your playing fields were baroque lobbies or concrete courtyards of apartment houses, wide sidewalks where you drew your potsy or skelly grids, sewer-studded gutters where legendary stickball games took place, steep stoops of four-family homes where the intricacies of Russian or Chinese handball were perfected.

You attended a neighborhood elementary school known only by its number preceded by the initials *P.S.* Then with thousands of students you went on to a high school that may have been named after a figure famous in American history, like Abraham Lincoln, Thomas Jefferson, Marquis de Lafayette, or James Madison. Your hangouts were cavernous cafeterias like the Famous or Dubrow's and massive movie palaces like the Kingsway or Loew's Oriental, where you spent the Saturday afternoons of your childhood and the Saturday nights of your teens.

Your favorite foods are still the foods of your Brooklyn childhood: a half-sour pickle straight from the barrel, a charlotte russe from the bakery in the wintertime, ice cream scooped by the man in the candy store into a sugar cone, long skinny pretzels, lime rickeys, and malted milks.

Trolleys glided under the McDonald Avenue el to Coney Island; safe and clean subways had names like the West End Local and the Sea Beach Express. For a seven-cent fare, you could go everywhere: to Bay Parkway, Ocean Parkway, and Eastern Parkway—expansive thoroughfares lined with luxurious "elevator" apartment houses suggestive of European promenades—to bustling Pitkin Avenue, chic Kings Highway, boisterous Thirteenth Avenue, or downtown Brooklyn, with department stores like Martin's, Russek's, and A & S. Or you could take the Flatbush Avenue bus and cut straight through the length of the borough, from the East River to the Rockaway Inlet shore.

In the fourth grade, you learned that the Dutch originally settled Brooklyn, and though you probably didn't give it much thought after studying about Henry Hudson and the *Half-Moon* and how they bought Manhattan from the Indians for twenty-four dollars worth of trinkets, your childhood was nevertheless stamped by the Dutch presence. Even modest walk-up apartment houses had the requisite front garden enclosed by a neat privet hedge. Towering maple and oak and sycamore trees drenched summer streets in greenery. Neighborhoods were punctuated by pastoral parks. And the calm uniformity of rectangular blocks gave to your vision a sense of order and predictability.

Manhattan was another world: "the city" where your father worked and your mother took you to buy clothes or see the Christmas show at Radio City Music Hall. The Bronx was some hilly terrain up north, Queens an indistinct wilderness, and Staten Island a place somewhere across the water that you had to take a ferry boat to reach. Whatever you wanted and needed was there, right at home, in Brooklyn.

By the time you grew up, nearly everything had changed. The 1960s brought Vietnam, civil unrest, riots, new rules, new games. The beloved Dodgers had done the unbelievable—moved away, and to California of all places. The few surviving movie palaces were divided into multiplex theaters. The old hangouts had closed down.

There are compensations enough. Your freezer has more delicacies than the corner candy store ever stocked. Watching rented movies on the projection-screen TV beats sitting near a stranger at the crowded Commodore. A steamy summer night is better spent in an air-conditioned bedroom than on a sweltering stoop. And how can the Coney Island steambath compete with the private pleasures of a sauna or Jacuzzi?

But for some reason, Brooklyn stays with you—that special time, that special place. It keeps coming back like a song.

The Voices

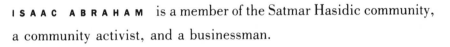

ISAAC ABRAHAM is a member of the Satmar Hasidic community, a community activist, and a businessman.

MARTY ADLER was an assistant principal at the Jackie Robinson Intermediate School, in Brooklyn.

SOLOMON AIDELSON is assistant rabbi and educational director of Temple Hillel, in North Woodmere, Long Island.

MEL ALLEN is the former "Voice of the New York Yankees."

BOB ARNESEN was a social studies teacher at Far Rockaway High School, in Queens, for many years.

PAT AULETTA was a longtime Coney Island resident who operated a sporting-goods business there.

ANGELO BADALAMENTI is a composer whose credits include the scores for *Blue Velvet* and *Twin Peaks*.

FRANK BARBARO is the state assemblyman for Brooklyn's Forty-seventh District.

JOEL BERGER is a professor of science education at the College of Staten Island, City University of New York.

JUDY BERGER is an assistant principal at FDR High School, in Brooklyn.

HERB BERNSTEIN is a composer, arranger, and musical accompanist.

KARL BERNSTEIN was an assistant principal at Meyer Levin Junior High School, in Brooklyn.

MARNIE BERNSTEIN is the pseudonym of an author who lives in Long Island.

POLLY BERNSTEIN was a longtime employee at A & S department store in downtown Brooklyn.

SAM BERNSTEIN is a retired furrier.

ALAN BLANKSTEIN is an associate at Kenneth-John Productions.

FRANCES BLUM is a paraprofessional in special education and a lifelong Bensonhurst resident.

TOM BOORAS is a Long Island businessman.

JULIE BUDD is a recording and performing artist who has sung on television, on stage, and in nightclubs.

MARCO CARCICH is a businessman who resides in Queens.

LOUIS COHEN was a longtime executive at Macy's Herald Square.

SYLVIA COLE is a writer and former English teacher.

LUIS COLMENARES is a Greenpoint resident and college student.

BETTY COMDEN is a writer of books, lyrics, and screenplays, along with her partner, Bronx-born Adolph Green.

PAT COOPER is a comedian and television, radio, and nightclub personality.

WILLIAM CUNNINGHAM is a well-known figure in Irish circles in Brooklyn.

ANNETTE DE LUCIA-CLARK is an administrative assistant at New York City Technical College, in Brooklyn.

JOHN DOWNIE was a ticket taker at Ebbets Field.

PAUL DOYLE was a professor of English at New York City Technical College, in Brooklyn, from its inception in 1947.

JACK EAGLE is a comedian who, for many years, was Brother Dominic in the Xerox commercials.

GAIL EISEMAN BERNSTEIN is a teacher at Samuel J. Tilden High School, in Brooklyn.

BOB ERTEL is a Long Island resident and Manhattan businessman.

PHIL FAGIN is an administrator at New York City Technical College, in Brooklyn.

BILL FEIGENBAUM is president and creative director of Bill Feigenbaum Designs.

IRVING FIELDS is a pianist, arranger, and composer of many songs, including "The Miami Beach Rumba."

BARRY FRANK is the longtime director of entertainment at the Raleigh Hotel in the Catskills.

HELEN FRIED GOLDSTEIN is a professor of speech at Kingsborough Community College and the Jewish Theological Seminary.

MORRIS FRIEDMAN is the rabbi of Temple Hillel, in North Woodmere, Long Island.

STARR FROST GOLDBERG is the owner of Trail's End Camp, along with her husband, Stan Goldberg.

PEARL GASARCH is the secretary of the Professional Staff Congress at CUNY and a professor of English at New York City Technical College.

RALPH GASARCH was an assistant principal at Shallow Junior High School, in Brooklyn.

DONNA GEFFNER is a professor of speech at St. John's University, in Queens.

BOB GERARDI is a television actor.

FREDDIE GERSHON is a producer of Broadway shows whose credits include *Evita* and *La Cage aux Folles*.

HENRY GERSHON is a retired garment worker.

STAN GOLDBERG is the co-owner of Trail's End Camp and was the inspiration for the character Alan in the TV series *Brooklyn Bridge*.

RICHARD GOLDSTEIN is an editor in the sports department of *The New York Times*.

ROGER GREEN is the state assemblyman for Brooklyn's Fifty-seventh District.

HERBY GREISSMAN is president and CEO of a wholesale produce company.

ELLIOT GUNTY is a talent representative and agent.

BILL HANDWERKER is senior vice-president of Nathan's Famous and a grandson of its founder, Nathan Handwerker.

DOROTHY HANDWERKER is an art collector and the wife of Murray Handwerker.

MURRAY HANDWERKER was, for many years, the CEO of Nathan's Famous, founded by his father, Nathan Handwerker.

CLIFF HESSE is chairman of the Speech and Theater Department at Kingsborough Community College, in Brooklyn.

CHARLES HYNES is the district attorney of Brooklyn.

LONNY IRGENS is an artist who lives in New Jersey.

HOWARD JONES is first vice-president of the Professional Staff Congress, CUNY.

MARVIN KAPLAN is an actor familiar to audiences for his role in the TV series *Alice*.

CAROLINE KATZ MOUNT is the director of immigrant services for the United Jewish Appeal—Federation of Jewish Philanthropies of New York.

RICHARD KEHOE is a priest and professor of speech at St. John's University, in Queens.

MATT KENNEDY is the executive secretary of the Coney Island Chamber of Commerce.

EVERETT KERNER was principal of Samuel J. Tilden High School, in Brooklyn.

DICK KITTRELL is an attorney and longtime Brooklyn resident.

MIRIAM KITTRELL is a professor of biology at Kingsborough Community College, in Brooklyn.

JUDITH KURIANSKY is a clinical psychologist and TV personality.

CLEM LABINE is a former Brooklyn Dodger pitcher.

ABE LASS is a writer and the former principal of Abraham Lincoln High School, in Brooklyn.

ALAN LELCHUK is a Brooklyn-born novelist whose works include *Brooklyn Boy* and *American Mischief*.

BOB LEVY is a Long Island businessman.

AL LEWIS is an actor best known for his role as Grandpa in *The Munsters*.

BOB LIFF is a reporter for the City Hall bureau of *New York Newsday*.

DAN LURIE is a former Mr. America whose stores specialize in physical fitness equipment.

JOEL MARTIN is a Long Island cable TV personality.

JOAN MAYNARD is the executive director of the Weeksville Society, in Bedford-Stuyvesant, Brooklyn.

ROBERT MERRILL is a star baritone of the Metropolitan Opera Company, in New York.

DORIS MODELL TIPOGRAPH is the daughter of Henry Modell, founder of Modell's, and the company's corporate archivist.

PETER NERO is an arranger, conductor, and pianist and the head of the Philly Pops Orchestra.

CLARENCE NORMAN, SR., is pastor of the First Baptist Church of Crown Heights.

TERRY PERNA ARNESEN was, for many years, a teacher of accounting.

IRWIN POLISHOOK is the president of the Professional Staff Congress of CUNY.

HOWARD RAPP is a partner in Charles Rapp Enterprises, the talent-booking agency.

JOAN RIBAUDO is district leader and state committeewoman for the Forty-seventh Assembly District, in Brooklyn.

RACHEL ROBINSON is the widow of Jackie Robinson and head of the foundation that bears his name.

ELIZABETH RONCKETTI is a longtime Greenpoint resident involved in community life.

IRVING RUDD is a former public relations director for the Brooklyn Dodgers.

TOBY SCHOM GROSSMAN is a teacher and interior decorator.

NEIL SEDAKA is a singer, pianist, and composer.

JOYCE SHAPIRO FEIGENBAUM is vice-president and executive producer of Bill Feigenbaum Designs.

JOE SIGLER is the CEO of a computer consulting firm.

WADE SILER is a former bartender and nightclub singer.

JIM SLEEPER is a columnist at *The New York Daily News* and author of *The Closest of Strangers: Liberalism and the Politics of Race in New York.*

MARTIN SPITZER is a community activist and court reporter for the office of the Brooklyn district attorney.

NORMAN SPIZZ is one of the principal partners of Steven Scott Music and Entertainment.

ROZ STARR is a celebrity sleuth.

JERRY STILLER is an entertainer and one-half of the comedy team Stiller and Meara.

STEWIE STONE is a comedian who has appeared on the nightclub circuit and television.

LARRY STRICKLER is an assistant principal at Edward R. Murrow High School, in Brooklyn, and director of activities at Kutsher's, in the Catskills.

SHELLY STRICKLER is a news broadcaster for WOR radio, in New York City.

WILLIAM THOMPSON is associate justice of the Appellate Division Second Department, New York State.

NORMAN TIPOGRAPH is a retired sporting-goods business owner.

ALBERT VANN is the state assemblyman for Brooklyn's Fifty-sixth District.

ELI WALLACH is an actor whose career spans many years on stage, screen, radio, and television.

MAX WECHSLER is the pseudonym of an author who resides on Long Island.

No sooner did *It Happened in Brooklyn* hit the bookstores than the calls and letters began to come in from people we hadn't seen or heard from in decades: childhood playmates, classmates, teammates, old boyfriends and girlfriends. They'd found it, read it, claimed it as their own. A long-time friend of Myrna's arranged a reunion of women who had reconnected by virtue of this book. From all over the country, they descended on a Manhattan (sorry, not Brooklyn) restaurant. It had been so long, nearly forty years. So much to catch up on, many tears, much laughter, heartfelt promises to meet again. And, of course, musings on how grand it had been to grow up in Brooklyn. But the funny thing was, out of the forty or so women who gathered that day, only two still lived there.

A few years later, we were talking to our editor about a literary agent whose attitude smacked of the aspirant avant-garde. "Oh well," he said by way of explanation, "he lives in Brooklyn."

Already it had become another Brooklyn, a new Brooklyn, intellectual, arty, fashionable, the kind of place where literary agents would choose to live. By now, we venture to guess, some of the children of the women who gathered for that reunion, who had grown up in spacious homes in leafy suburbs, reside in the throbbing, crowded environs—at once gritty and pastoral, dangerous and secure—that their parents, for all the declarations of affection, could not wait to escape. In all likelihood, they own condos in Fort Green or Park Slope, in (can it be possible?) Williamsburg or Red Hook, spend Saturday afternoons in neighborhood art galleries, dine in local restaurants that get reviewed in the *New York Times*. That is the new Brooklyn. But the old Brooklyn remains as well. There is still a Bensonhurst and Flatbush and Bay Ridge and Brighton—known for some time now as "Little Odessa"—and Sunset Park, the second largest Chinatown in New York, home to the city's most inspired Chinese restaurants, and all the other neighborhoods filled with new immigrants from places like Bangladesh, Lebanon, Nigeria, and Haiti mingling with and befriending each other as well as those who have been there for a generation or more, joining in the pursuit of what may be the most optimistic vision in the world: the American dream.

That is a major theme of this book; it is the spirit in which it was written. For all the changes, in its most essential aspect, Brooklyn remains the same today as it was in the middle of the twentieth century when *It Happened in Brooklyn* takes place. It abides as a dynamic center of life and humanity, a place of eternal possibility.

Lyme, New Hampshire
Fall 2004

It Happened in Brooklyn

A Future to Behold

PAT COOPER: *Red Hook, in South Brooklyn, was a nice Italian neighborhood near the Gowanus Canal. There were apartment houses, brownstones, yards in the back, trucks all over the place, garbage guys taking the garbage away, kids jumping rope, kids making their own skateboards and scooters by nailing a two-by-four to a pear box, breaking a skate in half, and putting two wheels on the front and two on the back. There were a lot of moms screaming out the window: "Come home, come on. The macaroni's on. Get up here." "Tony, where are you? Bring the dog in."*

You went to school, you had your three meals a day—that was the norm. When a woman had a package, you ran over and helped her. She offered you a nickel, you never took it. You respected the neighborhood cop. If the policeman said, "You—move," you moved. If he said, "Hey you, what are you doing out at seven o'clock?" and you answered, "None of your business," he'd throw you through the wall and take you to your father. And what would your father do? He'd beat your brains in for hurting the policeman's hand. The cop was worried about you. That was his job, for thirty-six dollars a week.

Every Sunday in the summertime, everybody had their windows open and their radios tuned to the same station. It was like a stereo, an Italian station with all the Italian songs playing—Cheno luna mezza mama . . . the melody Milton Berle sang as "Lucky lucky lucky me." Or songs like "I'll Be Seeing You in All the Old Familiar Places" during the war. You'd smell the aroma of the tomatoes cooking, the smoke of the cigars from the old men outside talking about the old hometown. Your father's sitting on the stoop, and you're eating a lemon ice. You thought you had nothing; you had everything. . . .

BARRY FRANK: December 7, 1941, a Sunday afternoon—we were visiting my aunt on Remsen Avenue when someone called with the news. We put the radio on right away. Everybody started screaming. Even though it was wintertime, we ran out into the street; it was filled with people. I was not quite sure of what was going on, but I understood something had taken place that would change all of our lives.

SAM BERNSTEIN: Somewhere I read that Brooklyn gave more men to the armed forces than thirty-eight states. I was one of them. My sister gave birth to a baby girl in a little hospital on Bay Parkway. They didn't allow any visitors, but since I was set to be shipped overseas, I got special permission to see the new mother and daughter and say good-bye.

PRECEDING PAGE
Streamers crisscrossing the streets and flags hanging from windows reflected Brooklyn's postwar euphoria.

No 824963-EZ

UNITED STATES OF AMERICA
ICE OF PRICE ADMINISTRATION

WAR RATION BOOK No. 3 Void if altered

dentification of person to whom issued: PRINT IN FULL

Blum
(First name) Richard (Middle name) Floyd Street (Last name)

Street number or rural route 165 Floyd street

City or post office Brooklyn N.Y. State N.Y.

AGE	SEX	WEIGHT	HEIGHT	
13	M	120 Lbs.	5 Ft. 3 In.	BLUM

SIGNATURE R.C.Ful
(Person to whom book is issued. If such person is unable to sign because of age or incapaci

WARNING
This book is the property of the United States Government. It is unlawful to sell it to any other person, or to use it or permit anyone else to use it, except to obtain rationed goods in accordance with regulations of the Office of Price Administration. Any person who finds a lost War Ration Book must return it to the War Price and Rationing Board which issued it. Persons who violate rationing regulations are subject to $10,000 fine or imprisonment, or both.

LOCAL BOARD

Issued by .... (Local board number)

Street address ....

City ....

(Signature of i

OPA Form No. R-130

RATION STAMP NO. 2
RATION STAMP NO. 3
RATION STAMP NO. 6
RATION STAMP NO. 7
RATION STAMP NO. 10
RATION STAMP NO. 11
RATION STAMP NO. 14
RATION STAMP NO. 15
...N NO.
RATION STAMP NO. 11
RATION STAMP NO. 10
RATION STAMP NO. 15
RATION STAMP NO. 14
RATION STAMP NO. 19
...ION AMP NO. 13
RATION STAMP NO. 18
RATION STAMP NO. 23
RATION NO. 17
RATION STAMP NO. 22
RATION STAMP NO. 21

ELIZABETH RONCKETTI: My aunt Eleanor joined the WACs and got stationed in North Carolina. It was quite unusual for women to be in the service then, but Eleanor had a mind of her own. We all thought she looked so smart in her uniform. She had a gorgeous pair of legs and loved to show them off.

The merchant ships let off at Noble Street in Greenpoint. The guys on the crews always seemed to find their way to our house—maybe because my grandfather had been in the Merchant Marine. Everybody had stories to tell, and I always got a lot of presents.

TOM BOORAS: We went down to the Navy Yard to watch the big ships being built. We stood at the docks and saw them going out to sea. I was so impressed. It was hard to believe something so big was sitting in the water.

FREDDIE GERSHON: You could see the aircraft carriers and destroyers moving out through the Narrows. In Brighton, where we lived, people patrolled the beaches for fear that German subs might try to land. Once a mine rolled onto the shore and had to be exploded.

BILL FEIGENBAUM: The boardwalk in Coney Island was filled with soldiers and sailors. Music blared from the penny arcades. Even though all those terrible things were going on, the mood was up, patriotic.

JERRY STILLER: Banners crisscrossed the streets. They put up plaques with the names of the fighting men. If somebody died, people put out a gold star.

BOB ERTEL: We played on this vacant lot on East Fifth Street that had some big trees, which made it great for war games. Farther down at the dead end was a trench called the cut. That was where the Long Island Railroad commercial spur ran from the Brooklyn Army Terminal out east to Long Island. When we'd hear a train, we'd drop everything and run to the cut to watch the troop trains carrying tanks and jeeps and army trucks. On our block almost every young man of military age was in the armed forces. The war was very close to home.

MAX WECHSLER: My father was a former boxer and a tough guy, but he spent the war working in the shipyards. "I was too young for World War I, and now I'm too old for World War II," he used to tell everyone. I guess he felt funny because so many other fathers were away. But he pasted an American flag on his black lunch pail to show his support.

POLLY BERNSTEIN: Our son couldn't remember his father. He would say, "All the children on the block have their fathers. Where's my father?" I told him, "He's in the army." I showed him a picture. Whenever I put him to sleep, he'd say, "Mommy, tell me a story about Daddy." And I'd say, "Some day your father will come home, and we'll buy a car, and we'll go any place that you want."

There was a drugstore on Bay Parkway. The owner was my friend, and every time I came in with Marvin, he'd say, "What a nice boy. Too bad your husband is away. Let's hope he'll come back." Mike, the neighborhood grocer, would call me up: "Polly, do you need something?" He felt sorry for me because Sam wasn't around.

JOAN RIBAUDO: My father became an air-raid warden. His hat looked like an upside-down washbasin. With flashlight in hand and a band around his arm, he and another gentleman in our building would go up to the roof every night.

The Brooklyn waterfront brought the war close to home.

Brooklyn dockworkers united behind the war effort.

KARL BERNSTEIN: As soon as the sirens sounded, we pulled down the black shades on all the windows and went into the dinette, the only room in the house without a window. My father had put a lamp with a blue light bulb on the kitchen table, and we sat around it until the all-clear. I was very frightened of the blackouts, the sirens, the searchlights in the sky.

BOB ARNESEN: My mother and I went to a Norwegian restaurant on Eighth Avenue in Bay Ridge. On the menu was a Norwegian flag and an American flag and the words "VEE VILL VIN" and underneath, in Norwegian, "Can you ever forget old Norway?"

JOAN MAYNARD: On Sunday afternoons, my mother would take me to the Brooklyn Botanic Garden. My favorite place had always been the Japanese Garden. How disappointed I was when they closed it down during the war.

KARL BERNSTEIN: Grandpa Louie and I would plant seeds that I got in packets from school in our backyard Victory Garden and in cottage-cheese boxes filled with earth. We grew grapes, carrots, radishes. For fertilizer, we would go to the bridle path on Ocean Parkway, just a block away, and shovel up the horse manure into a pail.

Grandma Yetta worked at a place called Economy Auto Fabrics, sewing seat covers for army vehicles. She brought home leftover material. It was real thick canvas, and at night working in the basement on the old treadle sewing machine, she made book bags for me. You couldn't get them during the war.

TERRY PERNA ARNESEN: I was one of the first of the fifty women hired by the Brooklyn Navy Yard. We worked among thousands of men, making templates.

JACK EAGLE: At the age of sixteen, I began my career as a trumpet player. The bands had kids my age, men over fifty, and no one in between. I became well known in Brooklyn because I could hit the high D on the end of "In the Mood" and hold it. If you could do that in those days, you were open for all kinds of jobs. I was a busy little kid.

MARVIN KAPLAN: To show you the kind of misfit I was, I belonged to the Interscholastic German Glee Club, which performed Strauss songs and German folk songs at concerts and outings. Later we found out the organization was really a Bundist front to raise money for the Nazi party.

JERRY STILLER: We collected fat from the butcher, melted it down, and put it in a can. Then we brought it to the entrance to Ebbets Field and got into the Dodger game for nothing. It seemed every kid in Brooklyn was there for Fat Day.

Victory gardens were all over Brooklyn, including these at the Brooklyn Botanic Garden.

KARL BERNSTEIN: We collected wire for the war from glass milk bottles, saved newspapers and fat, which we exchanged for additional blue ration stamps. My mother sent me to the store with the stamps. The grocer would raise the glass in the dairy cabinet and precisely cut the quarter-pound of butter you were allowed from a big wooden tub.

ALAN LELCHUK: At night, I'd sit on my father's lap, and we'd listen to Gabriel Heattor and H. V. Kaltenborn on the radio. We would go over the war map in *The New York Times*: the dotted lines versus the solid black lines, the Allies versus the Axis.

RICHARD KEHOE: In my second-year Latin class at St. John's Prep, we were studying Caesar's *Gallic Wars* at the same time the American troops were fighting their way through France. We read about Caesar's battles on the plains of southern France, following the same patterns the Allies were taking.

SAM BERNSTEIN: In the spring of 1945, we crossed the Channel from England to France and were moving on to Germany. All the news was out during the crossing, but as soon as we reached land, we learned FDR had died. For us, it was such a calamity. Who's Truman? We never heard of Truman. The war will never end, we thought.

KARL BERNSTEIN: My mother called out the window that Roosevelt had died. I was almost eleven years old, and in my short lifetime President Roosevelt was *the* president. There never had been another. President Roosevelt—the words seemed to fit together. During the 1944 election, every grown-up I knew was voting for him. All the kids were for him, too. The big rumor was if Dewey became president we would have to go to school on Saturdays and Sundays.

POLLY BERNSTEIN: When I heard the news on the radio, I got Marvin dressed and put him in the stroller. And I walked up Bay Parkway about two miles, all the way to the bay. "What's going to happen now?" I thought. "Is Sam ever going to come home? Will Marvin ever see his father?" Tears were just coming down my face. It seemed the world was over.

ALAN LELCHUK: My father was Russian-born, and although very left wing, he worshiped Roosevelt. He was the head of the Brownsville air raid wardens and had received a letter signed by the president encouraging the wardens' efforts. That gave me a sense that somehow this man Roosevelt was connected to Brownsville. I believed he was such a paragon of justice and optimism. When my mother came up Ralph Avenue to tell me he had died, the world as I knew it fell out from beneath me.

MARNIE BERNSTEIN: We had a book with a red cover from *The New York Post*, a picture history of America. At the end was a photo gallery of the presidents, four to a page, in chronological order. But the last one was President Roosevelt, and his face took up an entire page. I could not imagine a world without him.

About a month later, I was sick in bed, and my mother said, "You have to hurry up and get well in time for VE day." It was coming—VE day! I didn't quite understand what it meant—victory in Europe but the war not over, my uncles not coming home yet. Still, I could feel the momentum. On the other side of the building, the Rutts were planning a welcome-home party for their son Mel. All the furniture was moved out of the apartment into the hall. The big stairwell windows that faced the courtyard were open wide to the springtime air. My friend Barbara lived next door to the Rutts, and we went together into the foyer of their apartment. It was empty, big, waiting. There was so much anticipation.

POLLY BERNSTEIN: Our bedroom window faced Sixty-third Street. The night of September 2, we were asleep when all of a sudden I heard such a big commotion—you have no idea. I got up and pulled

A USO facility in Manhattan Beach.

up the shade, and I saw the street was full of people, yelling, crying, hugging each other. Everyone was shouting, "The war is over, the war is over!" It seemed whoever had someone in the army had come running out into the street. My little son, who was three years old then, woke up. "What's happening, Mommy?" I said, "The war is over." And he said, "Is Daddy coming home?"

"Yes," I told him, "your daddy is coming home."

KARL BERNSTEIN: When my Uncle Herb went away to the war, we all said good-bye in front of the house. Then we stood there and watched him walk down East Seventh Street toward Kings Highway. At the corner, he looked back once, waved, and turned the corner. Now he phoned and told us to wait in front of the house. So we all went out and stood there, and in a little while, there he was, turning the corner from Kings Highway onto East Seventh, coming back just the way he had left.

JOE SIGLER: Sometimes on Saturdays, my father took me along with him to his accounts. We were at a mirror place, and outside all these tanks and trucks were lined up, ready for the big parade to celebrate the end of the war. The soldiers took me inside the tanks. Thrills, these were thrills.

PAT COOPER: In the neighborhood, there was a block party every night for a year. Sackett Street and Henry, President Street and Henry, Clinton and First Place. They'd put up a little platform or we'd use the back of a truck. There was a festive feeling. Everybody kissed each other. People hung flags and signs from their windows.

I worked block parties seven nights a week. They'd give me a dollar, two dollars. People would say, "Get Pat up here." I'd do impressions of James Cagney, Peter Lorre, Sidney Greenstreet. My father would say, "You're makin' stupid again? Can't you sing opera?" But the crowd said, "Go get 'em Pat, we love ya." They didn't want to hear opera.

JOAN RIBAUDO: Christmas lights were strung across the streets. Tables were set up in front of the buildings and in the middle of the street. People shared all the different ethnic dishes. There was music, and everyone was dancing and singing.

MARNIE BERNSTEIN: I remember it as the first time I was out at night—it was odd to see the blocks lit by street lamps, the sky so dark. A parade came down Sixty-third Street: three people like a

Yankee Doodle Dandy pageant, with a fife-and-drum and a huge American flag. Then a woman in a short skirt twirling a baton, and behind her, a brass band.

The street was filled with people in costume. Mrs. Unger, who lived upstairs, was dressed in black Chinese pajamas and had strange-looking colors on her eyelids.

We moved with the crowd down the block and around the corner, onto Sixty-fourth Street. The porch of one of the houses was set up like a stage, with a little band and a microphone. People were entertaining. A few days before, I had been at a birthday party where someone sang "Don't Fence Me In." That gave me the idea. They put me up on a chair so I could reach the microphone, and I sang that song.

There were loudspeakers all over the area, and my father, walking past Feder's Drug Store a block away, stopped to listen. Someone told him, "Don't you know who that is? It's Marnie." He ran down the block and around the corner, and reached the porch just as I finished the song. And while everybody was applauding, they handed me down the steps over to him.

LOUIS COHEN: I came home at the end of 1946. On a Friday night, I was standing on a street corner in my uniform, with all the nice medals on my jacket. A girl walked by, pointed to one, and said, "Can I ask you what that medal is for?" We got to talking, and I walked her home. She lived in East New York. I started taking her with me when I played handball in Brighton. She would say, "Louie, you're some ball player." I ended up marrying that girl.

DOROTHY HANDWERKER: When Murray came home from the army, you couldn't get an apartment for love or money. There had been no construction at all during the war. We moved in with my parents; lots of people did that. It was a beautiful three-bedroom, two-bathroom apartment overlooking the ocean in Brighton. But we were seven people living together: my parents; Murray and me; my sister and brother-in-law, who just got out of the air force; and my nephew, who was just born. And I was pregnant. Still, we were so happy to be together.

NORMAN TIPOGRAPH: They built four "veterans' preference" apartment houses for young married couples on Ocean Avenue between Avenues X and Y. We got a three-room apartment for twenty-five dollars a room. Everybody in the place had served in a branch of the armed forces. Buddy Rich and Harvey Lembeck lived there.

ALAN LELCHUK: The boys coming home were treated like heroes. Some were given free suits on Pitkin Avenue and free meals.

NORMAN TIPOGRAPH: Henry Modell had sales day just for veterans at his downtown Brooklyn store. On Veterans Day 1948, he opened up the store only for veterans. He started a school under the GI Bill of Rights, training them in selling and merchandising. Some went on to work for him at Modell's, many others started their own businesses.

Henry bought merchandise that the government wanted to dispose of: underwear, insect repellent, shoes, sweaters, hats. There was no end to all the utility items available. One of the hottest numbers in Modell's was U.S. Navy shoes: a black oxford. Everybody and his brother bought them, they were so cheap and useful.

MATT KENNEDY: The Depression was over, and now the war was over. There was more money. The soldiers and sailors and Marines coming home helped bring about the resurgence of Coney Island. They'd come off the subway at Stillwell Avenue and rush to the places they frequented, spreading out to the rides. They loved the Cyclone —especially the Air Force people. They'd spend every nickel that they had, and the rides were a nickel then. If they didn't have any

Borough president John Cashmore presents diplomas to graduates of Modell's Veterans' Training Center.

money left for carfare, they'd go to the Sixtieth Precinct, where the police had a special fund to help them.

MURRAY HANDWERKER: At that time, Nathan's was just hot dogs, hamburgers, french fries, soft drinks, chow mein. I had just gotten out of the army, and I saw all the uniformed people coming to Coney Island. I realized the American soldier had been exposed to French food, his tastes had become more sophisticated. I wanted to put in a seafood counter. My father was afraid. Our frankfurter wasn't kosher, but it was kosher-style: all beef, no pork. He was afraid if I put in shrimp and clams, people wouldn't like it. After a while, he said, "All right, if you want to do it, do it. I'm not gonna be around. Do it while I'm away in Florida." So I tried it, and it was a success, and then I brought in delicatessen.

The postwar years were a turning point, you could say—a time of expansion. Tastes were changing. And I, coming home from the war and going into the business, was part of that scene.

PAUL DOYLE: February 5, 1947, was the first day of classes at the experimental New York State Institute of Applied Arts and Sciences. The students were primarily demobilized veterans. The war had made everyone aware we were living in a world of new inventions and sophisticated technology, and this school was designed to prepare people for the future with a combination of technical training and general education. Our slogan was: "Earn a living, and live a life."

P.S. 15 was the original site of what would become New York City Technical College of the City University of New York.

For the first few months, classes were held at P.S. 15, at the corner of Schermerhorn Street and Third Avenue. The GIs sat on top of the small grade-school desks. That spring we moved into our permanent site on Pearl Street. Most of our equipment was surplus war stuff. The only way you could get fifteen file cabinets was also to take twenty-five ship chronometers or maybe forty ship anchors. We had three radar trucks in our parking lot that we had to take in order to get inkwells. Young families moved into the trucks and set up house-keeping.

I taught psychology and sociology. Some of us were not totally familiar with our subjects and kept just a chapter or two ahead of the students. But none of that seemed to matter. We felt what we were part of would bring the benefits of science and technology to everyone, and that was going to make for a better future.

FRANK BARBARO: When I started working on the waterfront, the longshoremen and the sons of the longshoremen had come back from war. They remembered the tremendous oppression they or their fathers endured at the hands of the Mob during the Depression. Like, if you want to work, your daughter has to go to bed with me or your wife has to clean my house or you have to kick back. There had been open terror, subjugation.

Now the Second World War is over. The violence, the intimidation, the corruption—are still there, but different. The people are different. Many saw their friends die. All believe in democracy.

A boss on the pier gives a guy a hard time. The guy goes home, gets his gun, goes back and says, "You son of a bitch, you mess with me, and I'll kill you. You think I went to war to come back and take this from you?" The boss never bothers him again.

The men are cheated out of their time, and they walk off. Nothing striking at the heart of the power structure—just basic elements of common decency, a developing rank-and-file struggle for decency in the union. Coming off the Second World War, a lot of people were saying, "We just fought a war, and it's time for a better life for working people."

MAX WECHSLER: For a week or more, the word was going around the neighborhood: the candy store on Havemeyer Street was getting a shipment of Fleer's Double Bubble Gum. When it finally arrived, the line stretched almost a block and a half. Adults were there along with the kids. The price was at least ten times what it had been before the war. Still, people were jumping the line, bumping the line. They sold the gum direct from cartons stacked up outside the store, and people were in a panic to get to that sweet chewy taste. I guess it made us feel things were getting back to the way they used to be.

KARL BERNSTEIN: Bubble gum was so expensive, we would put it into a glass of water overnight so we could chew it the next day. Rubber came back into production, and so did Spaldings. We finally got rid of those hard balls that didn't bounce. We could get Duncan yo-yos again. Everyone was doing all kinds of tricks with them, like the Windmill, Around the World, the Walk. They became such a distraction that if a kid brought his yo-yo to school, he could get expelled. We had been through the blackouts, the rations, but now everything was coming back. My father even got a new car.

But best of all, the war was over. Now there was a United Nations to make sure there would never be another one. In school, we sang:

United Nations on the march with flags unfurled.
Together fight for victory, a brave new world.

Our teacher at Seth Low Junior High School took the class to Greenwich Village for a lesson in Esperanto, the universal language. Once everyone could speak the same language, they told us, there would be no more misunderstandings.

JOAN MAYNARD: With all the world upheaval, people had come into Brooklyn by the bushel, and there was hope and a spirit of optimism, a feeling we had made it, had come through the Depression and the war. We went out to Fulton Street to shop and left the iron gate to our brownstone in Bedford-Stuyvesant open. We went to dances and parties and came back at three in the morning, and there'd be singing in the street, and the milkman would wave to us.

WILLIAM THOMPSON: I came back to my family's home on Put-nam Avenue in Bedford-Stuyvesant after serving in the segregated Ninety-second Infantry Division. Bed-Stuy was a fabulous area then, an integrated neighborhood. I started Brooklyn Law School and joined the segregated United Action Democratic Club. When a judge died, we asked that a black man be nominated as his replacement, since the neighborhood was turning black. We were told power does not concede. They took a white man from out of the area, moved him onto

Macon Street, and said, "This is your candidate for judge." At which point a whole bunch of us got together and backed Louis S. Flagg.

They don't hand power to you just because you happen to be there. We spent a lot of money. It was a hard fight. And Flagg won. Then we started opening doors.

ROGER GREEN: There'd be a banging on the front door of our house on Madison Street, and us kids would come running. We knew it was my grandfather up to visit from North Carolina, smelling of Old Spice and his leather suitcase. We'd jump all over him, and he'd cry, "Great Gugga Mugga! Great day in the morning!" And next thing he would say was, "When are we gonna see the Dodgers? I gotta see my man Jackie."

Jackie Robinson breaking through the color line in the years following the war gave folks the perception that there was something different about Brooklyn, that it was a special kind of place.

ALAN LELCHUK: During Robinson's first season, a very close friend of mine named Burt would pick me up at P.S. 189 one hour earlier than the regular let-out time and take me to Ebbets Field. Burt had been shot down during the war and had a Purple Heart. As soon as the ushers saw this uniformed soldier with a Purple Heart, they immediately gave him a box.

Together with Burt, I watched the Brooklyn Dodgers, a team that had been one of comedy and futility now, suddenly, with the introduction and acceptance of Robinson and then other black players, become one of the two great teams of the postwar era.

In the years after the war, nothing symbolized the feeling of hope and optimism more than the Brooklyn Dodgers. By taking in blacks and making them part of the team, Branch Rickey made the Dodgers truly representative of the borough, which at that time flourished as a unique place. The team stood for aspirations at a time when the people of the city were ready for a future of rightness.

For us in Brooklyn, there was the feeling that not only had we made it through—we were on the way up. We had a lot of motivation, we children of immigrants. There was a tremendous amount of talent pooled together to be the smartest, the best, the wittiest, the most mischievous. We had the desire to work hard plus the belief we could do anything. The myth of invincibility was very important. After a great victory in war, there was a feeling that merit would be recognized. It was like coming into a bright light.

PART ONE

When We
Were a Couple of Kids

THE STREETS WERE OUR SANCTUARY

SCHOOL DAYS

LOOK, MA, I'M DANCING!

ONE BIG HAPPY FAMILY

The Streets Were Our Sanctuary

2 GOOD

+2 BE

4 GOTTEN

—Autograph album, J.H.S. 265

STAN GOLDBERG: Most of us came from blue-collar families, from fathers who had to give up college educations to go to work. My father was a mailman. "I don't mind being a worker," he would tell my brother, Gary, and me. "It's OK. I don't care that I'm not a leader. You two, I want you to do whatever you want to do." He made us really believe that we could be anything in this world that we wanted, that we could succeed in anything. But we couldn't go on the subway alone.

And we had to have our milk and cookies at three o'clock. School days, I came home, had my milk and cookies, and went back to the schoolyard. Weekends, my grandma brought the milk and cookies to the schoolyard. The score is tied? Bases are loaded, and Stanley is up? Grandma Jennie comes by and stops the game. That was bad enough, but she brought a napkin yet. And my grandfather would stop football games to bring me a jacket. In the middle of the play, he would call me to the sidelines. "Grandpa," I explained, "I'm the quarterback. The quarterback doesn't wear a jacket."

FREDDIE GERSHON: Every neighbor looked out for you. If your parents were away, you could not get into trouble, because twenty other mothers were looking out the window. I never experienced that again.

ALAN LELCHUK: It was a very tidy neighborhood life where I grew up, on the border of Brownsville and East Flatbush. For four–six blocks around, I knew practically every face. When I was about seven, my sister said she was not going to baby-sit any longer, and as my parents went out a great deal, I was on my own nearly every evening. If I needed something, I ran across the landing and knocked on a neighbor's door.

ROGER GREEN: When my parents were working and I was outside playing, Mrs. Haskins, who lived down the street, was always looking out for me. At night, I would get the litany from the intelligence network: "Well, Mrs. Haskins said so-and-so."

STAN GOLDBERG: Laura, one of my mother's friends, would have been great in the CIA. You climbed the fence to get the ball, and of course the spy saw. Immediately the word went out if you said the four-letter word. I'd walk in the door and my mother would say, "You cursed!"

"How'd you find out?"

"Laura said."

We knew all the grown-ups in the neighborhood and what to expect from them. Even Silvio, the kid who ruled the schoolyard, knew. Silvio was an older boy who took collections: two cents, three cents, whatever people would give him. He collected just because you were there—until we got wise and stopped going to the schoolyard with money. One day, I was playing third base, and Silvio came over.

"Goldberg, what you got for me today?"

I said, "Nothing."

He checked my pockets and found a quarter. "You lied to me. You have a quarter."

"My mother gave it to me for a rye bread."

"A rye bread's twenty-one cents." He took the quarter and gave me back twenty-one cents. He knew better than to risk my coming home without the rye bread; my mother or, worse, grandma would be after him. Still, I was surprised. I didn't think he knew how to make change.

JULIE BUDD: If my mother wasn't around, I knew the neighbors would take care of me. I could go eat at the Caracaffas', or Lilly Simon's, or Sandy Warren's. In the warm weather, they were all out sitting on their porches, and the kids would stay outside, wait for the ice-cream man, play in the street till eleven o'clock at night.

JUDY BERGER: We played on the streets till our mothers leaned out the window and yelled it was time to come in. The Prince spaghetti commercial that takes place in Boston is really a Brooklyn scene.

ANGELO BADALAMENTI: I had loads of friends—twenty, thirty really good friends, the kids on our block. We went to school together and then played outside together on the streets of the neighborhood.

ROGER GREEN: We played stickball, punchball, hide-and-go-seek, and of course, basketball and softball till after dark. Our block was known for that kind of street activity.

JERRY STILLER: We played ringolevio and kickety-can-hide-go, which means you kick the can and hide before the guy who's It picks up the can. And Johnny-on-the-pony, where guys would line up with their heads against each other's tushes, and someone would take a flying leap, trying to get as far as he could over the line of backs. Then the last guy on the line would try to get on top of the first guy. It ended up a pile of kids.

LUIS COLMENARES: We played "kings" with a Spalding ball in the alley between the houses. If you lost, you were the target. You got your ass up against the wall, and everybody had five throws at you with the ball. I got whacked pretty good.

MARTIN SPITZER: With a piece of chalk, we would draw a big geometric grid on the sidewalk. We'd fill bottle caps with clay or gum or melted crayons and flick the caps into boxes on the grid. That was skelly. Or we used a cigar box and a marble. You'd cut out holes and each hole would be worth so many. People would come with their

marbles and if they got it in the hole, I'd have to pay them off, and vice versa. That was the first type of gambling. I made a lot of marbles.

ANGELO BADALAMENTI: We played "heels" with heels gotten off old shoes or from the shoe store. The idea was to throw the heel so it landed on a line of the sidewalk. If it did, the next kid would try to get his heel on top of it. We played "land," flipping a knife onto the strip of earth that lined the sidewalk.

JOYCE SHAPIRO FEIGENBAUM: We played potsy and hop-scotch and jump rope and double-dutch jump rope—the stuff that kids who spent all their time in the streets did. I lived in this crowded little apartment that was so small and stifling. I remember the yelling and all that. I spent every moment I could outside, even in the win-tertime. The streets were my sanctuary.

HELEN FRIED GOLDSTEIN: Winters seemed so fierce when I was a kid. There would be so much snow. They didn't clear it for weeks, and it would be piled up in high mounds on the edge of the streets. Bay Ridge, where we lived, has a lot of hills. We all had sleds, some big enough for several kids, and we would toboggan down the big hill on Forty-fifth Street from Seventh Avenue to Fourth Av-enue. At the bottom of each street, we had a monitor posted to watch the traffic. If it was clear, he'd signal us to go through. If not, he'd motion for us to get over to the ash pile on the left. The hill continued below Fourth Avenue, but we stopped there, because we had to carry our sleds back up the hill. We were a crowd of boys and girls, different ethnic groups, all friends, playing outdoors in the cold, brisk air. It felt so healthy and invigorating. Except if Mike, a very fat kid, was on your sled. We bellied, one kid laying on top of another. No one wanted to be under Mike.

HERBY GREISSMAN: On rainy days, we sat on the hard marble steps in the building, flipping baseball cards off the wall, trading joke books, playing cards, pitching pennies, shooting dice. We'd steal two or three cigarettes from our parents' packs, go under the steps by the mailbox, and smoke.

MARNIE BERNSTEIN: The halls of the apartment house were like a theater. Marble staircases led up to tile floors—a stage, perfect for performing. The audience sat on the steps below. Acoustics in that old building were wonderful; your voice bounced off the walls, echo upon echo. The hallways were also great for playing hide-and-seek.

There were so many entrances and alcoves and stairwells where you could hide.

TOBY SCHOM GROSSMAN: We played a game on the lobby floor we called alligator. Most of the floor tiles were white, but there was a green border going around. You had to walk on the green tiles, and if you fell into the white tiles, the alligators would get you.

On Halloween, we got dressed up in costumes, but we never left the building. We'd go from one side of the building to the other. Everyone knew us and gave us treats.

JOYCE SHAPIRO FEIGENBAUM: We avoided the cellar. It was a dark and forbidding place, with many locked rooms. Still, it held a certain fascination.

CAROLINE KATZ MOUNT: The cellar was one of those foreign and frightening elements that intruded every once in a while into my otherwise safe and circumscribed world. When we had to go from the courtyard to the backyard through the corridor that divided the cellar in two parts, we ran in a blind panic. A man named Jeffrey, who did odd jobs for our super, lived down there. Sometimes he hung around with his friends. I'd see them laughing and drinking. None of them ever so much as spoke to me; still, I was very afraid of Jeffrey and the cellar.

FRANCES BLUM: The big courtyard that separated my building from the one next door had benches along the walls and a couple of trees. The mothers would come out with the baby carriages, and all the little toddlers would be running around. There were children of all ages. We never lacked for friends. In the summer, my mother would let us out early in the morning, call us in for lunch, and let us out again to play till suppertime. In the middle of the afternoon, the ice-cream truck came along. You could get chocolate or white—I didn't know it was called vanilla until years later. We bought dixie cups with pictures of movie stars on the lids. After you licked off the ice cream, you had a picture for your collection. We used to trade them: a June Haver for an Alan Ladd. I would trade everyone but Betty Grable. I loved her. I think I saw every Betty Grable picture there was.

We played house with our dolls and doll carriages and toy dishes and pots and pans. We put on talent shows. The kids who took lessons dressed up in their costumes and tap-danced. I mostly used to watch. If the boys didn't have enough for their punchball game, they'd grab one of us: "You're on first base, you're on second base, you're in the outfield."

IRWIN POLISHOOK: I used to explore the old apartment houses in the neighborhood, climbing in the narrow spaces between the buildings—crevices barely wide enough for a child to crawl through. At the end of the war, there were a number of empty buildings we used for war games. I crawled through one, fell down, and cut my hand. I still have the scar.

JOYCE SHAPIRO FEIGENBAUM: In back of my apartment house was a labyrinth of alleys, and beyond them, the backs of other houses. They were two-family or private houses—a whole other world to me.

MIRIAM KITTRELL: We used to play in the alley that runs a full block between the backs of the houses on East Second and Third streets between Quentin Road and Avenue P. Someone planted a row of magnolia trees there. I remember the pink blossoms in the springtime. Occasionally, there was such a scent of magnolia.

KARL BERNSTEIN: The trees on our block were part of our punchball games. When we were younger, if the ball hit a tree, you were out. If the ball went into Mrs. Capricilli's garden across the street, we never saw it again—even during the war, when Spaldings were treasures. Mrs. Capricilli would be out the door in a flash and cut it up.

HELEN FRIED GOLDSTEIN: There must have been at least twenty steps on the stoop of our brownstone, perfect for stoopball. You tried to hit the ball off the corner of the step and catch it before it bounced.

STAN GOLDBERG: We lived and breathed to play ball. If I wasn't in the schoolyard, I was in the backyard. I left the house in the morning, the ball was in my hand. I'd walk down the block and hit every stoop along the way. All my friends were ball players. My mother wanted me to be friends with Gary Stein. "Ma," I said, "I can't. He doesn't like to play ball." She said, "Don't worry. Someday he'll be something." Today he's a heart surgeon in Boston.

In the schoolyard—P.S. 205, Twentieth Avenue between Sixty-sixth and Sixty-seventh—you were on your own. You developed a code that was a great carryover to later life: covering up for each other in certain situations, sharing—whether sharing for a game, or sharing a stickball bat, or sharing a Spalding ball that everyone chipped in for. You didn't want to lose that ball. When it rolled down the street and went into the sewer—that was it, you were finished. You didn't have a quarter for another one. You got a wire hanger, made a loop in it, and fished down to get the ball in the loop and bring it up. Sometimes, you put gum on a stick. No one thought of how to wash it off.

MARTY ADLER: We broke a broom or mop handle under a car's wheel to make it the right length for stickball. It never came off clean, and we were always getting splinters. But that was it. There was no such thing as a store-bought bat.

STAN GOLDBERG: Some women in the neighborhood spent a little more money for a better mop. We cased them. Mrs. Aronowitz bought a very good mop. She hung the mop out the window. It was so tempting. I took it, passed it to my friend Billy Levine. He cut it off at the curb, and Billy and I shared it.

PETER NERO: None of us had the money for a football, so we improvised. We played association football—that was touch football with a Spalding. Aluminum foil was becoming popular just then. We would save it, bunch it up until we got something the size of a golf ball, maybe a little bigger. We'd hit that with our bare hands. It was easy to hit long fly balls that would hang up in the air and not break any windows, either.

ROBERT MERRILL: We scrunched the cellophane and silver paper from cigarette packs into a ball and wrapped electricians' tape around it. That became the ball for a stickball game.

MARTY ADLER: Choosing sides for a game, we would toss the bat vertically. One of the guys would grab it as high up at the top as he could. You added your hand on top of his. The person who was able to hold on to the highest part while turning the bat around his head three times, have his opponent kick it, and still hold on to it was allowed to choose sides first.

FREDDIE GERSHON: I was a fat child and not a great athlete. I was always the person least desired on either team, so I was made to play home plate.

ANGELO BADALAMENTI: Our favorite game, "sewers," was played at an intersection with sewers at each of the four corners. The ball would be thrown to the batter at home plate—one of the sewers —on a bounce, and he would try to slap it through the infielders, run around the other three sewers, and literally slide on the cement of the gutter into home. I can't remember how many times I ripped my pants and ended up with my legs down the sewer. On Sunday mornings, when the fourteen- and fifteen-year-old boys played, it was serious business, with a little side betting for sodas or malteds.

MARTY ADLER: If we had four guys, the sewer was home plate in our stickball games. The pitcher would throw fast to a catcher, who played without benefit of mask or glove. If you hit the ball as far as one sewer down the block, it was a single; two sewers, it was a double. Another kind of stickball was one-on-one, where the batter stood in a box drawn in chalk, and the pitcher threw fast against the wall behind. Another kind was where you hit the ball yourself down the block. Since you were generating your own power, you could get a three-sewer hit.

STEWIE STONE: People from Brooklyn ask, "How many sewers could you hit the ball?" A sewer was every sixty or eighty feet. Anyone who tells you he could hit two sewers is either King Kong or a liar. Ted Kluszewski couldn't hit two sewers.

We played on a narrow street and made up markers—ground rules. If the ball went a certain distance on the sidewalk to the left, it was good. If it went under the sewer, it was a foul ball. If it went past the Chevrolet on the fly, it was a double. If you could hit past the Ford, a triple.

"We lived and breathed to play ball."

JOEL BERGER: If a car came down the street, we'd yell, "Ship ahoy!" If a guy tried to park, we'd say, "Hey mister, could you move your car? You're on second base." He'd always move.

HERBY GREISSMAN: The cars didn't bother us much because not too many people had cars in those days. If someone drove a Lincoln Continental, it was like the end of the world. We would stop and stare.

MARTY ADLER: The Blumberg brothers from East New York came to play stickball against me, Larry Freidman, Harvey Kaufman, Herbie Young, and Renato Guidice. We set up the game on Fiftieth Street, off Eleventh Avenue. Somebody scrounged up a piece of chalk so we could keep score in the gutter. In the second inning, Larry Freidman hit one smack into Mrs. Myers's window. She came out screaming. Her husband, who happened to be home because he worked nights in the post office, came out, too. Everybody scattered. The cops came. Mrs. Myers pointed her finger and screamed—we're loafers, we're hooligans. A fire engine came driving down the block. People were looking out of their windows, crying, "What the hell is going on?"

When it was all over, every one of us had to chip in for the broken window. The Blumberg brothers never returned. That was the first shot heard round the world.

ALAN LELCHUK: We had a regular team, with club jackets. They were purple and white, and reversible—wool on one side, satin on the other. The club's name, the Charantes—which we got from an Indian tribe in the "Dick Tracy" comic strip—was on the back, and our own names were on the breast pocket. We saved for about four years to get those jackets. They cost about eighteen or twenty dollars—a monstrous amount of money in those days.

BOB LEVY: We had kelly-green-and-gold jackets and basketball shirts and shorts. The club's name was the Deuces, and each of us had nicknames. Mine was "Bread," for Levy's bread. We played basketball and schoolyard softball and challenged all the schools in the area. Right next to P.S. 161 was the Crown Heights Yeshiva. We played basketball against the yeshiva kids, and they beat us all the time.

BOB ERTEL: We played football, baseball, or stickball against kids from other neighborhoods. The whole team would ride on bikes halfway across Brooklyn to play those games. Those kids who didn't have a bike sat on the handlebars.

IRWIN POLISHOOK: I explored all over Brooklyn on my Schwinn bike. It was an adventure. I rode to Red Hook and the Navy Yard, where my friend's grandfather owned a junk yard where my father

worked during the war. I bicycled ten miles down Shore Parkway to Coney Island.

I had a yen to know what all the different areas of Brooklyn were like. Even as a little boy, I would go around on the subway. I used to wonder what was above me. What kind of people lived there? What kind of neighborhood was I riding underneath?

KARL BERNSTEIN: You'd begin riding the trains and buses and trolleys by yourself when you were a little kid—seven, eight years old. Before I knew how to read, I could identify all the subway trains by the colored lights at the front. The West End line was green and white, the Sea Beach was red and white, the Culver was green and orange, the Brighton was red and green, the Fourth Avenue Local was green and green. I loved the elevated subway trains; you could open the top windows, stand on your knees, look out and feel the wind on your face. They were the old brown trains with rattan seats that stuck to your legs in the summertime when you wore short pants.

JUDY BERGER: The Culver line didn't link up to the rest of the system, so we always had to change trains. Our station had a floor-to-ceiling turnstile, like a revolving door. A family of three could squash into one compartment for a nickel—which a lot of people did, as there was no agent at that station. I was never one for looking down from a height, and when you looked down from the elevator platform, you saw right through to the street. My little sister used to stand at the edge, and I would panic.

CLIFF HESSE: On Sunday afternoons, my sister and I went for these long walks. We picked a direction we never had been before and walked that way. We wandered into new neighborhoods and never worried about it.

LUIS COLMENARES: I lived on Pineapple Street in Brooklyn Heights, and my friend Tommy Antanasio, a Greek kid, lived on Henry Street. We were playing poker. I had taken him for a couple of dollars, and we had nothing else to do that night, a beautiful clear summer night, so we decided to walk over the Brooklyn Bridge. I used to see the city across the river, but I had never gone there. Manhattan was a strange land, a forbidding place. I wondered what it would be like.

So we walked and talked and got to the other side of the Brooklyn Bridge. It was no big deal. All we saw were some official-looking

buildings that didn't seem so interesting. So we headed back to Brooklyn, which was our world. We came home close to midnight, and my mother whipped my ass. I found out later on that Tommy's father punched him in the mouth. The walk wasn't worth it.

ANNETTE DE LUCIA-CLARK: My friends and I would walk from the community center on Baltic Street in Gowanus up to Court Street and all the way down the promenade in Brooklyn Heights to the end, somewhere around Pineapple Street. We'd get off and go over to downtown Brooklyn, where we'd go shopping at A & S, Martin's, the big stores. Not real shopping, just looking around. The only thing I ever bought was a lipstick.

ELIZABETH RONCKETTI: In Greenpoint, all the kids rollerskated together, great bunches of us skating down the streets. Some went long distances, all the way into Queens.

HELEN FRIED GOLDSTEIN: I was the best roller skater around. My mother gave me money to take the trolley to my piano lessons. I pocketed it and roller-skated all the way instead. How many times would I come to my piano teacher all out of breath, with a scraped knee. But what a great trip, so free and out in the open.

JOEL MARTIN: In the summer, my friend Warren and I rode our bikes at crazy speeds around Greenwood Cemetery. It was a wonderful place for bike riding—long and pretty and peaceful, with all those big trees. Some of the old gravestones went back hundreds of years. Occasionally, we would get chased by a caretaker or someone in uniform. We'd move out fast, not knowing what they would do to us if they caught us.

I biked only up to a certain point. I had boundaries in my mind. I knew there had to be a Seventeenth Avenue, an Eighteenth Avenue, but I never went past Sixteenth Avenue. Like the guys who sailed with Columbus, I always had this feeling that I would fall off the earth if I went beyond.

When I was about eleven, we ran away from home to Prospect Park, taking along boxes of sugar-coated cereal and a canteen of water. We stayed till one or two in the morning. When we got home, don't ask what happened. They beat the hell out of my friend. Me they just yelled at. My mother said, "Why didn't you tell us you were running away? I would have packed you a good lunch."

FRANCES BLUM: In the springtime, we spent nice Saturday or Sunday afternoons at Prospect Park. We went in one of my uncles' cars, or we met my aunt and cousins and took the train. There were different ways to enter the park. One way, we passed the band shell, and we'd stop off and listen to the band play marching music. Another way took us through the zoo. My aunt would bring along a wicker picnic basket lined with red checkered cloth that she filled with sandwiches and fruit. We brought along big blankets that we spread out on the great lawn. While the grown-ups lay down and relaxed, we ran around on the grass, or played ball. My mother would take us out on the lake in one of the swan boats. Sometimes my father or one of my uncles would rent a rowboat and let us try the oars.

WILLIAM CUNNINGHAM: Donnegal Hill, right near the main gate of Prospect Park off Flatbush Avenue, was named after a county in Ireland. On a Sunday it would be filled with people from all over Ireland. Kids would run up and down the hill, young people would meet and walk around.

JOE SIGLER: Prospect Park was my playground, my front yard and my backyard. When I looked out the window of our apartment, I saw the park, the trees, the grass. Right across the street were the toilets, in a nice big stone building. In those days custodians took care of it, and there was no graffiti. Right down the street, three blocks away, were the Parade Grounds, at the southernmost tip of the park. Everybody came there to play baseball.

A pair of crowd pleasers at
the Prospect Park zoo.

MARTY ADLER: Officiated, organized league games were played at the Parade Grounds. There were all these leagues: Babe Ruth, Ty Cobb, Gowanus International. Koufax played there, the Aspromonte brothers, the Torre brothers.

CHARLES HYNES: The Parade Grounds were broken up into thirteen baseball fields. Diamond one and diamond thirteen were the major fields, because they were enclosed.

MARTY ADLER: You had to wear a uniform to play on fields one and thirteen. When I got to play there, it was the first time in my life I put on sanitary whites. My mother said, "You're putting socks on socks."

"That's the way they do it in the big leagues, Mom."

A family spending a blissful Sunday afternoon in Prospect Park.

JOE SIGLER: When I went to P.S. 92, on Parkside Avenue, the schools were crowded, and there were split sessions. If you had the morning session, it was great. We'd have lunch and then meet in Prospect Park. We'd race down the hills. We'd roller-skate on the asphalt-paved playground, play stickball, go look at the animals in the zoo. We rowed on the lake in the summer, ice-skated on it in the winter. When it snowed, we'd go sleigh riding down Lookout Mountain.

My aunt Florence had a brother Nat who was in the cavalry in the First World War. He decided his sons, Sid and George, and my cousin Jay and I should take riding lessons. We took indoor lessons every

Saturday for five dollars an hour in the winter, and by the spring we were riding the bridle paths in Prospect Park. We learned to handle the horses English-style. It was beautiful, but we weren't interested in the trees, only in how fast we could go without getting caught. There were mounted police to keep everybody calm, and the instructors were watching us. We couldn't go off by ourselves, but of course we tried to break away a little.

DORIS MODELL TIPOGRAPH: On Saturdays I took the train from Brighton Beach to Prospect Park wearing a beautiful riding outfit that I got from the Modell Riding Store in Manhattan. I'd rent a horse from the Black and White Stables and take the bridle path on Ocean Parkway, beginning at Prospect Park and going all the way down to Brighton Beach. When I reached the end, I'd turn the horse around and ride all the way back to Prospect Park. Then I'd buy a pretzel for a penny and an ice cream for a nickel, and take the subway back to the Brighton Beach stop.

JUDY BERGER: Riding horses through Prospect Park was pretty passive; we just followed the guide through the trails. I preferred roller skating at the Park Circle rink, right outside the park. They had organ music, and you rented shoe skates instead of the iron skates you used on the streets, the ones with keys that expanded as your feet grew. Of course, we'd have to wait outside on a long line for the two o'clock Saturday afternoon session, but it was worth it.

JOE SIGLER: Most Saturday afternoons, my aunt got rid of us by packing up lunches and candy bars and sending us to the movies. Within walking distance were the Flatbush Movie Theater (which also had big bands performing, and the last of the vaudeville acts) and the Kenmore on Flatbush Avenue, the Paramount, the Patio (which had fish ponds in the lobby), and the Parkside farther down. Near Erasmus Hall High School, there was the Astor, which showed foreign movies; past that, the Albemare; and past that, the Rialto. They were unbelievable: art deco, gorgeous.

HERBY GREISSMAN: My mother used to give me a dollar on Saturday afternoons to go to the Marboro Theater, on Bay Parkway. I walked up Sixty-fifth Street with my friends, and we would stop off at the delicatessen, where we each got a hot dog, a knish, and a soda. We got enough change from that for the movie and a piece of candy.

When they raised the price to get into the Marboro to twenty-six cents, a bunch of maybe ten guys would go, and one guy would go in

for twenty-six cents. He'd go to the exit doors and open them, and all nine of us would run in and scatter in all different directions. The matron would come after us with her flashlight, but she couldn't run after everyone.

BILL FEIGENBAUM: Every Saturday we went to the Surf Theater, in Coney Island. We'd buy our candy before we went in because it was five cents in the candy store and seven cents in the theater. Admission was a quarter—fourteen cents during the week—for a main feature, a western, a newsreel, cartoons, and something called the weekly races, usually bicycle races. They used to give out free tickets based on having the right number on your stub. Howie Shumsky, whose big brother was the head usher, won all the time.

CHARLES HYNES: Because my mother was working, her drill most summer weekdays was to drop me off at the Beverly Movie Theater, on Church and McDonald, in the morning and pick me up after work. I think I knew every line in *Guadalcanal Diary*. On Wednesdays there was a drawing. Since I was there so often, I had more chances than others. Twice I got to go up on the stage and collect a Monopoly set.

ALAN BLANKSTEIN: The movie theaters were the first places to be air-conditioned. In the summer we stayed there the whole afternoon. I'd come out from the cold, dark theater into the blinding sunlight, and it felt like I was being hit by a brick of hot air.

FRANCES BLUM: I went with my friends to the Walker Theater, on Eighteenth Avenue, every Saturday. Then we'd come home and play the movie we had just seen. Once we saw Esther Williams and Ricardo Montalban in a movie about bullfighters. Sandra wanted to play Esther Williams. This one time I put up a fight: "I'm tired of playing the mother. I'm going to be Esther Williams."

KARL BERNSTEIN: In those days before television, our entertainment was from either the movies or the radio. My cousin Bill and I loved the radio mystery programs: *The Shadow* and *The Green Hornet*. There was a large brick fireplace in the basement of our house, and we spent countless hours tapping every brick in that fireplace, looking for one that would open the secret panel.

PETER NERO: My grandfather had a little tailor's shop right across the street from Junior High School 149, on Sutter and Vermont, and sometimes I'd bring a lunch from home and eat with him. But most of the time, I would run home and gobble down my sandwich. Neither of my parents were at home at that hour, and I had the radio all to myself. My friends also ran home to listen to the programs, and we compared notes.

MARVIN KAPLAN: I lived inside that radio tube. On Sunday night, there were all the comedy shows: Jack Benny, Fred Allen, Edgar Bergen and Charlie McCarthy, George Burns and Gracie Allen.

MIRIAM KITTRELL: The radio was on all the time. We had a big radio in the living room and a small one on the table in the kitchen. We'd be having dinner when Stan Lomax came on at 6:45, and there'd be a big silence. We lived for the Texaco broadcasts of the Metropolitan Opera on the radio on Saturday afternoons.

CAROLINE KATZ MOUNT: My father heard Ezio Pinza singing "This Nearly Was Mine" from *South Pacific* on the radio, and he couldn't get over how beautiful it was. He bought a new victrola with the 33⅓ LP speed just so he could play the record from that show. And then he decided we had to see it. That became a tradition. Every year, my mother, father, sister, and I, and usually a relative and friend or two, went to see a Broadway show. We saw *Kismet*, *The Pajama Game*, *Can-Can*. We went by subway to a Saturday matinee, and afterward we had a bite at Chock Full O'Nuts.

JULIE BUDD: My sister Jill took me to see my first Broadway show, *Fiddler on the Roof*. That was the beauty of it. We were two kids— Jill was thirteen and I was nine—and we just got on the subway, the

Number 2 express to Forty-second Street, and then got out and walked. I was so impressed that there were kids in it. After that we saw a whole bunch of shows, Broadway, off-Broadway.

BETTY COMDEN: My parents loved music, and we had the traditional records: the Caruso, the Galli-Curci, the Misha Elman. The Metropolitan Opera and the Philharmonic gave performances at the Brooklyn Academy of Music at that time, and that's where I saw my first opera, heard my first symphony. You could have a very rich cultural life without even going across the Brooklyn Bridge.

Our apartment on Park Place and Kingston Avenue, in the Bedford section, was opposite a small park where the Brooklyn Children's Museum is situated. At that time it was in an old Victorian building that was quite wonderful. It had a library, stuffed animals and birds, wonderful dioramas of different periods of history, rooms depicting the way people lived. They showed old silent movies. Since it was right across the street, I went there all the time.

JOE SIGLER: One of my favorite places in Brooklyn was the library at Grand Army Plaza. I was always reading, always curious, and that library had every book, every magazine that you would want. Often I went there all by myself, and then I'd go over to the Brooklyn Museum, which is right down the street. That was another world. The Flatbush Avenue trolley car dropped me off right in front of the library, and in those days it was a nickel. I could have taken the subway, but with the trolley you could see things.

JOEL BERGER: I could take the trolley or the bus, but usually I took the Brighton line and switched to the Franklin Avenue Shuttle to get to my favorite place in all of Brooklyn: Ebbets Field. I'd walk out of the train station, and immediately I'd be hit by the aroma of baking bread from the Taystee factory. It would follow me all the way to the ballpark. I'd see the crowds descending, hear the yelling and screaming, and smell the bread—a total sensory experience.

CHARLES HYNES: We got off at the Prospect Station of the BMT to go to Ebbets Field. The voice of the guy selling programs would get stronger as we came closer: "The Dodgers are going to win. . . . The Dodgers are going to win."

JOE SIGLER: We'd walk seven long blocks on the other side of the Botanic Garden to Ebbets Field and wait outside the main gate. Friday was businessman's night. If a businessman had tickets for

somebody who didn't show up, he'd give them to us kids. And not only that, he'd treat us so nice—buy us hot dogs, soda.

DICK KITTRELL: Our apartment house, on President and Bedford, was so close to Ebbets Field, we snuck in on a regular basis. We dearly loved the Dodgers, except when people who drove to the games parked their cars on our block and interfered with our punchball games. There were no parking lots around Ebbets Field, so people had to park in the streets.

AL LEWIS: I was a great walker and would walk home from Ebbets Field on Bedford Avenue, straight down Eastern Parkway to Brownsville. You know what kind of a walk that is? But when the Dodgers won, it wasn't walking. It was flying.

What did I want when I was a kid? I wanted the Dodgers to win the pennant.

JOEL BERGER: During the 1950 baseball season, the Philadelphia Whiz Kids took the lead and were holding on. The Dodgers were something like seven games out with nine games to play. There was a doubleheader; I didn't get to hear it, but the Dodgers won both and picked up a game and a half. The next day, again I didn't get to hear the game, and again they won, and the Phillies lost. This convinced me if I had anything to do with the game, it would be a loss. But if I did not hear it, the Dodgers would win.

The pressure started to mount. The Phillies came into Ebbets Field for the last two games of the season. If the Dodgers won, they'd win the pennant. Everybody, everywhere was listening to the game. But

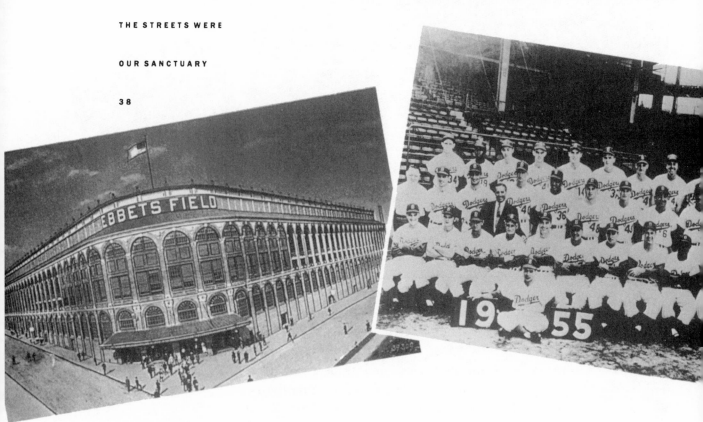

LEFT: That great little bandbox of a ball park where so many "waited for next year."

RIGHT: The Brooklyn Dodgers in their glory when "next year" finally arrived.

I went to the movies. There I was with a bunch of old women in the Claridge Movie Theater on Avenue P. I came out:

"What happened?"

"The Dodgers won."

The last game, I went to the Kingsway Movie Theater. That was the game in which Cal Abrams was thrown out at the plate. At least I knew I was not responsible.

Why was I a Dodger fan? Naturally, all the good people were Dodger fans. If a guy was a Yankee fan, you knew he was a nerd, out of touch. He was probably anti-union, not for good causes, had a rich uncle somewhere. If someone was a Giant fan, he was mixed up, like an anarchist, a nihilist—he was doing it to spite his family, his friends. A Giant fan. Who could be a Giant fan? Dodger fans were the salt of the earth, the common folk who believed in social progress, the American way, the underdog. Where did Jackie Robinson come to if not to Brooklyn? The Dodgers lived in Brooklyn. They could be your neighbors. You actually got to see them out of uniform, on the streets, doing things ordinary people did.

CLEM LABINE: After the kids were out of school, my family came down, and we rented a house in Bay Ridge. Quite a few of the Dodger contingent lived in that area: Pee Wee Reese, Duke Snider, Carl Erskine, Russ Meyer. Preacher Roe lived in the Seventies. Gil Hodges lived on Bedford Avenue.

BILL FEIGENBAUM: We used to see Gil Hodges on the way to junior high school. We saw him wash his car. His wife complained to the principal to please have the kids stop coming around.

JOEL MARTIN: Walking by Gil Hodges's house on Bedford Avenue, we'd jump up and try to look in the windows, which we never could; or walk back and forth; or stand across the street for hours waiting for someone to come out.

MAX WECHSLER: When school was out, I sometimes went with my father in his taxi. One summer morning, we were driving in East Flatbush, down Snyder Avenue, when he pointed out a dark red brick house with a high porch. "I think Jackie Robinson lives there," he said. He parked across the street, and we got out of the cab, stood on the sidewalk, and looked at it.

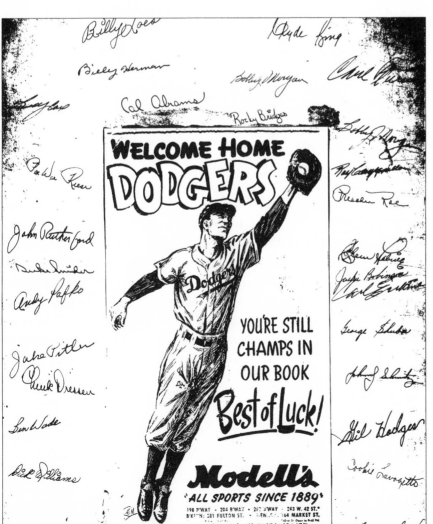

Suddenly the front door opened. A black man in a short-sleeved shirt stepped out. I didn't believe it. Here we were on a quiet street on a summer morning. No one else was around. This man was not wearing the baggy, ice-cream-white uniform of the Brooklyn Dodgers that accentuated his blackness. He was dressed in regular clothes, coming out of a regular house in a regular Brooklyn neighborhood, a guy like anyone else, going for a newspaper or a bottle of milk.

Then incredibly, he crossed the street and came right toward me. Seeing that unmistakable pigeon-toed walk, the rock of the shoulders and hips I had seen so many times on the baseball field, I had no doubt who it was.

"Hi Jackie, I'm one of your biggest fans," I said self-consciously. "Do you think the Dodgers are gonna win the pennant this year?"

His handsome face looked sternly down at me. "We'll try our best," he said.

"Good luck," I said.

"Thanks." He put his big hand out, and I took it. We shook hands, and I felt the strength and firmness of his grip.

I was a nervy kid, but I didn't ask for an autograph or think to prolong the conversation. I just watched as he walked away down the street.

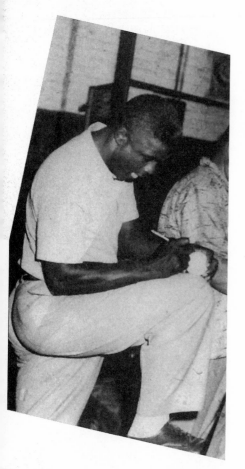

HERBY GREISSMAN: It was a tremendous treat if my father would give up his time and take me to a baseball game. Once we were next to a priest. My father struck up a conversation with him, and he ended up buying beers for everyone in the whole area. There was that kind of feeling at Ebbets Field. Except when the Giants came. Then it was war.

STEWIE STONE: It was like your father's a Democrat, you're a Democrat. My father was a Giants fan, I was a Giants fan. Sal Maglie to me was scary, with that beard. But I loved him; he was a Giant. Until they traded him to the Dodgers. Then I hated him.

It was great to argue with the kids in the neighborhood because they were all Dodger fans. If the Giants lost, they would all come into the alley and yell up to my window, "Hey Stewie, we really got you today, ha-ha-ha." When Bobby Thomson hit the home run that gave the Giants the pennant in 1951, I ran down the street to my father's dance studio to tell him. I was the only one in the street who was happy. Brooklyn was dead.

JOHN DOWNIE: It was the rare kid in Brooklyn who wasn't a Dodger fan. They knew everything about them, felt so close to them they called them by nicknames: Oisk for Erskine, Skoonj for Furillo, Ski for Hermanski, Cookie for Harry Lavagetto.

MAX WECHSLER: In those days, before baseball encyclopedias and readily available stats, baseball knowledge came from newspapers, scorecards, baseball cards. The facts were stored in our heads. On the steamy summer nights, we played all kinds of baseball word games. "Initials" was a game where one guy would stand on the top of the stoop, and a bunch of kids on the sidewalk would shout out initials: "JR" (Jackie Robinson), "VR" (Vic Raschi)—that was the easy stuff. The more rabid baseball types would have a supply of the same initials for different players and would fire them off to the kid on the stoop: "DL" (Don Liddle), "DL again" (Dick Littlefield). One set of initials referred to fourteen players. Then there were the variations. One was "reverse initials": "RJ" (Ransom Jackson, John Roseboro). Another was replacing initials with nicknames. Virtually every Dodger player had a nickname. "The Reading Rifle" (Carl Furillo), "Shotgun" (George Shuba). In another version, "geog-

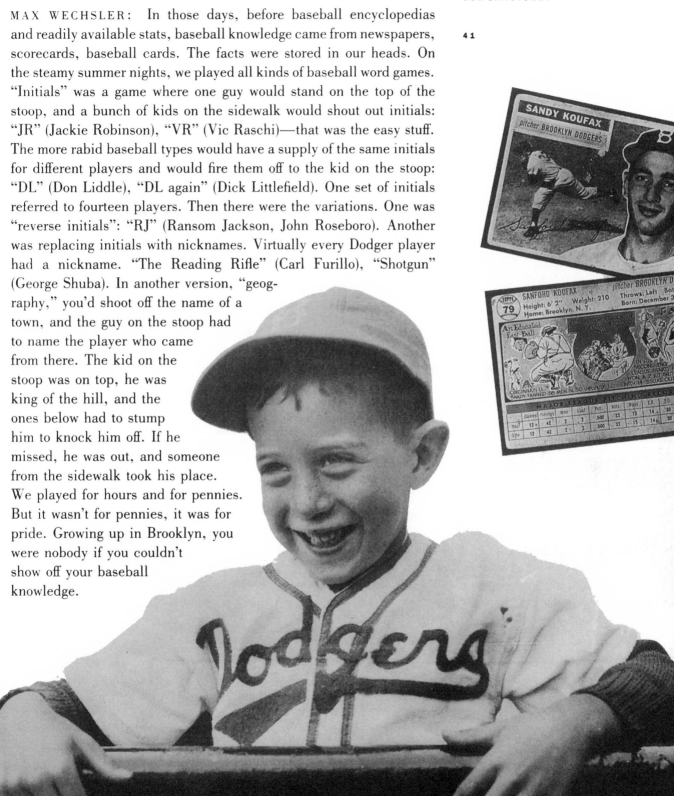

raphy," you'd shoot off the name of a town, and the guy on the stoop had to name the player who came from there. The kid on the stoop was on top, he was king of the hill, and the ones below had to stump him to knock him off. If he missed, he was out, and someone from the sidewalk took his place. We played for hours and for pennies. But it wasn't for pennies, it was for pride. Growing up in Brooklyn, you were nobody if you couldn't show off your baseball knowledge.

CHAPTER 2

School Days

**REMEMBER THE ROW,
REMEMBER THE SEAT,
REMEMBER THE WAY
WE USED TO CHEAT.**

—Autograph album, P.S. 226

CAROLINE KATZ MOUNT: Every spring, my father was worried and unhappy. He was a furrier, and that was his slack season. But one spring morning when I was seven years old and he was at home because there was no work, he decided to walk me to school. Our neighbor Frieda leaned out her kitchen window, which faced the street. We stopped off to say good morning, and my father said, "Look how pretty Caroline is." He held my hand all the way, down the block and around the corner, past the two-family houses with their neat front gardens. Then we crossed Sixty-fifth Street and walked by the big empty lot that was filled with spiky little daisies and dandelions and other wildflowers. All the children were walking to school this beautiful morning, carrying their books; the boys fooling around, the girls giggling with each other. And there I was in a little white sun dress with red flowers and a matching jacket, walking hand-in-hand with my father, who suddenly seemed very happy.

JOAN RIBAUDO: There were no school buses, and no one was driven to school by car. You'd see a march of mothers with children in hand, walking to school.

STEWIE STONE: You'd meet kids along the way, wait on the corner for your friends from down the block. Everybody would gather and walk together in a little crowd. If during the school day it started to rain, the mothers showed up at dismissal with umbrellas and galoshes.

BOB LEVY: P.S. 161 was directly across from our apartment on Crown Street. Our living room faced the schoolyard. I was in that schoolyard every Saturday and Sunday morning at 7:00 A.M., because if you didn't get there early you weren't chosen into the games. But school days, I had to walk all the way down to the corner and wait to be crossed by the crossing guard. I was late every day.

MIRIAM KITTRELL: P.S. 177, on Avenue P and West First Street, was typical of the schools built in the 1920s: four or five stories, dark red brick. The roof was enclosed by some kind of iron latticework, like a big dome. On nice days we had gym classes up there, and when we looked out, we could see as far as the parachute at Coney Island.

My mother took me to kindergarten class the first day of school and saw the children playing. "What do the children do here?" she asked.

"They play, and they learn," the teacher told her.

"Play? She could play at home," said my mother.

I never went to kindergarten.

Out of the classroom but still in uniform, elementary school teachers enjoy moments of rare repose.

CAROLINE KATZ MOUNT: My sister started school before me. I was terribly jealous. My first day, my mother and I walked up this great marble staircase. It was so beautiful. We went into the principal's office. I said, "What's my teacher's name?"

The woman said, "If I tell you, will you say good morning to her?"

I said, "Of course." It was funny because my mother was very quiet, and I was four and a half years old. But I felt very much at home. There was nothing scary about it.

Yet, at the same time, school *was* scary. The teachers could be intimidating; they had so much power. In first grade, my job was to set the table in the back of the room. I kept forgetting which was my right and which was my left, and sometimes I put the fork on the right side. One day the teacher yelled at me, "If you do this one more time, you'll lose this job." The next day was the only day in my life that I played hooky. I told my mother I had a stomachache, because I was so afraid I would not remember which was my right and which my left. Later, when I banged my finger in the door and one of my right nails became misshapen, I was glad, because now I had a sign for which was my right.

MARNIE BERNSTEIN: In the second grade, I had a teacher who had just come into the school. Mrs. Winters was young, tall, and attractive, but I felt there was something cold about her. One afternoon, we were lined up to leave, standing along the wardrobe wall, and my friend Ruthie said to me, "You called me a lucky dog." I said, "I did not." Mrs. Winters heard me talking, and she made me get off the line and go back to my seat. "You wait there till I come back," she said. She marched out with the other children, and I remained behind.

Back then, I was very much afraid of being left alone, and there I was, all alone, I thought, in the whole school. It was very quiet.

I must have panicked, because I bolted from the room and raced down the single flight of stairs and out the door. My mother was waiting for me by the schoolyard gate with my sister in the baby carriage, puzzled by why I wasn't there with the rest of the class. Mrs. Winters was nearby, seeing the children off. When she noticed me, she came over and made some kind of explanation to my mother. There was never anything said or done about it afterward. But for Christmas, my father bought Mrs. Winters a box of handkerchiefs. She was very nice to me after that.

CAROLINE KATZ MOUNT: I wore glasses, and in fourth grade, the teacher sat us alphabetically. I ended up in the back and told her I couldn't see the board from there, but she didn't seem to care. My mother wrote her a note, and she still didn't do anything. Finally, my mother went to see her. "Of course we'll change her seat," the teacher said. "You know, we teachers are not monsters."

In sixth grade, our teacher taught us to make an *X* without lifting the pen. There was a little boy from Czechoslovakia in our class, and one time she chided him for lifting his pen. He said, "But Mrs. Fisher, you do it." And she said, "I do not. Do I, class?" We all said, "No, Mrs. Fisher." But we lied. She did lift her pen. We were afraid to tell the truth.

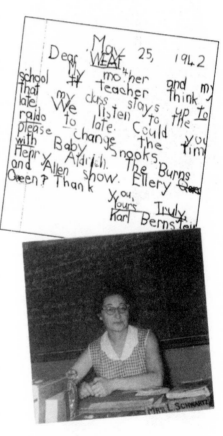

DORIS MODELL TIPOGRAPH: P.S. 99—"It stands for all that's helpful and everything that's fine"—was on East Tenth between Avenues K and L. In the eighth grade, all the girls had to sew their graduation dresses. I had gotten this beautiful organza material at Namm-Loeser's, but I had trouble sewing the French seams. You had to stitch it, turn it over, and stitch it again. So my grandmother did the first stitching on the machine, and I did the other stitching by hand. Miss McCarthy, my gray-haired, pinched-faced teacher, who always wore black, examined my work and spotted the machine stitch. She made me stand in front of the whole class while she ripped the dress open.

JUDY BERGER: Woody Allen named the character Mia Farrow played in *Zelig* after Eudora Fletcher, the principal of P.S. 99, and the photographer in the movie after the husband of Mrs. Degay, who taught sixth grade. Miss Fletcher must have been at P.S. 99 for forty years. She wore bolero-type jackets with frog fasteners. Her hair was pulled back into not one but two buns. She ruled that school with an iron fist. All the teachers were in fear of her.

MARNIE BERNSTEIN: P.S. 177 was run like a military academy. It was right after the war, so that was the influence. We were put through marching drills: right-face, left-face, mark time in place. The whole system of student monitors was based on the military. There were the line and stair guards, and then the officers: sergeant, lieutenant, and captain; separate sets for boys and girls. We had badges. It was a prestigious thing to be in the guards, and most prestigious to be one of the officers. I was Sergeant of the Girl Guards in the sixth grade and got to blow a whistle and say, "On line!" and the kids had to assemble on lines. And then we'd say, "Lines forward," and the lines would proceed from the gym or, in nice weather, the yard to their classrooms—in total silence. If you spoke, one of the guards might spot you and give you a Guard Report, which was noted on your Permanent Record. I was never quite sure what the Permanent Record was, but I knew it was something very significant that would stay with you for your entire life.

TOBY SCHOM GROSSMAN: The times I felt bad at school were when they did census reports. This woman would go around to each class and say, "Anybody not born in the United States, please stand up." I was usually the only one.

STAN GOLDBERG: Unlike a lot of my friends' parents, both my parents were born here. In fifth grade, when my mother came up on Open School Day, the teacher said to her, "I'm surprised to see you're one of the American mothers. From your son's handwriting, I'd never know it."

MARNIE BERNSTEIN: Many of us were first-generation Americans, and we were given strong doses of patriotic indoctrination. We sang songs like "Columbia the Gem of the Ocean," "Our Flag Is the Flag for Me," and "This Is My Country." Assemblies began with a color guard processional, with one of the bigger boys carrying a huge American flag set into a holder strapped around his waist.

Miss Harrington was the assistant principal of P.S. 177. She had silver hair that was perfectly waved and wore a lace handkerchief pulled through her wristwatch. "I wish I had a camera so I could take

a photograph of you," she would tell us as she stood on the stage of the auditorium, with a picture of George Washington on one side and Abraham Lincoln on the other. We were dressed all alike for assembly day: girls in white middy blouses with red ties and navy pleated skirts, boys in white shirts, red ties, and navy pants.

LONNY IRGENS: I felt the sense of being American through the assemblies every Thursday. I loved singing the patriotic songs and dressing up in red, white, and blue.

MARNIE BERNSTEIN: Each assembly, one class put on a play, and another class did a choral reading of a psalm. In addition to the patriotic songs, we sang a lot of hymns: "The Lord's Prayer," "The Lord Is My Shepherd" set to music, and "We Gather Together" at Thanksgiving. We also sang all the Christmas carols, even though at least half the children were Jewish. But no one seemed to mind.

ANGELO BADALAMENTI: All the teachers at P.S. 177 loved my playing of "Argonnaise." It was my piece, one of the numbers I performed regularly at assemblies. But one day, in the middle of the piece, I looked up into the auditorium and saw all the kids, all the white shirts and middy blouses and red ties, and I stopped. "I can't perform," I said, and ran out of the auditorium crying. Mrs. Doyle, my sixth-grade teacher, came after me. "Angelo, you have to go back," she said. She wouldn't let me give it up. The next week, I went back, played it through, and got a standing ovation.

Every morning I would walk up to the corner and wait for Mrs. Mary Doyle. She'd come down Avenue P from the Stillwell Avenue

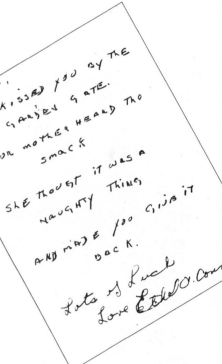

P.S. 177, the school run like a military academy.

bus stop, passing my corner at 8:20 A.M. We would walk the next seven blocks to school together, talking about this and that. She was very Irish, not terribly warm in her approach. But I loved her.

MIRIAM KITTRELL: Many of the teachers were Irish women. There was Miss O'Donald the art teacher, Miss Williams, Mrs. Cunningham, Mrs. Doyle. After I graduated and moved on, I realized they all wore the Hunter College ring. And they all loved baseball and the Brooklyn Dodgers. World Series time they would bring in radios, and we would stop classes to listen to the games.

"The teachers knew their job. Whatever they said was right."

JUDY BERGER: Sometimes the whole game was broadcast over the PA. At the very least, we'd get the score at the end of each half-inning.

MAX WECHSLER: Nobody could take my job away during World Series time: putting the score up, half-inning by half-inning, on the blackboard. I'd get the boards ready by washing them with water and black ink, so the chalk would show off, and I'd use two different colors to distinguish between the Dodgers and the Yankees. That gave the teachers something nice to say about me when my mother came up on Open School Night.

MIRIAM KITTRELL: My parents did not come on Open School nights. They didn't want to be bothered. The teachers knew their job. Whatever they said was right. I just had to bring home a good report card. PTA meetings—forget it. I had to pay the dues myself. The teachers used to make us crazy. They had to have 100 percent PTA so they could hang up those pennants in the window of the classroom door. I used to save up the nickels I got to buy Mounds bars to pay the dues.

JOEL BERGER: In first grade, the teacher sat behind the piano and called you up one at a time to sing while she played a little song. You were pronounced either a robin or a sparrow—a singer or a listener—a judgment that followed you all through elementary school. Most of the people I knew were listeners.

IRWIN POLISHOOK: I was a sparrow. I didn't sing. But I would whistle a lot.

GAIL EISEMAN BERNSTEIN: I was a P.S. 181 listener. I couldn't carry a tune. I also have a dead ear. The robins sang, "Remember your name and address and telephone number too. . . ." or "Let the ball roll, let the ball roll no matter where it may go. . . ." We learned a lot of those safety songs. The teacher walked around the room. "One of the robins or sparrows is not doing what he or she is supposed to," she said, trying to catch the singing sparrow. That was me. When she came near, I shut up. As soon as she moved on, I sang along, off-key.

MARNIE BERNSTEIN: We were three robins who regularly sang the same songs, party after party, term after term. I did the World War II ballad "Mamselle." Ruthie Freedman, a dynamic little brunette, did "The Rich Maharaja of Macador," and Barbara Sanders—who was cool, blonde, and beautiful even in fourth grade—sang "Ah, Sweet Mystery of Life" in a lovely, lyric soprano voice.

Mrs. Marcus, who played the piano for all the assemblies, was our fifth-grade teacher. She was tall and pretty and wore her short dark hair in what they used to call the feather-cut. She dressed in "New Look" outfits—long, swirly skirts and blouses with ruffles around the neck and sleeves. For Christmas, we put on a musical play in which the children represented toys from all over the world. Barbara Sanders was the nurse doll, Ruthie Freedman was the French doll in gorgeous pink organza, and I was the Dutch doll in an authentic costume—courtesy of the Netherlands Board of Trade—right down to the clunky wooden shoes.

ANGELO BADALAMENTI: Emma Marcus was the wife of Colonel Mickey Marcus, the only American buried at West Point who died in the service of another country. He was killed in the Israeli War of

Form 77-6725 (2A-6B) 750M-2-47

P.S. *181*   Borough *B'Klyn*

Board of Education
City of New York
—
Report Card

In the development of these traits, the home shares responsibility with the school.

TRAINING IN PERSONALITY Desirable Traits	Nov.3½ Dec.3½ Mar.15 May 15	Jan.31 Jun.30	
1. Works and plays well with others	S	S	S
2. Completes work	S	S	S
3. Is generally careful	S	U	I
4. Respects the rights of others	S	S	S
5. Practices good health habits	S	S	S
6. Speaks clearly	S	S	S
7. *Behavior*		S	S
8.			

MEANING OF RATINGS
S—Satisfactory   U—Unsatisfactory
            I—Improvement is shown
A—Excellent   B—Good
C—Passable   D—Failing

When per cent ratings are used, ... % is the passing rating, except in Spelling, where .... % is required.

Independence. I remember reading about it in the papers that morning, and when I came into class, there she was with all the other teachers around her, hugging her and crying.

MARNIE BERNSTEIN: Mrs. Conan was another music teacher, and a great lover of Gilbert and Sullivan. In sixth grade, we had club periods. She was in charge of the glee club. For graduation, we put on *The Pirates of Penzance*. Imagine, an operetta in elementary school.

BETTY COMDEN: I went to a wonderful school that no longer exists: the Brooklyn Ethical Culture School, begun by the people who started the Ethical Culture Society. They were pacifists, gentle and wonderful people. The school was new when I entered at the age of five. I was in the first class. They added a class every year, so I was always in the top class. The school was across the street from Prospect Park, on Prospect Park West and First Street. We did our athletics in the park and had spring festivals there. We didn't celebrate Christmas or Easter, since this was an ecumenical school. Instead we had a winter festival, a spring festival—like Old England: yule logs, that kind of thing.

We were encouraged to express ourselves. I was excused from arithmetic if I felt like writing a poem. We studied things in themes. If it was Greek history, for example, we had a Greek festival, studied Greek art and literature. One teacher I remember clearly, Delia Stebbens, encouraged us to take different books and dramatize them. I did *Ivanhoe*.

JOE SIGLER: I had tough, motivating teachers in elementary school. We had to read "The News of the Week in Review" in *The New York Times* every Sunday, and we were tested on it every Monday. For the most part, the teachers lived in the neighborhood. They had a neighborhood interest in us. It was like a small town in that way. You didn't cut school, because someone would see you and tell your parents; you couldn't go to the movies, because no kid was allowed in the movies until after three o'clock.

KARL BERNSTEIN: When he discovered I could play the cello, Mr. Levy drafted me into the Seth Low Junior High School orchestra. It was made up of thirty trumpets, four violins, a clarinet, and now, a cello. Mr. Levy played the violin and conducted at the same time. The setup offended me. I spent the better part of my two and a half years at Seth Low hiding from him. In front of my class, he would say I had no school spirit.

STAN GOLDBERG: The black teacher on the TV show *Brooklyn Bridge* is modeled after Mr. Webb, who was an English teacher and later an assistant principal at Seth Low Junior High. Here we were, all white, mostly Jewish kids, and our two role models were Mr. Webb and Jackie Robinson.

CAROLINE KATZ MOUNT: Mr. Webb was so smart, he made literature so exciting. Also, he was much younger than most of the other teachers, and tall and thin—a handsome, elegant man.

I was active in student government at Seth Low, and Arnold Webb was the faculty advisor. It was the time of Little Rock. We had a meeting in the principal's office about it. We must have had an assembly program or some kind of protest, but all I remember is wondering whether Mr. Webb wasn't embarrassed over the whole situation. Here we were so concerned that something bad was going on in Little Rock. Yet nobody seemed to notice that aside from Mr. Webb, there wasn't one black person in the whole school.

CLARENCE NORMAN, SR.: I moved up from a small town near Fort Bragg, North Carolina, to the Williamsburg section of Brooklyn. I really suffered from culture shock coming from a segregated southern school to P.S. 122, on Harrison Avenue, which was nearly all white.

The children were friendly. The teachers, who were all white, were friendly too. They really bent over backward to try to involve me. They made me a hall monitor. Needless to say, the entire time I was in elementary school, I got As in conduct. I was the nicest kid in class, but I was very unhappy. The first summer I went back to North Carolina with the intention of remaining. It had been too much of a sudden change, going from a small rural farming community to Brooklyn. But the irony was that after the summer, I realized that I liked Brooklyn more than I thought I did. I actually begged my mother to bring me back.

ROGER GREEN: I always felt, from first grade on, very oppressed and repressed in the public school system. When I attended P.S. 44, on Madison Street in Bedford-Stuyvesant, all the kids were black, but the whole power structure was white except for one African-American teacher. The class categorizations in the school were almost always color-conscious even within the context of an African-American population. We had 1-A, which might have been the smartest, and those children were the lightest-skinned, etc. When I went to P.S. 221 in Crown Heights and Winthrop Junior High School, it was the same kind of thing: the white students were always in the smarter classes and the black students in the so-called slower classes. It really implanted in the minds of some of the children this subliminal message that you're just not as bright.

I took the IQ exam and scored poorly on it. As a result of that one test, they wanted to put me in one of the slower classes. My mother was a fighter, and she challenged it. She said, "I don't know if one test can determine intelligence. At home he's reading everything. Maybe he just can't take tests."

CLARENCE NORMAN, SR.: I was sent to George Washington Vocational High School because it appeared on paper, from my test scores and grades, that I might have been rather slow, that I was not college material. I was looked upon as one of those children who was going to be a failure. The best thing for me, according to the guidance counselors, was to take up a vocational trade. I was to be relegated to the trash pile. What did I say about it? I felt they were the experts. They knew more about what was best for me than I did.

ROGER GREEN: I was in the second or third grade when some young folks broke into the school building, got into an office, and stole some materials. The following week, my class was getting ready to go on a trip when I was pulled out of the class line and sent into a classroom where there were three white police officers. At first I wasn't scared, because I didn't know what it was about. But I will never forget it. They sat me down, surrounded me, and were very abusive, shouting and cursing. It frightened me very much. I told my father, and he was very upset. He came up to the school and challenged the principal and the teacher. He said if there was any question as to whether I had done anything wrong, he should have been notified.

What happened was that a student in what we would now define as a Special Ed class had said I was part of the group that broke into the school. It was interesting because he was in Special Ed because, among other things, he was visually impaired. Earlier I had been in the playground when some kids were belittling and demeaning him. Now I have a clear understanding of the anger and frustration that he must have felt. At that time, though, I was so traumatized that for about two to three weeks I played hooky. My parents didn't know.

PAT COOPER: The teacher at P.S. 242 said, "All right, Pasquale, get up here. Tell us about Christopher Columbus." I got up in front of the room. "The guy had bloomers on," I said. I made Christopher Columbus so funny that she hit me.

Your father and mother always found out. "Did you say Christopher Columbus wore bloomers? What kind of respect is that?" my father said.

Next day, I'd be black and blue. "What happened?" the teacher asked.

> If all the boys were across the sea
> What a swimmer Gail would be

> Ivan Bernstein
> Today we saw a movie about Santa Claus. I liked the picture very much. I saw it three times. The best part was when the postmen brought a few million letters into the court. The letters were sent to Santa Claus by all the children. This showed the judge that there must be a Santa Claus but I don't believe in Santa Claus.

CLASS
OF
JUNE 1952
P.S. 181
6-1

"My father threw me out the window."

"Oh," she said. "OK."

"Just make sure the teacher don't call me to come to school and I lose a day's work," my father would say. "Or I'll electrocute you. Get a chair, a nice wire, and boom!"

ANNETTE DE LUCIA-CLARK: In the late 1950s, when my parents separated, we moved from the Bronx to the fourteen-story Gowanus Housing Project at 417 Baltic Street. We didn't live well in the Bronx, but moving to the projects in Brooklyn was going down in the world.

My older sister and I were placed in the CRMD class at P.S. 6 —that's for children with mental and medical disabilities. We shared the same clothes even though she was larger than me. Nothing ever fit. The clothes would be basted, or I'd wear a belt around the waist, or a rope. At night we'd wash what I wore, take out the basting, and my sister would wear it the next day. Most of the time at school we slept on cots and did recess. Miss Henry, one of the good teachers there, taught arts and crafts to a class of forty. She taught us how to sew. Guys would ask, "What do we need this for?" And she would tell them, "One of these days you'll thank me for giving you a skill." Some of those guys became tailors. Some of those girls became seamstresses.

The Catholic church felt we shouldn't be in that type of surrounding. St. Agnes Church, on Hoyt Street, took us for a year. Sister Margaret seemed very tall, but I was only four-foot-nine, and anyone seemed tall to me. One day she took a young man who was causing trouble, threw him against the wall, and beat him up. But she did not terrify me. What could scare me? I was a prisoner of life.

CHARLES HYNES: I went to Immaculate Heart of Mary, on Caton Avenue and East Third. I used to think the street was named after Father Caton, the pastor. We were taught by the St. Joseph sisters, who wore the old traditional habit and were very strict. Sister Jeanne DeLourdes, who taught fifth grade, hit very hard. I complained to my mother. But even though she was so protective she took me to and from school every day, she let the sister complete whatever discipline cycle was started. My mother's youngest sister had died shortly after her birth, and Sister Jeanne would have been the same age, which is maybe why my mother became very fond of her. By the time I left Immaculate Heart, in sixth grade, Sister Jeanne had become a fixture in our family.

TOM BOORAS: We were parishioners of St. Charles Borromeo, on Sydney Place in Brooklyn Heights, and I attended its grammar school, which was directly across from our house. I was taught by the sisters, who wore the long black habits and covered their hair with big winged headdresses.

Under their capes, they carried little metal castanets, the kind you used to get as prizes in Cracker Jack boxes. The class would go into church and all the kids would be finding seats in the pews, and you'd hear this *CLICK*. Everyone froze. *CLICK* again. Everyone stood up. *CLICK* one more time. Everyone genuflected. The nuns were very big on group discipline. They liked it when everybody did the same thing at the exact same time.

They were also big on penmanship. Your handwriting had to have this perfect slant. And if you were a lefty, forget it. To this day I write with my right hand although I was born a lefty. While we practiced our penmanship, the nuns would walk up and down the aisle with a ruler. You'd sense this black figure hovering over you as you struggled to get the correct slant. Sometimes you'd get a smack right across your knuckles. What for? You didn't dot your *i*.

But out in the yard, the sisters were terrific. We were seven, eight years old; they were twenty-two, twenty-three. They played everything with us: basketball, volleyball, handball. And some of them were great athletes. Running across the court with their big habits flapping around, the sleeves of their capes wide as wings, they looked to me like giant black birds.

A bevy of "little brides" dressed for their first communion.

JOAN RIBAUDO: Two o'clock on Wednesday afternoons, we were dismissed from P.S. 247 to go to St. Anthanasius for religious instruc-

tion. We were maybe twenty kids running the fourteen blocks up Bay Parkway to get there on time. No matter what the weather—there could be four inches of snow, our feet could be frostbitten—we made sure we got there before the bell.

The reason was the principal. She'd stand in the doorway—a stern, short woman, no more than five feet tall. Behind her, the hallway was dark. All you would see was this little figure in the black habit with a ruler in her hand. If you came late, she'd give you a whack across the knuckles with the ruler.

We had only one hour of religious instruction a week in preparation for our communion and confirmation. There weren't too many explanations given or answers to questions. Whatever it said in the Bible, that was it.

I could never understand why so many of the nuns had men's names, like Sister Thomas Aquinas. They took saints' names, I guess, because they sounded holier than their own. Some of them were nice, though. One was young, very sweet to everyone. She used to tell us to be on our best behavior when she thought the principal was roaming the halls. She didn't want to get reprimanded either.

My communion was on a beautiful spring day. There were over a hundred of us, little brides dressed in white dresses and veils. The custom was that after your communion, your parents presented you with a little bouquet of nosegays. But I remember coming out of the church and seeing my father, his arms filled with a massive bouquet of orange gladioli. I ran over to him, and he put this enormous beautiful bouquet in my arms. It was almost as big as I was, and I thought to myself, "Look at this. Aren't I swell?"

Seth Low Junior High School's 1948 graduation ceremony included the transfer of the colors to the new color guard.

Look, Ma, I'm Dancing!

**PLAY IT ON THE PIANO,
BANG IT ON THE DRUM,
LOOK OUT, MISTER,
HERE I COME.**

—Jump-rope rhyme

KARL BERNSTEIN: All over Brooklyn there were kids banging away on pianos, blowing horns, scratching out melodies on violins, singing up and down the scales: "do-re-mi-fa-sol-la-ti-do."

NORMAN SPIZZ: Every kid on my block played an instrument. When you walked down the block after school was out, you would hear them all at the same time: trumpets, saxophones, clarinets, drums, pianos, accordions, cellos, violins—each playing something different. I took up the trumpet. The very first song I learned was "You Belong to Me."

LARRY STRICKLER: The immigrant parents wanted to enhance their children's lives and believed that culture was the way. Not that they wanted their children to become artists or musicians; they wanted them to become doctors and lawyers. But they had a picture of a successful person, and that included culture.

FREDDIE GERSHON: My mother bought an old upright piano for a dollar. I picked out the melody of "Buttons and Bows," which I'd heard in a Bob Hope movie. I was able to get it because the melody is the five black notes. My mother thought Mozart had been reborn in her home. A local music teacher was not good enough for me—I had to go to Juilliard.

NEIL SEDAKA: I was fascinated with an accordion that one of my uncles brought back from the war. When I was in the second grade, I was picked to lead the class in singing, and the teacher told my mother she thought I had musical talent. Then my mother saw I could play melodies by ear on a neighbor's piano. So when I was eight years old, I started taking piano lessons, together with my sister. We practiced on Myra Auerbach's piano in her sixth-floor apartment. But after a while, my mother got a job as a saleswoman at A & S for a year and made enough money to buy me a secondhand piano.

I practiced the piano five hours a day. I loved it. I was a shy and introverted kid. I didn't play ball, I was always playing music. I planned to be a concert pianist. After my first year of lessons, my teacher said I was too advanced for him and that I should go to a school that could really develop my talent. So my mother started taking me on the subway up to Juilliard every Saturday.

FREDDIE GERSHON: I'm not sure I would have stayed at Juilliard if not for my buddy Neil Sedaka. After a while, we started traveling alone, and every Saturday became an adventure. Neil was so small and frail-looking that he actually was able to get in under the turnstile and not pay the nickel to get on the BMT. We counted stops on the train. Sometimes we stood in the front car and watched the tracks and lights. But mainly we looked at faces to keep ourselves occupied. We tried to imagine who each person was and made up stories about them.

PETER NERO: I picked out tunes on a one-octave toy xylophone my parents bought me—which probably cost eight cents in those days. At night, I'd sing myself to sleep tapping on the bed with my knuckles. I did not come face-to-face with a piano until I was seven years old. We were visiting a relative, and I just started to play on their upright the way I had played the xylophone. My grandmother convinced the relatives they didn't need the piano anymore. It barely fit into our apartment.

When I was seven, my father bought a forty-year-old reconditioned Steinway on the advice of a teacher for one hundred dollars. We lived in a four-family, two-story dwelling, and it was impossible to get the piano up the stairs. It had to be hoisted up to the second floor by a lift anchored on the roof of the building.

From the time I was seven until I was eleven, my father went with me for my lessons every Saturday. We took the subway to either the Grand Army Plaza station or Kingston Avenue. After, we visited the Brooklyn Botanic Garden, the Brooklyn Museum, Prospect Park. I don't know how many pictures were taken of me as a child in Prospect Park. In 1945, at age eleven, I made my official concert debut at the Brooklyn Academy of Music.

ROBERT MERRILL: My mother wanted me to grow up and be a big fat opera singer. She was careful of what I ate. In those days they would buy boiled beef on the bone. She'd not only have the beef, she'd make a big soup with the marrow of the bone melted in. It was quite nourishing. My mother could feed my kid brother, my father, and me for five bucks a week.

We lived in a tenement flat in Williamsburg with no heat except from the stove. My mother didn't like me breathing the polluted air; she thought it would harm my voice. She gave a tugboat captain a couple of dollars to take me out on the water with him so I could breathe the fresh air of the East River.

She sang around professionally under the name of Lillian Miller. She brought music into the home, got a piano for peanuts that someone was throwing out. Once she borrowed a hand-pumped Victrola and got a Caruso recording. I used to shut the windows when she put those records on, so my friends downstairs wouldn't hear. They would have

"All over Brooklyn, there were kids banging away on pianos, blowing horns, scratching out melodies on violins, singing up and down the scales."

called me a fag, because listening to classical music was considered a sissy thing to do. But when I listened to "O sole mio" or "Vesti la giubba" from *Pagliacci*, instinctively I felt something. I tried to imitate it. I did not want to tell anyone how I felt, not even my mother, because I wanted to play baseball—that was the big thing in my life. But listening to Caruso, something stirred in me.

ANGELO BADALAMENTI: I grew up listening to Enrico Caruso, Carlo Buti, all the Neapolitan and classical songs on the old 78-rpm, twelve-inch records. There was always music in the house. My father was an amateur singer. My older brother played the trumpet. It was his idea that I take up piano. We could barely afford the old upright, a player piano with the works taken out.

I started lessons when I was eight. When I was eleven, I wanted to stop, because practicing interfered with stickball games. My father was thrilled that he could save the three dollars a week, but my brother insisted I continue. Then, in the first year of junior high, I began to notice the girls would come over and sit next to me on the piano bench when I played. After that you couldn't get me away from the piano.

KARL BERNSTEIN: First I took piano lessons from Miss Leitman, who came to the house. When I was in fifth grade, I went to the Brooklyn Music School, on St. Felix Street. Then I stopped the piano and took cello lessons. My father was a violinist, although a lousy one, and my mother was a very fine pianist. They needed a cellist in order to have a trio.

LEONA ANTEL DANCE STUDIO

presents

VARIETY REVUE

Thursday Evening, June 7th, 1951
at 7:30 o'clock

BROOKLYN ACADEMY OF MUSIC

---•◆•---

PROGRAM

Entire production created by Leona Antel

ACT ONE

1. OPENING — Song _____ Frank Alesi and Rochelle Brodsky, Lavern Brown, Patricia Brown, Norma Farca, Ilene Greisman, Carolyn Katz, Angela Panarello, Annette Passamonte, Adrianne Passamonte, Susan Kunen, Gloria Polansky, Karen Sorci, Lila Goldstein, Cynthia La Rocca
   Words of Opening song by James Selva _____ Gae Blau, Joyce Fantelli
1A. DANCE _____ Angela Friscia, Marie Anne Friscia, Yvette Jaeger, Carolyn Saiya, Barbara Gellerman, Joan Winston, Joan Legrand, Brenda Kaftal, Sheryl Shapiro, Barbara Pasternack
2. GOOD MORNING _____ Cynthia La Rocca, Joyce Shapiro
3. SONG AND DANCE _____ Barbara Trepidie,
4. WILAMENIA — Song & Dance _____ Joseph Trepiedi, Frank Alesi
5. DAINTY MISSES _____ Dianne Glatzer, Judith Wollock
6. PRESCHOOL TAP _____ Marylin Frectman, Betty Giaruso, Sharon Kaplan, Barbara Kreisman, Anna Pantrello, Ginger Rollo
6A. TWO GOBS _____ Carol Poppiceno, Charles Marmo
7. MODERN MOOD _____ Sheryl Shapiro
8. LET'S DO IT AGAIN — Song & Dance _____ Beginners Tap Rochelle Brodsky, Lavern Brown, Patricia Brown, Carolyn Katz, Norfca Farca, Ilene Greisman, Susan Kunen, Angela Panarello, Annette Passamonte, Adrianne Passamonte, Gloria Polansky, Karen Sorci, Lila Goldstein, Cynthia La Rocca
9. CLAP YOUR HANDS _____ Arlene Ryman

PROGRAM - continued

9A. PONY BALLET _____ Angela Friscia, Marie Anne Friscia, Dianne Glatzer, Adv. Toe Group Marylin Silverberg, Maxine Richland, Yvette Jaeger, Carolyn Saiya, wiex, Joan Winston, Laurel Sikorowiez
10. DIANNE
11. TEA FOR TWO
12. SOME OF THESE DAYS — Song _____ Joan Legrand
13. TAP DANCE _____ Debra Roth
14A. PIZZACATO _____ Ellen Kaufman
15. CHALLENGE _____ Susette Haber
    Carol May, Joan Epifania, Gae Blau, Joyce Fantelli, Angela Friscia, Marie Anne Friscia, Yvette Jaeger, Friday Adv. Tap
16. LITTLE BIT OF HEAVEN _____ Carolyn Saiya, Barbara Gellerman, Joan Winston
17. IRISH JIG _____ Chris Salvo
18. AIR DE BALLET _____ Lila Gutfeld
18A. PURPLE BUTTERFLIES _____ Pearl Dee Lichtman, Joan Ackerman, Lorraine Boriello, Barbara Elbaum, Gloria Krieger, Rosylin Golding, Arlene Ryman, Myra Schaer, Carol Sokol, Dianne Sokol, Joyce Cohen, Susan Wollock
19. LOVER — Tap Dance _____ Brenda Kaftal
20. RHYTHM DANCE _____ Roberta Golding
21. MOONLIGHT SONATA _____ Saundra Steinbrecker
22. SHIEK OF ARABY _____ Judith Holtzman, Harriet Barcon, Ronnie Kemilhor & Joy Belleti, Joan Epifania, Elaine Genger, Lila Gutfeld, Sandra Josephthal, Debra Roth, Marylin Silverberg
23. TAPS IN TIME _____ Yvette Jaeger
24. HINDOO SCENE — Persian Market _____ Monday Semi-Adv. Tap Barbara Pasternack, Joan Legrand, Terry Mizrachi, Sarah Soloway, Sheryl Shapiro, Dianne Glatzer, Joyce Shapiro, Brenda Kaftal
24A. LAZY RIVER _____ Barbara Gellerman, Bertha Abadi, Josephine Rosenblatt
24B. TAHITI NATIVE DANCE _____ Monday Semi-Adv. Tap Barbara Pasternack, Joan Legrand, Terry Mizrachi, Sarah Soloway, Sheryl Shapiro, Dianne Glatzer, Joyce Shapiro, Brenda Kaftal
24C. WHIRLING DERVISH _____ Carol Poppiceno, Arlene Scofield, Mathilda Waldron, Ruby Winston
25. HUNGARIAN CZARDAS _____ James Krieger, Angelina Calo, Joseph Calo, Charles Marmo
25A. TAP ACROBATICS _____ Pat Parks
26. YOU LOVE ME — Song _____ Marylin Silverberg
27. TAPPING MISS _____ Henry Jim
28. PIANO ROLL BLUES — Song _____ Francis Fallon
29. HAMP'S BOOGIE WOOGIE _____ Barbara Pasternack Betty Lynn Jensen
30. ABA-DABA HONEY MOON _____ Advanced Tap Group Angela Frisca, Marie Anne Friscia, Gae Blau, Carolyn Saiya, Yvette Jaeger, Joyce Fantelli, Barbara Gellerman, Joan Winston
31. NEVERTHELESS — Soft Shoe _____ Carol Poppiceno, Arlene Scofield, Mathilda Waldron, Ruby Winston Tues. Inter. Group Roberta Barandes, Mary Anne Celono, Catherine Curley, Susette Haber, Shiela Kantorman, Patricia Borden, Arlene Ryman, Anita Schwartz, Rose Weiss, Lida Wunderlich
32. VALSE BLUE _____ Maxine Richland
33. THRU THE YEARS — Song _____ Dorothy Carley
34. HAWAIIAN WAR CHANT _____ Terry Mizrachi
35. I LOVE YOU — Tap Dance _____ Gae Blau
36. BE A CLOWN — Song & Dance _____ Pat & Stanley Parks
37. INTERMEDIATE BOOGIE _____ Friday Tap Joy Beleti, Joan Epifania, Elaine Genger, Lila Gutfeld, Sandra Josephthal, Ronnie Kemilhor, Debra Roth, Marylin Silverberg

---

HERB BERNSTEIN: When I was four years old, I saw a violin in a store and fell in love with it. My mother bought me one, and I took lessons, a dollar a lesson, till the age of ten. We never had any money. I think his best year, my father earned $150 a week. But you know how parents are: I wanted music lessons, I got them.

JACK EAGLE: My parents didn't have me until they were married thirteen years. As they say in Yiddish, I was an *ain in aintzika*—one of one. They were very protective, didn't want me to play ball or roller-skate for fear I would get hurt. Instead, they bought me a trumpet. I took lessons from the New York Band Instrument Company, near the St. George Hotel, starting with a little mouthpiece. I moved on to a bugle and started doing bugle calls. Then my mother got me a really good horn.

MARNIE BERNSTEIN: At one time, I took accordion lessons from Mr. Haber, who came to the apartment. I was an advanced student then, and he gave me a difficult arrangement of "Begin the Beguine" that had different rhythms for the left and right hands. He told me, "You know, if you play both hands with the same rhythm, no one may notice. But that's the difference between someone who takes the easy way and the real musician."

My first accordion teacher was Laura Petri, who together with her husband gave music lessons out of their house. She taught piano and accordion in the living room; Mr. Petri taught everything else in a converted closet. I was invited to join the Petri band, and once, when I was about eleven, I went over on a Saturday afternoon. It was a hodgepodge of brass, woodwind, percussion, and one accordion playing "Winter Wonderland." I was the only girl out of about twenty musicians, but just a little too young to appreciate what a nice situation that was.

Mrs. Petri taught from a book called *Everybody's Favorite Accordion Pieces*. She'd assign a different song each week, and as soon as I learned it, I had to perform it for my father. He waited and waited for me to learn "Ave Maria." Finally, he asked Mrs. Petri why she kept skipping it. She explained it was a Catholic hymn. "So what?" my father said. "It's beautiful music."

HOWARD RAPP: My mother heard someone play "The Anniversary Waltz" on the accordion, and she loved it. She wanted to be able to hear it whenever she liked. So she decided my brother would take accordion lessons and learn to play that song. Since we couldn't afford two instruments, I had to take accordion lessons, too. Our teacher came by subway. He got off the train and walked ten blocks to our house. My brother hated the accordion and begged my mother to stop the lessons. But she wanted him to play. Finally, he arranged for a bunch of his friends to meet the teacher on his way and beat him up. The teacher refused to come back again.

Our dancing lessons were another thing. We took tap at the Fred Astaire Dance Studios right under the el on Broadway, in Williamsburg. They got you to pay a year in advance, and they placed you on *The Merry Mailman Show*. I was on three times, once with a bunch of eight other guys, all of us dressed in top hats and canes, singing the Johnny Ray hit "Walking My Baby Back Home."

One day the people who ran the studio absconded with everybody's money. Fred Astaire came down to straighten things out; his name on the line. He taught a class or two to us. Imagine, Fred Astaire in Brooklyn, teaching Howard Rapp to dance.

CAROLINE KATZ MOUNT: In our one-bedroom apartment, there was no room for a piano, so my sister got to take accordion lessons. Since I was little, they decided the accordion was too heavy for me, but my parents felt I had to do something. That's how I wound up at Leona Antel's Dance Studio on Bay Parkway.

Leona Antel was a tough-looking, heavily made-up blonde who gave lessons in every kind of dance you could imagine: ballet, tap, acrobatics, and flamenco with castanets. For advanced students there was Mrs. Antel's specialty: tap-on-toe, where a tap was affixed to the bottom of a toe shoe. I can still hear the *tap-tap-tap* on the wooden floor of that long, narrow, mirror-lined room.

The big event of the season was our recital at the Brooklyn Academy of Music. Mrs. Antel, in the spirit of Busby Berkeley, had choreographed a spectacular opening. All eighteen of the girls in my troupe were positioned in a horizontal line. The curtain was supposed to rise in three stages. First it would reveal just our dancing feet in silver tap shoes doing a shuffle step, then up to our knees, and finally the rest of us. We got through the first stage all right. But when the curtain stopped at our knees, somehow, in the pressure of the moment, we thought it got stuck. In a panic, we crawled under and out in front of the partially raised curtain. There was a jumble of arms and legs. We all bumped into each other. The music played on, but all through the number we couldn't manage to get back in line and step. Maybe I should have taken the accordion after all.

STEWIE STONE: My father, who had been a hoofer in the George White Scandals and the Ziegfeld Follies, ran the Robert Stone Dance

The program for the Leona Antel Dance Studio's annual recital. As noted, the program was always subject to change.

Studio for tap dancing and ballroom for more than forty years. It was only a little place with a linoleum floor, but he taught people like Jeff Chandler and Susan Hayward, as well as all the kids in my high school who took up tap.

He said, "Listen, we have no money. But I can give you five dollars a week to go for drum lessons."

I said, "What's that gonna do for me in my life?"

He said, "You play drums and you practice, every summer you can go away and have a free vacation playing in a band. You'll have enough money to put yourself through college. No matter what you do, you can always augment your income playing on weekends. Playing the drums will open a lot of doors for you."

I started on a practice pad. Then he bought me a snare drum, then a bass drum, then the high hats, then the cymbals. I practiced in the apartment. The neighbors threw rocks through the window. Finally, my father cut a deal. They allowed me to practice from 3:30 to 5:30. After I got a full set of drums, I joined a band. We'd go to one guy's house, and we'd all practice together. It sounded a lot better.

You hear a guy practice the drums, you hate it. You hear a guy practice the trumpet, you hate it. But put it all together in a band, it's not that bad.

JULIE BUDD: When I was four or five, I had a lemonade stand. My father was in the soda business, so I figured I knew how to do this. There were construction workers putting up some houses on Avenue J, and I thought I could do some business. There was no problem going away from the house in those days. The only thing I couldn't do was cross Utica Avenue—that was the big street. When I was finally allowed to cross it, I knew I was a mensch.

Anyway, the first day I made a few dollars. That gave me an idea. The next day I put on my holiday dress, the one I was only supposed to wear on Rosh Hashanah and Yom Kippur, with forty-seven crinolines. I put on my patent leather shoes and ruffle socks. And I went around the neighborhood door-to-door, ringing the bells.

"What are you doing all dressed up today?" the neighbors asked.

I said, "I'm here to sing a song for you, but if I sing, you've gotta give me a nickel."

The next day, different dress—I knew, even then, give the audience a surprise. They said, "Are you back?"

"This time," I said, "it's two for a quarter."

BARRY FRANK: I began my career singing for ice cream. Neighbors asked for a song, and I would do "Amapola" or "Zippity-Doo-Dah." I ate so much ice cream, I became a little chubbette. From the streets, I moved on to the department stores in downtown Brooklyn, where they had amateur contests that were broadcast over the radio.

IRVING FIELDS: I began playing the piano when I was eight years old. We moved from Coney Island to Bensonhurst around then, but I had gotten my taste for show business from Coney Island, from hearing the singers and musicians in the Bowery saloons and the bands that played at Steeplechase.

I entered those amateur contests that used to be held in movie theaters all over Brooklyn. They were terrific openings for people who had talent. Then I hit the big one: the Fred Allen Amateur Contest, which was coast-to-coast on radio. I won first prize playing my arrangement of "The Continental" and got a week's engagement at the Roxy for fifty dollars plus fifty dollars prize money. I took all single bills, came home to Brooklyn, threw them all in the air, and said, "Mama, Papa, it's all for you."

PAT COOPER: The boys on the corner would wait for me. "Where's Pat? When's Pat coming down?" I'd do impressions of the instruments of Glenn Miller, Charlie Barnett, Tommy Dorsey. I won the Fox Theater's Monday Night at the Amateurs in '48 or '49. I beat my sister, knocked her brains out.

She sang "Ave Maria." While she was on, everybody was very quiet. People said, "She's gonna win." Then I went out there and did my impressions. Tore the house down.

Productions on the stages of school auditoriums gave Brooklyn kids like "Fidgety-Ben" a chance to show their stuff.

I got the twenty-five dollars. My sister got the watch that never worked. My father got mad at me. "Your sister sings about Jesus Christ and Mother Mary. You, stupid, make the noise. You had to go and beat your sister." They didn't speak to me for six months.

I worked the Bedford Theater Amateur Night, on Bedford Avenue and Bergen Street. Joey Adams was the MC. Sometimes they gave me a dollar, three dollars. My sister quit. "I'm not gonna work with him no more."

Like James Cagney, I said, "Cause you can't touch me."

My father said, "Go to confession. Tell God what a skunk you are."

I go into the confessional booth. The priest said, "Yes?" Like James Cagney I said, "I ain't tellin' you nuttin'. I don't squeal on nobody. Who do you think I am, you dirty rat?"

MAX WECHSLER: Every year Junior High School 50 put on a big talent show that gave the kids in the neighborhood a chance to show off their performing ability. My friend Benjamin Gordon was constantly frustrated. For years, he had tried to get a big part in the show, but to no avail. Benjamin was into everything. He collected war memorabilia, stamps, and soda bottles. He raised gerbils and kept a flock of pigeons in a coop on his roof. But even though he took piano, drum, and tap-dancing lessons for years and walked around with a book on his head to perfect his posture, "those teachers," as he told me, "never give me a tumble when it comes to show business."

Now, Fidgety-Ben, as we called him because he couldn't stand still, was one of the most persistent kids I ever met, and finally, in eighth grade, he pushed his way into a starring role in the show. "Maxie," he said, "it took a lot of effort, but they finally recognized talent. I'm going to show them everything I have."

Although I had no talent, even I got a part in this show. For the big Indian dance number, I got to wear a costume and stand on the stage with a long spear and look out at the audience.

Opening night was packed with students, parents, relatives, and friends of the cast. The teachers who directed the show and the performers felt the pressure. I had nothing to worry about. All I had to do was stand on the side of the stage holding my spear.

Benjamin's time came about thirty minutes into the show. And he was ready. I caught a glimpse of him backstage with a book on his head practicing his balance. He was wearing a colorful Indian outfit: a blue fringed shirt, a yellow loincloth, and a feathered headdress. Then there was a big drumbeat. The lights dimmed, a single spot came on, and Benjamin bounded out to the middle of the stage. They didn't call him Fidgety-Ben for nothing. He was loose out there, bouncing up and down. It took a few seconds before everyone realized he was wearing nothing under his loincloth.

The teachers went berserk. I heard them screaming in the back, "Drop the curtain, drop the curtain!" The audience was *ooh*ing and *aah*ing. But Benjamin was having a ball. It was his moment in the spotlight, and before they dropped the curtain, true to his word, he got to show off everything he had.

CHAPTER 4

One Big Happy Family

FUDGE, FUDGE, CALL THE JUDGE.
MAMA'S GOT A NEWBORN BABY.
WRAP IT UP IN TISSUE PAPER,
THROW IT DOWN THE ELEVATOR . . .

—Jump-rope rhyme

STAN GOLDBERG: My brother Gary came back from visiting a friend who had moved out to Long Island. "It's terrible there," he said. "They have to sleep in their own room. They don't share with the brother."

NEIL SEDAKA: I shared a room with my sister, Ronnie. I used to put on shows, make up radio programs, keep her up to all hours entertaining her. When she left to get married, I cried bitterly.

We lived in a two-bedroom apartment on the second floor of a building in Brighton. At one time, it was my parents, Ronnie, me, my father's parents, and his five sisters. As each of my aunts got married, they moved out. My grandfather died when I was little, but my *nonni* (Spanish for grandmother) lived with us till she died when I was thirteen.

We were the only Sephardic people in the building. We had different foods, different customs, a different language—Ladino. My mother was Ashkenazi, but she learned how to speak Ladino because she wanted to understand what her in-laws were saying about her.

JOAN RIBAUDO: My parents, two brothers, and I lived in a three-room apartment. But other people always lived with us: an aunt and uncle, my grandmother, another aunt. When relatives came from Pennsylvania, we put a drawer on top of the dresser, put some towels in it, and the baby slept there. Another child slept in a drawer on the floor. One time, my brother was sleeping in the kitchen across two chairs. He slid off the chairs onto the floor under the telephone table and slept right through it.

TOBY SCHOM GROSSMAN: When we first came to this country, we lived with my aunt and uncle and their two sons in their little two-room apartment, although sometimes neighbors took us in for a night or so because it was so crowded. But after a while, we got our own apartment in the building.

My parents were Holocaust survivors. My father was in the ghetto on the way to the camp, and my mother was able to get him out. They hid in the woods in Poland for two years. Their little son died. My father was the only one of ten brothers and sisters who survived. My mother lost everyone but two sisters. They tried not to talk about the war too much. Still, I remember my father waking up screaming, howling in the middle of the night.

Being an only child and the child of survivors, I was very protected. I never learned to roller-skate or ice-skate, to swim or ride a bike. I guess they were afraid. Once I went to Washington Baths with my friends, and they all jumped into the pool, so I jumped in, too. I almost drowned.

My mother was from the old school. She set basins out on the fire escape to collect rainwater that we used to wash our hair. On Fridays, she'd bake challah, and the apartment would be fragrant with its aroma. She was an excellent seamstress. At one time, she wanted to get a job, but I said, "You can't. I don't want to come home from school and not find you here." She listened to me. They wanted to move to a bigger apartment. I said, "I can't leave this building. All my friends are here." They didn't move.

PAT COOPER: I lived with my parents and three sisters in a five-family building in Red Hook. The luckier families were on the floor with the one bathroom in the whole building. I was a bed wetter. I felt terrible about it. Instead of helping me, they beat the daylights out of me. There was never "I love you" in that family. The only time you got a smile was when you brought in money. Everybody grabbed theirs.

I was considered the rebel because I had imagination. My father loved opera. But if you had humor, he thought that there was something wrong with you. He was a cold but very bright and handsome man. I don't think he thought I listened, but I picked up on things. He was a bricklayer and worked on the first housing project in the country. They used him to do the foundation so the rest of the building was straight. He had such a sense of balance that if he wore a hat on top of a brick wall on a windy day, the hat wouldn't blow off.

JOAN RIBAUDO: The whole neighborhood thought my father was Italian, including me. It wasn't until after he passed away that we looked through his papers and discovered he was really Portuguese. The immigration people had taken the *dos* out of his name, Ventura dos Santos.

Everyone called him Sam. He was a plumber and the super of our building on West Eighth Street. At four in the morning, he was up putting coal in the furnace. He dragged the heavy pails of ashes out to the curb for the garbage pickup and carried cast-iron sinks and bathtubs on his back. He worked until he was eighty-two years old.

In their wedding picture, both my parents are the same height. But my mother was only fifteen then, and she continued to grow to be five-eight, while my father remained five-three. He had to get on a chair to be eye-to-eye with her. When they had a heated discussion, he'd look up at her and say, "If I knew you'd be this big, I wouldn't have married you."

HERBY GREISSMAN: I came home from school one day, and it was snowing. I said to my father, "I'm not going to work." He said, "You've got an obligation. You've got to go." I peddled the bike through the snow to deliver the grocery orders. You couldn't dodge the bullet with my father.

He was a fruit-and-vegetable broker. In 1951, when things began to pick up for him, he bought a two-door black Dodge. One afternoon that summer, he drove onto the block, and the car was filled with watermelons: the back seat, the passenger seat, the trunk couldn't close. He brought enough watermelons for almost all the people in the building.

HOWARD JONES: We were playing stickball on the street one afternoon when one of the fellows hit the ball into a neighbor's window and it broke. Everyone ran except for my brother Basil and me.

Mr. Baptiste came out and accused us of breaking his window. One thing led to another, and my father came down. "I *saw* your son break the window," Mr. Baptiste told him.

"You're a liar," my brother shouted.

At that, my father hit my brother. "I'll pay for the window," he said to Mr. Baptiste.

"I don't doubt that you were telling the truth," he later told Basil, "but you spoke back to an older person, you called an adult a liar. I cannot allow my son to be disrespectful."

My father, Lynton Mac Jones, came from Jamaica, and he never lost the British influence of his youth. He was a formal man, a meticulous dresser. He bowled in a cricket league and played tennis on

More than trees grew in
Brooklyn. This brownstone
backyard was a verdant
vegetable garden.

the grass in Prospect Park dressed in white flannel. In the back of
our brownstone, he kept a garden where he grew lettuce, green pep-
pers, tomatoes, and calilou, which is a stringy, spinach-type plant.

My father was a baker for Ebinger's, and the smell of cloves and
cinnamon always seemed to cling to him. The summer I was fifteen
and Basil was eighteen, we heard Ebinger's was hiring kids. We asked
our father if he could get us jobs. "Yes, I can," he said, "but I won't."

We were so surprised. He knew how much we needed to work.
"Why not?" we asked.

"Years ago, when I began my job, the foreman told me that not
only would I be there for the rest of my life, but my sons would come
on and do the same thing," he said. "I may still be there, but I will
keep the promise I made to myself that day: no matter what, my sons
will never work at Ebinger's."

NEIL SEDAKA: My father drove a cab for the Rio Taxi Company
in Manhattan. Even though it was cheap back then, he never wanted
to own his own medallion. "I don't want no headaches, Skinny," he'd
say to my mother (he called her Skinny because she was so thin). "I
want to be able to sleep at night."

In the sixth grade, my friend Freddie Gershon moved. His father
was an insurance man and could afford a twelve-thousand-dollar home
in Bayside, Queens. My mother cried to my father. He said, "No,
Skinny, no headaches. I can't afford twelve thousand dollars for a
house." He was from poor people and held on to a buck.

STAN GOLDBERG: My father would come home after working nights, pop in, give us the hugs and kisses, be very warm. He gave us values too. But he had another job. Our family was female-oriented; my mother and grandmother directed what was going on.

The phone was in Grandma's apartment. Once I was going with a girl Grandma did not approve of, because she wasn't Jewish. She telephoned, and Grandma told her, "Stanley moved."

My mother was one of the first women in the neighborhood to drive. She took us to the JCH [Jewish Community House], to Lafayette, to the Mapleton Park library in her '47 Nash. She knew if I was doing a project in science or social studies. While I was out playing ball, she'd go to the library. I'd come home, all the books would be lined up and ready. "Took charge" is an understatement.

LARRY STRICKLER: My mother did not look at the thermometer. She looked at the calendar. Come Labor Day, out came the winter coats. One Veterans Day it was unseasonably mild. A friend and I went out of Brighton Baths across the sand and into the ocean. The water was warm, and I was feeling really good. Here I was, seventeen years old, swimming in November. Walking back across the beach— it must have been about 70 degrees—I hear a great shriek followed by cries about influenza, pneumonia, polio. I look up to see who's screaming. There on the boardwalk is a figure bundled up in a winter coat. It's my mother.

STAN GOLDBERG: I think Brooklyn neighborhoods in the fifties were run by women. They went to the PTA meetings. They went up to school. Very few of them worked.

STARR FROST GOLDBERG: There was so much house-work. My mother shopped for food every single day. And she always was there when I came home for lunch. There were no wash-and-wear fabrics. She would stand over the ironing board for hours.

JOYCE SHAPIRO FEIGENBAUM: My mother washed clothes with a washboard on the deep side of the kitchen sink and hung them out to dry on a clothesline. Later, they installed a washing machine in the basement of our building, and she would lug the heavy bags of laundry up and down two flights of stairs, like she had dragged the baby carriage when we were little. We were so crowded in our little apartment, there was so much stuff.

MORRIS FRIEDMAN: We never ate out in a restaurant, never bought cake in the bakery. My mother prepared every meal and baked every cake we had. She made her own kreplach, all the specialties. She knew how to stretch a dollar.

CAROLINE KATZ MOUNT: In addition to all the housework, the cooking and cleaning, my mother did a lot of handiwork. She took knitting instructions from a store on Bay Parkway. From that, the word *instructions* became associated in my mind with knitting. When the Catholic children got out early from school for religious instructions, I thought they were going for knitting lessons.

My mother had grown up in a rural area in the Ukraine, and although she had been here since she was a teenager, she never got used to city life, to living in an apartment that looked out on a concrete backyard. She talked about how she would bring the ducks down to the water as a little girl and see the frogs jumping about, how it felt to run around on the grass in bare feet, how beautiful the changing seasons were. It bothered her that we were missing the pleasures of a bucolic childhood. Our neighborhood was not particularly beautiful. But on Saturday and Sunday afternoons, we would walk down to Ocean Parkway, and she would point out the trees, the flowers in the little gardens. In the summer, she would pick wild daisies that grew in the empty lots and twine them into a crown for my hair.

My mother was different from the other women in the building. She didn't play mah-jongg and kept mostly to herself. She had this elegant, erect carriage, which made people think she was snobby. But actually, she was very modest and shy, comfortable only with her own family. Her mother, sisters, and brothers and their families all lived in the neighborhood, and her whole life was bound up in the family.

STAN GOLDBERG: We lived in the upstairs apartment of a four-family semiattached house in Bensonhurst, and my mother's parents lived downstairs. My father's parents lived two blocks away, and aunts and uncles lived nearby. The whole extended family made a big deal out of the children. They made me feel I was special. I'd be in the schoolyard and Joe Feiffer, an elderly man and a cousin of my grandfather's, would pass by. "You have money?" he'd ask, and give me a quarter for a soda.

My mother's father had a great effect on my life. He was into the humanistic things: taking care of an animal, noticing how beautiful nature is. My grandfather didn't like that I played ball a lot. He wanted me to go to yeshiva, but it ended too late to play sports, and there weren't any girls; sports and girls, the two most important elements.

The nation got to know Gary David Goldberg's grandparents in the TV series *Brooklyn Bridge*. Here they are with Gary at his bar mitzvah.

CHARLES HYNES: My grandfather Charles Drew was the replacement for my father in every sense of the word. He was very tall, an imposing kind of guy who was still jumping horses at the age of seventy-five. He had come to Boston from Ireland. But after he made some money, he moved to Brooklyn and opened up a riding academy off Ocean Parkway. It catered to an elite clientele who dressed in beautiful riding clothes and drove up in luxurious cars. Irene Dunne was one of them. My grandfather gave me a pet pony, which I walked more than rode. People kidded me about that. But I looked at the pony as a large pet and didn't want to hurt it by riding it.

CLIFF HESSE: We lived on Ridgewood Avenue near Cyprus Hills cemetery, about midway between my father's parents and my mother's mother. Having all that extended family about was a very comforting part of my childhood.

Every Saturday night, we'd pick up crumb cake from the local bakery for Sunday morning breakfasts before church. To this day, crumb cake is my version of Proust's madeleine. I take a bite, and the whole experience comes flooding back: Sundays after church, walking up New Jersey Avenue, crossing Liberty onto Atlantic Avenue (being very careful of the traffic) and heading for my grandfather's

drugstore. Sunday dinner was in the large kitchen–dining room of my grandparents' apartment upstairs. It was big and warm, the old stove was there.

My father's mother was English-Scotch—the only one in the family who wasn't German—very much a turn-of-the-century Victorian lady, quite tall, statuesque. She had a proud, noble look, could have been royalty. But how she loved to throw parties for crowds of people. My father's two brothers were musicians who played with the big bands in the forties. All their musician friends would come over, and they'd jam way into the night. You'd go down into the dark drugstore below and the ceiling would be shaking from the music.

MAX WECHSLER: My grandfather Jacob came here from Austria and made enough money as a roofer to buy a three-story brownstone on Vernon Avenue off Willoughby, in Bedford-Stuyvesant. He was short and wiry but incredibly strong. Once I saw him bend a penny between his fingers. The years of working as a roofer had hardened his body and developed his agility. Also, it had given him the opportunity to collect all sorts of things, which ended up in the deep, narrow yard behind his house.

Whenever we visited him and his wife, I would spend the time out in the backyard, exploring the collection of objects along the walks, in the shed and the greenhouse. Years later, when I read *Look Homeward, Angel*, it evoked those times. There were stone lion heads that were incredibly heavy; I wondered how he had the strength to carry them home. There were dozens of plants and shrubs, some planted in plain clay pots, others in elaborate copper and concrete urns. There were bottles of all different colors, pottery pitchers and figurines, watering cans, windowpanes, and copper and brass spheres that may have been plumbing fixtures. There were tin boxes within tin boxes, like matryoshka dolls. There were ladders of various sizes and kinds and big spools of rope, and a lot of tools. Every once in a while, I'd find a Spalding ball or some colored marbles, which I'd bring home.

My father looked upon all this as junk. My grandfather never took the time to explain or show off any of his things to me. He was a cold and silent kind of man. Although I wanted to, I never had much of a relationship with him. Maybe that explains why I spent so much time with the objects he collected, content to be by myself, wandering down the slate paths, picking up and putting down all the different things. My grandfather's yard was a private universe for me.

JUDITH KURIANSKY: Sunday was Grandma's day. Everybody came to her Bensonhurst apartment: her nine children and all their

kids. Sitting in the kitchen, sitting on the stoop, playing jump rope. All the generations just hanging out on the corner of a Brooklyn street, the nieces and nephews, the aunts and uncles, the older people, the rows of houses all looking alike, just a few trees and some small gardens.

JOEL MARTIN: When the weather was nice, my father and aunts and uncles would sit on the benches in front of the house and listen to the Dodger game on an old Philco portable. They called anything that had a handle a portable. Like my old Webcor tape recorder, which weighed more than I did. But it had a handle, so it was a portable.

We lived in a four-family house owned by my uncle. One apartment was for transients, the rest were for family. My grandmother, the matriarch of the family, lived downstairs. They called her Tanta Chai, which meant Aunt Ida. She was a beautiful, beautiful woman. I loved her like crazy.

My father was one of six children, four boys and two girls, and they all had families. Every Sunday everyone came over. If one of them didn't, it was noted. They kept track. There must have been a book hidden in a secret room that documented the Sunday attendance: "You know it's been three weeks since Uncle Izzy was here." "You know it's been four weeks since we saw Aunt Rose."

But if Uncle Lester didn't make the Sunday gatherings, he was excused, because he was the youngest and the busiest. He looked exactly like Jack Lemmon and was a big practical joker. In those years, the men wore big overcoats. We'd go to Garfield's Cafeteria, and Uncle Lester would fill my father's pockets with silverware. My father would walk out, and the silverware would start clanging. I never decided whether he wanted to get my father arrested, make me laugh, or both. Sometimes Uncle Lester would go into a restaurant, flash his wallet, and say he was a reviewer. He ate for free at lots of places. Later on he moved to Westchester, which I thought was a place somewhere between Asia and Siberia.

RICHARD KEHOE: Great-Aunt Del lived somewhere in Flatbush in a huge two-family house with six rooms on each floor. She was what we called lace curtain Irish, had more money than my grandmother. We never liked going there for our once-a-year visits. I found out later my father didn't either, because you had to sit there with your hands on your lap so you wouldn't scratch the furniture. My father would take us out for a walk and an ice-cream cone, and that would make the trip bearable.

KARL BERNSTEIN: We often went to Great-Aunt Freida's on Sundays. It was a lot of bodies and legs, a lot of children who were my second cousins. The kitchen table was crammed with people. There was hot tea and wonderful cinnamon cookies that Aunt Freida baked. After she died and I discovered she never learned to speak English, I was so surprised. I always understood everything she said.

FRANCES BLUM: People came and went to Bubbe Freida's all afternoon. The kids would read joke books or play Monopoly in the bedrooms, play in the street or on the stoop, run in and out of the house, up and down the steps. The women would sit in the kitchen, sipping glasses of tea through sugar lumps they held between their teeth, reading out loud the letters they received from the family in Israel. The men would play pinochle in the living room. Uncle Abie, my grandmother's youngest brother who married her oldest daughter, arranged the Sunday games.

MARNIE BERNSTEIN: I used to wonder what Uncle Abie was doing in our otherwise sober and serious family. He worked in the china trade, and his little apartment was cluttered with useless objects ("tchotchkes" my parents called them) that he accumulated for no other reason than that he liked them. He had a small white piano, which he played by ear. His favorite song was "*H-A*-double-*R-I-G-A-N* spells Harrigan" which he rewrote as "*S-U-S-S-M-A-N* spells Sussman." He did magic tricks for the kids, like pulling nickels out of his sleeve or from behind our ears. He played practical jokes; spent money freely on things the others considered frivolous, like magazines; had sweet cream instead of milk in his cereal; and was often in debt. When people asked him what he had put away for a rainy day, he'd say, "I got a big umbrella." My father disapproved of him, I know. But he was a lover of life, and somehow it seemed like a good thing.

MARCO CARCICH: I lived in Queens. But every summer, instead of playing stickball with my friends or hanging around in the streets, I went to stay with my grandparents in Brooklyn. I never brought any of my friends along. Family life was very important, and I wanted to keep it private. I wanted to relish it all by myself.

I would take the subway to Hoyt-Schermerhorn, change to the Brooklyn line, and get off at Avenue J. My grandparents lived in a six-story building near the elevated train, in a high-ceilinged apartment that seemed massive to me. I would lie in bed, staring for hours at the ornate plasterwork on the ceiling-light fixture—it was an old one that had been converted from gas to electricity.

My mother's father, Marjain Sarunich, was born in what would become Yugoslavia. He was about five-six and very stocky. His head was bald as a cue ball. There was no hair even on the sides of his ears. The story was that he walked into a barn when he was about fifteen and saw his aunt in a sexual embrace with the devil. As he turned away, the devil reached out and ripped his hair off.

The gathering of the generations. It was a lot of bodies and legs.

The men who played pinochle "would argue and fight back and forth for pennies."

He came to this country with no papers. Along with Manny, a Russian Jew he met on board, he jumped ship in the Ambrose Channel, where the big ships and tankers enter New York harbor. They swam a mile and a half, maybe two miles, all the way to Coney Island. They were lucky; it had to have been between tide changes. Both ended up working in Coney Island. Manny opened up a knish place, and Matteo (as they called my grandfather) became a masseur at Bushman's Baths.

He got up at 5:30 every morning. If I was still sleeping, he'd splash a glass of cold water on my face. For breakfast, he would have a shot of J&B and a raw egg—to get him going. He brushed his teeth with Clorox. They were gleaming white against his deep tan, which he had twelve months a year. He was a member of the Polar Bear Club—about fifteen men and women, mainly from Eastern Europe, who went for a swim out beyond the breakers every day or every other day, no matter how cold it was.

When the family would gather for dinner at Uncle Georgie's house on Shore Boulevard, we couldn't sit down and eat until my grandfather arrived. Sometimes he was late coming back in the middle of the winter from his swim. He had a favorite fork and would not eat dinner without it. Wherever he ate, he brought that fork along.

After dinner, Matteo, my father, and my mother's brother Georgie would play pinochle in the kitchen. The women sat in the living room, listening to the radio or watching the test patterns on the eight-inch television screen. The men would argue and fight back and forth for pennies. The next time we got together, they might not be talking to each other, because they were still angry over something that happened in last week's game.

I must have been about nine years old when they sent me to the bar to get beer. "Take the stick," they said. I got this long stick and two buckets, went to the bar, and got the buckets filled with beer. Nobody told me I was supposed to carry the stick like an ox across the back of my neck and over both shoulders. I put it across one shoulder, and of course, I spilled most of the beer.

Matteo did not drive. He did not trust cars, never owned one. He did not trust telephones, never spoke on one. He thought the witches listened to his conversations. About six months after my grandmother died, a giant mosquito—the biggest one I've ever seen—flew into the window. I went to roll up a newspaper to hit it. "Don't," my grandfather said. "It may be Grandma." And with that, the mosquito disappeared.

PART TWO

Living Together

EVERY CUSTOMER WAS
A HALF-HOUR

EVERYBODY KNEW EVERYBODY
ELSE'S BUSINESS

FROM SWELTERING STOOP TO
SHIMMERING SHORE

CONEY ISLAND

ONE NATION—UNDER GOD

AMERICANS ALL

CHAPTER 5

Every Customer Was a Half-Hour

B MY NAME IS BARBARA
AND MY HUSBAND'S NAME IS BOB.
WE COME FROM BROOKLYN,
AND WE SELL BANANAS.

—Bouncing-ball rhyme

MARNIE BERNSTEIN: Summer mornings were very quiet on our block. Hardly any cars were parked along the curb, hardly any people were around. Then, from out of nowhere, this big truck would come down the middle of Twenty-fourth Avenue. It would send out great noisy jets of water on both sides, soaking the whole gutter. After, the asphalt would sparkle, and all along the curbs would be puddles edged with rainbows big enough to jump into and make a big splash.

JOAN RIBAUDO: The street cleaner, dressed in a brown uniform, came down the block wheeling a garbage pail in front of him. With a broom and shovel, he'd sweep up any bit of debris.

The policeman on the beat walked down the block. He knew every kid who lived there. If he found you on the street when you were supposed to be in school, he'd take you by the hand back to your house. We called him Tarzan, because he was so tall and muscular.

MARTIN SPITZER: The pony ride would come up and down the streets. People dressed up their kids in cowboy vests and hats and spats and took photos of them sitting on the ponies.

All kinds of peddlers came around selling clothes, small appliances. You'd give one an order. And he'd say, "Okay, I'll bring it to you next Tuesday."

JOAN RIBAUDO: A man used to come around to sharpen knives and fix umbrellas. He rang a bell: two rings meant knives, one ring meant umbrellas. And people would yell out of their windows: "I have an umbrella." "I have a knife." A man with a pushcart sold roasted chestnuts and baked sweet potatoes for a nickel. You could smell them up and down the street.

MARTIN SPITZER: A little peddler wheeled a little cart up the block. Inside were round hot knishes, potato or kashe with onions, seven cents apiece. Another came around selling hot chick-peas in little brown bags for a nickel or a dime. He'd salt-and-pepper them, and I'd devour them.

MARVIN KAPLAN: The lady with the orange pushcart sold "shoe-leather"—dried apricot that was tough and sour.

ROZ STARR: Joe came around the school pushing a wagon with a big copper pot. He dipped apples, marshmallows, and shoe leather into the hot jelly in the pot. Oh those jelly apples! In the summer he switched to Italian ices.

A Brooklyn version of
Orchard Street: pushcarts,
peddlers, and stores.

ROBERT MERRILL: The iceman came up the six floors every day with the ice on his back.

KARL BERNSTEIN: Just one family on the block, the Laudeuchers, still had an icebox. When the iceman came, he would busy himself chopping a slab off a block of ice, and we would hang around waiting for a piece to fall so we could suck on it.

Blue Coal was the sponsor of my favorite radio show, *The Shadow*, but our coal man delivered black coal in a big truck. He wheeled barrels of coal onto the sidewalk, opened up the chute, and poured the coal down into the basement into the bin. I would beg my father to get the big coal instead of the little coal, not realizing big coal was for industry.

JOEL BERGER: If you didn't want to walk to the store and carry the packages back, you could just sit on your stoop and everyone would come to you: the milkman, the bread man, the fruit-and-vegetable man, the fish man.

ELIZABETH RONCKETTI: The pie man in his open-back truck clanged his bell so loud you knew he was coming. How we waited for his fresh-baked fruit pies and the hot chestnuts in the wintertime.

BILL FEIGENBAUM: The Dugan's Bakery Man, a cool guy with a mustache in a white uniform, drove up in a shiny white step-in truck. He was always very friendly with the women.

JOAN RIBAUDO: The fruit man rang his bell, and the people looked out their windows. They knew him by name, and they'd yell, "What do you have today?" "How much are the stringbeans?" If he had what they wanted and they agreed on the price, they came down to buy. While this was going on, a neighborhood man hung around near the wagon. When the horse made a deposit, he'd shovel it up for his garden.

WILLIAM THOMPSON: My friends and I made some extra money peddling. We'd buy fruits and vegetables and rent horses from one of the stables on Dean Street.

KARL BERNSTEIN: Abie the fish man sold fish off his dilapidated truck with the dropleaf—but only on Fridays. He hollered, "Fish man!" and everybody on the block came out. He would clean the fish, scale it open, throw out the guts.

The rest of the week, he was Abie the fruit man. I saw red bananas on his truck. "Why don't you buy some?" I asked my mother. "Only the Italians buy red bananas," she told me.

"You could just sit on your stoop and everyone would come to you" — even the man who sold pots and pans.

ROBERT MERRILL: The banana man was a heavyset Italian guy with a huge voice who sold them off his truck, a penny apiece. He would yell out, "Banan-yol, banan-yol" in an operatic voice. You could hear him all the way up the six floors and around the block. People waited for him; they'd run down and buy as many bananas as they could, because they didn't last long. And if you bought more than five, he'd give you an extra one for free.

NEIL SEDAKA: In the courtyard, there were these street singers —they were so wonderful. There was a black lady who sang for years and years. She had a gorgeous voice. I would wrap a nickel in a tissue or a piece of newspaper and throw it down from the second-floor window.

JOEL BERGER: Early in the morning, I'd be wakened by the songs of the old-clothes men. They walked up and down the alleyways with packs on their backs, singing in two different cadences: "Clothes-old, clothes-old, I cash, I cash" or "Cash-clothes, cash-clothes, cash-clothes." What do they do with their packs, I wondered? Where do they go?

The elevated train would rumble overhead as you went from store to store.

LUIS COLMENARES: You'd hear the song "Fuller Brush man, Fuller Brush man," and you opened up the door. There was this guy in a short-sleeved striped shirt who had climbed up the six stories of the building. On his back, he carried maybe twenty sweep brooms and a bucket, and in a cardboard box every kind of brush and mop you could imagine.

CHARLES HYNES: The Hegeman man sang a lyrical song: "Hegeman man, Hegeman man." And the responses were like part of the song: "I want three bottles, bring me Fox's U-Bet."

RICHARD GOLDSTEIN: The seltzer trucks all seemed to come from East New York. Everyone took it by the case, a dozen blue or clear bottles in a long slotted wooden crate.

ELIZABETH RONCKETTI: A guy came around with bleach in glass jugs, the strongest in the world. One drop could burn a hole in any piece of material. Talk about recycling. He'd come back and pick up the empty jugs.

JACK EAGLE: For those who preferred going out to shop, Brooklyn had its own version of Orchard Street: Thirteenth Avenue, in Borough Park. It used to be filled with pushcarts and peddlers. Guys sold sweet potatoes and *hasha arbus*—hot chick-peas—from little carts. My poor aunt had a little stand and stood out in the freezing cold. There was a pickle man on the corner of Fortieth Street. He'd sell sour and half-sour pickles, sour tomatoes, fresh horseradish. You'd ask for a pickle, and he'd dig his hand right down to the bottom of the barrel and pull one out. And if you didn't like that pickle, he'd dig his hand down again and schlepp out another one. He was as sour as his pickles. All of that ended when the public market was built on Thirty-ninth Street and the stands went into the market.

Thirteenth Avenue also had a lot of famous stores, like the Majestic Chicken Market and Rothstein's, a department store that attracted fancy ladies who would come with their limousines and chauffeurs to shop for pricey items at bargain prices. Old man Rothstein, the grandfather with a torn sweater, would come out and chase the kids: "Bastards, get away from the store."

BOB ARNESEN: Eighth Avenue in Bay Ridge was called Lopskaus Boulevard, after the Scandinavian stew into which all the leftovers are thrown. It was the shopping area for Finntown, which was on Eighth Avenue around the Forties, and the Scandinavian community.

The stores were reminiscent of Europe. People shopped every day for fresh food. Bay Ridge was a mixed neighborhood. There were Scandinavian bakeries, delicatessens, and fish stores, but the candy stores were mostly owned by Jews, the ice-cream parlors by Germans, the fruit stores by Italians, the bars and grills by Irish. It was an island of small stores.

Behind our house was the Denyse nursery, which went back to the original Dutch settlers. From my bedroom window, I could see acres of plants, flowers, and trees. There was a barn, horses and wagons, even chickens.

My father managed the A & P in Bay Ridge, which was one of the biggest at the time, employing about thirty people. I worked there for forty-five cents an hour, packing the shelves, running the cash register. I knew every price in the store.

HERBY GREISSMAN: My father supplied the produce stores on Eighty-sixth Street between Twenty-third Avenue and Bay Parkway, in Bensonhurst. Every other store was a fruit market. They had no cash registers. The storekeeper would put the produce in a paper bag and add up on the bag. The pencil was always behind the ear. Forty-nine cents, thirty-nine cents. These guys who had no education, they knew more math.

BOB LIFF: My father had a grocery store on the ground floor of a four-floor walk-up on the corner of Union Street and Albany Avenue, in Crown Heights. The cans and boxes were on shelves that went up the ceiling. He got stuff out of reach with a long pole that had a grip on one end and grabbers on the other. He'd grab a can off the top shelf, flip it off, catch it, stick it into a brown bag, write the prices on the side of the bag, and swiftly add the order up.

Years before, my grandfather had a tailor's shop next door to the grocery. But in my time, it was a telephone operators' store, where women sat and plugged in your calls.

AL LEWIS: Pitkin Avenue was a major shopping area in Brownsville, which had been the largest Jewish ghetto in the world. The delis served the best corned beef and pastrami anywhere. A guy who called himself the Kishke King did a thriving business.

At one time the circus paraded down Pitkin Avenue to the railroad yards in East New York. It was a tremendous event; school was let out. There were all the circus wagons, the elephants, the clowns and acrobats—just like they used to do it in the small towns.

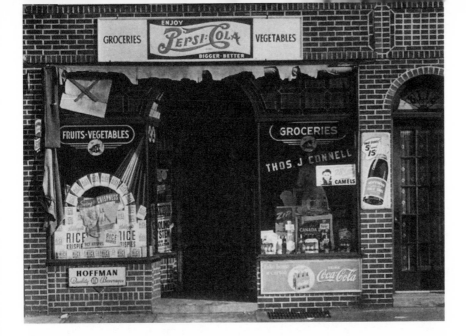

"The stores were reminiscent of Europe. People shopped every day for fresh food."

DAN LURIE: On Saturdays, I'd put on a nice shirt and tie and stroll up and down Pitkin Avenue. It was the Fifth Avenue of Brooklyn, with stores like Abe Stark's men's clothing, Fisher Brothers' ladies' coats and suits, Dubrow's or Diamond and Cooperberg furniture.

PEARL GASARCH: My mother had her furniture custom-made in Pitkin Avenue shops: the sectional sofa; the wing and club chairs all upholstered in damask; the massive mahogany-veneered Philco console that held a television set, high-fi, and bar; the bulky credenza she filled with china and collectibles. Our house in Sea Gate was furnished with Pitkin Avenue's best.

DAN LURIE: Mayrock's, which was the fancy store of the Fortunoff family, was on Pitkin Avenue. Fortunoff's, which catered to the poorer customers, was on Livonia Avenue under the el near Firkey's gym. A little guy named Max was the manager. He knew the price and location of any item in the store.

PHIL FAGIN: Fortunoff's was spread out over maybe a dozen stores. The elevated train would rumble overhead as you went from one to the other along the darkened street, shopping for dishes, glasses, linens, toasters, irons, pots and pans. The stores stretched from the end of Brownsville to the beginning of East New York.

CLIFF HESSE: The drugstores of East New York were scattered up and down Atlantic Avenue. My grandfather's, Hesse's Pharmacy, which he opened in 1904, was right near Pennsylvania Avenue. If my grandfather didn't have something, he'd send me down three blocks to the next store, and the owner would say, "Sure, take it." They exchanged things all the time.

Hesse's Pharmacy was a small place, about the standard city lot of twenty-by-one-hundred. It had wooden floors (which my grandfather liked scrubbed very clean), slanted glass cases with candy for the kids, two wooden phone booths, and a counter with the old crank cash register. Behind it was a higher counter, where he made up prescriptions with the mortar and pestle, the pill boards with tiny holes. He'd pour the medicine on the board, push it into the holes, knock it out —and that would be the tablets. Like making pancakes.

In back was a little yard trapped between two buildings. You couldn't see out of it at all. At the beginning of the summer, I'd go out with a scythe and hack down the grass, which had grown to a foot and a half high. My grandfather had put in a little trellis for a rose bush, and it was filled with roses all the summers I was there.

There was a little electrical repair shop on Liberty Avenue, a nondescript kind of place. I don't remember ever buying anything there. But every Christmas, the owner put an electric train set in the window and surrounded it with little lights. It was O-gauge—the very big old trains, like the British model trains. The engine and cars were about a foot long and six inches high. The rails were two inches apart, and the train ran around a circle that was maybe four feet wide. How I loved standing outside the window watching the train go around and around.

I also loved the smells in the neighborhood: the pungent odor of ozone from the electric generating plant that served the local area and the aromas from all the Italian and German bakeries.

ANGELO BADALAMENTI: Every Sunday morning, my father went to the Danish Bakery on Tenth Street and Kings Highway to buy the most delicious confections. My favorite was the "cake with pimples"—crumb cake filled with rich custard cream. Lovely ladies with pale, pure skin and flaxen hair in nets waited on you. Everything was so fresh and good. It was better than Ebinger's.

DORIS MODELL TIPOGRAPH: Throughout the Bedford and Snyder Avenue area, the aromas from Ebinger's baking plant filled the air. It supplied all the Ebinger bakeries in Brooklyn with daily deliveries of breads and cakes. My favorite were Othellos: little mounds of buttercream-filled white cake smothered with chocolate.

TERRY PERNA ARNESEN: Ebinger's goods were so nicely presented, with extreme cleanliness and fine taste. By two o'clock in the afternoon, the Eighteenth Avenue store would not have anything left to sell.

JUDY BERGER: Getting an invitation to relatives who moved to Long Island depended on the supply of Ebinger's in their freezer. Each of us would walk out of the bakery carrying cakes, one piled on another to the top of our heads.

JOEL BERGER: I did Ebinger's for my mother's Saturday night get-togethers. Early Saturday morning, I'd walk down Kings Highway and try the Ebinger's near Coney Island Avenue. If it was too crowded or out of what I wanted, I'd go on to the Ebinger's on East Seventeenth Street; from there, to the one on Avenue M; and then on to the one on Avenue J. If need be, I'd go to all four in order to get the "blackout cake."

Doc Hesse with the tools of his trade in his Atlantic Avenue pharmacy.

During the war, there were rumors that Ebinger's was run by Nazis, but we managed to put them aside. The saleswomen didn't look like Nazis. They were nice old ladies with blue hair pulled back into hairnets.

MARNIE BERNSTEIN: The woman in Block's ice-cream parlor wore her blue hair in a bun. Her skin was ashy white; she wore no makeup, was always in a white apron. Her ice-cream parlor, on the corner of Bay Parkway and Sixty-third Street, was a long and dark and very cool place with a turn-of-the-century feeling. The floor was black-and-white tile. The tabletops and counter were black marble, and the wall behind the counter was lined with mirrors and inserts of stained glass. You'd sit on a high stool and stare at the panels of flowers and fruit trees or watch yourself sipping a cherry soda that was so foamy it ran over the sides of the glass, and so full of fizz the bubbles went up your nose.

POLLY BERNSTEIN: Mrs. Block had a son who became a dentist on Bay Parkway. He died young. After that, Mrs. Block was inconsolable. She'd serve you an ice-cream soda, and the tears would be running down her face.

SAM BERNSTEIN: New stores opened up on Bay Parkway after the war, on Sixty-fifth Street too. Bensonhurst got more crowded. People had more money. Some groceries became what we called self-service; they were our first supermarkets.

HERBY GREISSMAN: The grocery store on Sixty-fifth Street was so active it required four delivery boys over and above the full-time help: me and my three friends. Every afternoon, we would race home from school to take out the orders. We walked up four flights of stairs

An active Bensonhurst shopping street after the war.

with two boxes of groceries, one on top of the other, so we wouldn't have to make the same trip twice and would be able to get back to the store quicker for the next order. We hustled for tips.

One day my friend delivers to this woman on Avenue P. She's not home. He's pissed because she's never home when he delivers so she doesn't have to tip him. He picks up a milk bottle and breaks it on the threshold of her apartment. When the woman came in to complain the next day, the owner said, "Well, if you would be home, this kind of thing wouldn't happen."

There was someone on Sixty-third Street who was cheaper than free lunch, and that's pretty cheap. He'd make believe he didn't hear the doorbell ring. One day, he asked for a delivery and the owner said, "No." He said, "Why not?" "Because you don't tip." The owner was on our side.

A dime tip was fair. Somebody gave you a quarter tip, it made your day. Mr. Katz, who lived in our building with his lovely wife and two daughters, was a quarter tipper. Strange as it may seem, everyone, no matter what age they were, called him Mr. Katz, including my father. For Passover, Mrs. Katz would come into the store and shop for her order, whatever that might be. Everyone's Passover order was more than one box in those days, so you had to schlepp pretty good. But we literally fought over who would deliver the Katz order, because Mr. Katz would give us a one-dollar tip. I guess it was in the spirit of the holiday. Nobody else did that. A dollar was a lotta, lotta money.

STARR FROST GOLDBERG: Morris-the-sweater-man was a refugee who peddled sweaters from a stand on Sixty-fifth Street. When it rained, he'd open a pair of iron cellar doors on the sidewalk and take his sweaters down the steps to the basement under one of the stores. That's where he stored his stock. He liked the girls, and he'd always want you to come down to the basement where he said he kept his special sweaters. The "busty" look was in then. We all wanted to look like Marilyn Monroe or Jane Russell, and Morris was only too glad to oblige. He did so well that after a while the cellar became like a regular store. Then he rented the space above it, and it became Morris' Boutique.

HELEN FRIED GOLDSTEIN: In those days, everyone wore hats. Men wore the fedoras and Stetsons. Women did not consider themselves dressed without a hat and a pair of gloves. So Jonas Millinery on Fifth Avenue in Bay Ridge was a thriving business. I was still in school when my grandfather got me a part-time job there. They used to call me "the kid." There was such a thing in sales known as the p.m., for *postmortem*, which referred to a hat that had been lying around since last year or the year before. If someone sold a postmortem, they earned another fifty cents. The experienced salespeople didn't want to be annoyed with the p.m.s, so they became my baby. If a woman walked in who didn't look very sophisticated, the others would say, "Let the kid take that one." I would take the hat, retrim it with a feather or flower, and make the sale.

DORIS MODELL TIPOGRAPH: The original off-price boutique was opened by Frieda Loehmann in Brooklyn in 1921, on the site of a former plumbing store. She haunted the wholesale houses, picking up high-fashion samples and overstock, paid cash, and passed the savings on to her customers. Like the ones that followed, the first Loehmann's, on Bedford Avenue and St. John's Place, attracted smart shoppers—very elegant women who had salesgirls call them when a special shipment was due. Then the news would spread like wildfire. Once I got a Pauline Trigère with the label cut out, but I recognized it.

GAIL EISEMAN BERNSTEIN: Loehmann's on Bedford Avenue was ornate, rococo, with banquettes done up in striped zebra material, like the ones in El Morocco. Frieda Loehmann held court on the second-floor landing. Unapproachable, she sat in a thronelike chair observing everything that went on. She wore a black dress, black stockings, black shoes. She had one pat of rouge on each cheek— two absolutely perfect round circles. Her hair was red in the style of Jane Avril, the model for Toulouse-Lautrec. Her money was in her garter. Everybody knew that she had hundreds of dollars there.

The imperious queen of off-price high fashion: Frieda Loehmann.

DORIS MODELL TIPOGRAPH: There were no dressing rooms. You tried on clothes right there on the floor. Men sat on gold thrones on the landing between the stairs. They couldn't walk around where the women undressed.

NORMAN TIPOGRAPH: Some tried.

KARL BERNSTEIN: As kids, it was a treat for us to sit there and watch all the women in their underwear.

GAIL EISEMAN BERNSTEIN: The fancy part of Loehmann's was the upstairs room. The downstairs was for the hoi polloi. You hung your clothes over your pocketbook over the rack and hoped nobody stole anything. And you ran around in your undies.

ELIZABETH RONCKETTI: Schroeder's Butcher Shop, in Green-point, was not for bargain customers. But if you didn't have the money, they would trust you. Come back tomorrow, come back when you can, they would say, letting you take all the goulash, pork chops, chicken fricassee that you wanted.

TOBY SCHOM GROSSMAN: I'd go with my mother to buy a chicken from one of the kosher butchers on Sixty-fifth Street. She'd pick one out, and we'd go in the back to the little chicken-flicking room, where she'd flick the chicken. Then they'd cut it up and give her the insides. Later on, I found out I was allergic to chicken feathers.

FRANK BARBARO: My father's butcher shop, the Majestic Meat Market, on Hamilton Avenue and Nelson Street in Red Hook, was sort of a community center, a social center—like the general store with the cracker barrel in New Hampshire. When La Guardia was running for mayor, the Italians were on a mission. The night of the election, everyone had gathered in my father's butcher shop, listening to the radio on the butcher block. They were ecstatic when he won.

On the sawdust-covered floor were maybe ten metal chairs where the women would sit, waiting their turn to buy meat. It was cut to order like a new suit, a little thicker, a little thinner. My father, in his apron and straw hat, would talk to the customers in Italian. Every customer was a half-hour.

"Before everyone had TVs, the barber shops and beauty parlors gave people a place to go where they could talk with other folk."

Because my father could speak English, he was a kind of a community service person to the Italian immigrants. When they had problems, he could direct them here and there. People like him were the conduits to the Anglo-Saxon community. The real estate broker around the corner, who could read and could notarize something, was called the Professor.

JOAN MAYNARD: Barber shops were in their flower during my childhood. They were centers of communication, places where men exchanged ideas. Younger men were in company with older men, where they could learn the mores of the community. Beauty parlors served the same role for women. We went to a sparkling pink-and-while salon on Ralph and Marion streets, in Bedford-Stuyvesant, to have our hair washed, pressed with an iron, and curled. That was standard procedure. Thelma, the owner, came from North Carolina. Holiday time, her family down south would send her country ham that was prepared in a special kind of way. She gave out slices to all the customers. Before everyone had TVs, the barber shops and beauty parlors gave people a place to go where they could talk with other folk.

RICHARD GOLDSTEIN: In 1951, someone offered Abie, the neighborhood barber, a year's use of a television set in exchange for a year's free shaves and haircuts. In that way, Abie's Barber Shop, on Howard Avenue in Crown Heights, became a neighborhood gathering place. He drew quite a crowd.

KARL BERNSTEIN: People got together outside of stores that sold TVs and watched them through the windows. The first TV I ever saw was at Rugby Radio on Linden Boulevard, just above Utica Avenue. It was the time of the World Series, and they had a Philco projection TV which projected the image onto a screen.

BOB ARNESEN: When my grandfather came to live with us, he spent his days in the bars and grills of Bay Ridge, where he drank his schnapps and enjoyed the camaraderie. The bars were something like the English pubs, gathering places for primarily the Irish and Scandinavian men.

MARNIE BERNSTEIN: Sam Germaine's candy store, on Twenty-fourth Avenue, was the gathering place for the men in the neighborhood. Once it had been a garage, and inside it was small, dark, and dusty. There was only enough room for a little soda fountain; a big

red ice chest you would open from the top, stick your hand in, and come up with a wet, cold bottle of Coke; and shelves filled with cheap toys, comics, and coloring books. All the kids bought their daily ice-cream cone or Melloroll at Sam's for seven cents. Sam was a gruff but good-natured guy who spoke in a raspy voice through a big fat cigar clamped between his teeth. His assistant was a silver-haired old gentleman named Harris who came from England, the only Englishman any of us knew. Once he was crossing Twenty-fourth Avenue, and a gust of wind blew his hat right off his head. He took off after it, ran like a sprinter, and caught it.

Because the inside of Sam's was too small to hold more than three or four people, all the action took place on the driveway out front. There was a newsstand, penny machines for Indian nuts and Chiclets chewing gum, and a rickety bench along the apartment house wall next door. The men would come out on a Saturday morning, pick up a newspaper from the stand, buy a pack of Chesterfields or Camels, and hang around, kibitzing till lunchtime. Or at night, after dinner— especially before everyone had television sets—they'd get together outside of Sam's, even in the wintertime.

JUDY BERGER: The radio was always on in the small candy store on Avenue M, and people sat at the fountain listening to the event of the day or the baseball game. The penny candy was behind a sliding glass case. You stood there forever with your two cents or nickel, deciding between the red licorice whips and the dots stuck to strips of paper, or leafed through the comic books that cost ten cents apiece. My favorite was *Superman*.

JOEL BERGER: My favorites were Classic Comics. The first one was *The Three Musketeers*, then *A Tale of Two Cities*, then the one I remember best, *Les Misérables*.

ELLIOT GUNTY: Saturday nights we hung out at the candy store on East Ninth Street and Avenue H until the news truck came. The guy would yell, "Yo!" The candy-store owner would give me two dollars, I'd pick up maybe fifty papers and bring them to the store. In no time, we'd be cleaned out.

JOEL BERGER: Schechter's candy store, on Avenue P, was filled with a jumble of pens and pencils and pads and all kinds of different little toys and games, plus an ice-cream fountain where the ice cream was sold hand-packed into little cartons that looked like the kind you get for Chinese take-out food.

A reason for reading the last page of the newspaper first: the time the Dodgers won the World Series.

But the important event at Schechter's was the arrival of the *News* and *Mirror* about 9:30 in the evening. There would always be a group of men waiting, talking about the game that day. The truck would throw the pack out on the sidewalk, one of the kids hanging around would bring it in, and the owner would cut the rope with a razor. For a nickel, you got the two papers and a penny change. The *Mirror* was second-rate to the *News*, but it was there and it was two cents, so you might as well take it. It had Walter Winchell.

The *Brooklyn Eagle* was sold on a home-delivery basis. It covered local events, gave a voice to the whole community, and had a fantastic sports page that covered not only the Dodgers, but everything that went on in the high schools. In my home, every day we got the *News* and the *Mirror* at night, the *Brooklyn Eagle* delivered by a newsboy, the *New York Sun*, and the *New York Post*. Sometimes we got the *Times*, but never the *Tribune* or the *Journal-American*. My father liked newspapers; he believed that for a few cents you found out something you didn't know before.

MIRIAM KITTRELL: In my house, no one read any paper from the front to the back. The sports news began on the back page, and the Jewish papers were read from back to front: *The Tag, The Forward, The Morning Journal.* The candy store on McDonald Avenue and Avenue P sold them all. It also sold *The Freiheit,* the Jewish communist newspaper, under the counter.

STEWIE STONE: The candy store on Church and Nostrand was the place for egg creams and long salt pretzels. Egg creams, for some strange reason, are only good next to a subway station. There was also the cherry lime rickey—that was the best. When I started traveling, at the age of twenty-three, I still had the taste for it. I thought I could get one like I got in Brooklyn. But no cherry lime rickey. And the egg creams—forget about it.

LUIS COLMENARES: The candy store in Brooklyn Heights on the corner of Orange and Fulton streets sold dates rolled in powdered sugar to make them soft and all kinds of trinkets, like automatic flints to start fires.

ELI WALLACH: My parents owned a candy store in Red Hook called Bertha's, which was my mother's name. My father made the two cents plain seltzer and sold charlotte russes, little rounds of sponge cake set into cardboard rings and topped with a mound of whipped cream that looked like the crown of a king. I swept the Indian nut shells off the floor.

As in all candy stores, people hung around. Some of them were Mafia guys. I've played these tough-guy roles, like the one in *Godfather III*, and based my characterizations on the people I used to see hanging around Bertha's.

ALAN LELCHUK: We all knew the history of gangsters in Brooklyn, people like Bugsy Siegel, Dutch Schultz. The lore about the local barber shop was that Bugsy used to slice up troublemakers while they were taking a shave there.

AL LEWIS: Brownsville was the home of Murder, Inc. I knew guys who were for hire to kill. I used to see them in the street—no big deal.

Abe Reles, allegedly a member of Murder, Inc., used to go to the Loew's Pitkin. Henrietta Kamern, who was the organist for the Dodgers before Gladys Gooding, played the organ while the people were walking in and out. Reles used to request his favorite song: "Be Sure It's True When You Say I Love You, It's a Sin to Tell a Lie." Every time she played it, he sent her a twenty-dollar bill.

NORMAN SPIZZ: There was a Mafia presence in the Brooklyn nightclubs in the fifties, although I didn't know it back when I got out

of high school and was playing in nightclub bands for Pat Cooper, who was still a part-time bricklayer, and a whole bunch of singers: Al Hibler, Jerry Vale, the DeCastro sisters, the DeJohn sisters.

ROZ STARR: When I began my singing career at a small club, an elegant gentleman came in wearing a suit that in those days must have cost close to a thousand dollars. He asked me to sing "Melancholy Baby," which is the song every singer hates, because they're always asked to sing it. This was the kind of place where people were always talking, but while I sang "Melancholy Baby," no one made a sound. The guy tipped me ten dollars; I was getting twenty-five dollars for the whole evening. The next day, I open the paper and his picture is in it; he's dead. It was Albert Anastasia. Me and gangsters—they love me.

WADE SILER: The Krulick brothers, owners of the Baby Grand in Harlem, also owned the Brooklyn Baby Grand, at Nostrand and Fulton. The audience was mostly black. They drank straight whiskey in a shot glass or scotch and milk, which was supposed to put a lining in your stomach.

JOAN MAYNARD: It was the kind of nightclub where ladies felt comfortable.

Dressing up and going out: the Oriental Beach employees in Tappan's Restaurant at Sheepshead Bay.

WADE SILER: A lot of big celebrities started out there, on the bandstand above the bar. My song was always "Body and Soul." They called me another Billy Eckstine.

HERB BERNSTEIN: Brooklyn had major places for live entertainment then. Shows ran all week. The whole thing was the going out, the dressing up. People drove up in terrific cars that cost three or four thousand dollars and gave the keys over to valet parking. The four-hundred-seat Elegante on Ocean Parkway, right next to the Washington Cemetery, had performers like Patti Page, Mel Tormé, Joni James.

BARRY FRANK: The Suburban Supper Club, across the cemetery from the Elegante, was chic and intimate, with a candlelit dining room. I sang "Zing Went the Strings of My Heart" and "Unchained Melody" and thought I was doing great making about $150 a weekend. Ben Maksik's Town and Country was the Copacabana of Brooklyn. It had the Copa attitude. Tony Bennett, Judy Garland, Milton Berle worked there.

HERB BERNSTEIN: It was a Las Vegas–type operation on Flatbush Avenue. With about twelve hundred seats to fill, it was so large that it started to lose business. They couldn't afford the big acts, and

the people wouldn't come to see the lesser acts. So, as a kind of lark, Town and Country put a group in called the Jewel Box Revue. They were a bunch of transvestites, gorgeous. It was unusual for those days, especially for Brooklyn. People came out of curiosity, and it kept the club going for a while.

STEWIE STONE: When I MC'd at the Airport, I dreamed I'd be lucky enough one day to cross Flatbush Avenue and work at Town and Country. But I never did. It closed down.

I used to go to a coffeehouse in Sheepshead Bay called Pips to watch guys work. It was the forerunner of the comedy clubs. David Brenner got his start there. All the stars would come out to practice before they did the *Ed Sullivan Show* Sunday night. You could sell your late Saturday night spot to whoever was doing Sullivan the next night. Like Joan Rivers would pay you to let her try out before that live audience. Every performer worked at Pip's.

"At Sheepshead Bay, you could eat at one of the restaurants, buy fish fresh off the boats, or throw a line off the wooden bridge connecting Sheepshead Bay and Manhattan Beach."

MARTIN SPITZER: Eating out was a Sunday ritual. My father came back from playing handball at Brighton Beach about 12:30, and we'd all go out for lunch. If friends were there, we took them along. Out of a month, three weekends we would go Chinese, and the fourth weekend we would go Italian.

There was a good Chinese place on Eighty-sixth Street upstairs, right near the elevated trains, and also the New Deal, on Bay Parkway and Sixty-fifth Street; later, it changed its name to Tang Fong. There were always lines outside and people we knew from the neighborhood inside. They didn't have all the fancy dishes they have today, just chow mein and chop suey, wonton soup, spareribs, egg rolls, and fried rice.

For Italian, we went to one of the restaurants in Coney Island. Stella's was a little family-owned storefront. You walked in and sat yourself down. They'd come over with their menu—not a big folded thing, but a paper sheet. I don't even think they had tablecloths. There was a big potbellied stove in the kitchen that you could see from the dining room, and you could overhear the family arguing in there. It made you feel like you were one of them.

KARL BERNSTEIN: Gargiulo's was and is the fanciest of the Coney Island Italian restaurants, with high ceilings, ornate decorations, and tile floors.

The Carolina used to have a little garden that was an outdoor dining room in the warm weather. You had to walk through the kitchen to get to it. After they paved the garden over, you still had to walk through the kitchen to get to the dining room.

MARTIN SPITZER: For pizza, there's no place like Tortone's, on Neptune and Fifteenth, just a little storefront with no signs. They use a little brick oven, all fresh ingredients, and make just so much dough. When the dough is gone, they close for the night; so if you're not there early enough, forget it. If you take a pizza out, they put it on a round cardboard and wrap it in brown paper. The aroma was unbelievable. People would come from all over; they still do.

LARRY STRICKLER: For seafood, everyone went to Sheepshead Bay. There was Pappas and there was Tappan's, but Lundy's was the tops, the apex. It was a beige stucco, two-story Spanish-style building with a red tile roof and green shutters on the windows that took up a whole block. The gigantic parking lot went all the way back to the Belt Parkway.

MARTIN SPITZER: They'd open up the cherrystones and littlenecks and sell them a half-dozen or a dozen. You could put your hand in this jar and take out crackers—they weren't wrapped up, just loose—and eat them while you watched the fishing boats in the bay.

SHELLY STRICKLER: There were so many entrances to Lundy's, and it was mobbed, especially on Sundays. There was no such thing

Lundy's was the tops, the apex of Sheepshead Bay dining.

as a line. You looked for a table that was finishing, where they were having dessert, and stood behind it, waiting, ravenous.

NORMAN TIPOGRAPH: Patsy, a head waiter, was a handsome black man, very dignified looking in his black jacket and pants, black bow tie with a white shirt. He had been at Lundy's for many years. Henry, my father-in-law, would walk up to him: "I'm here with the family."

"All right, Mr. Modell."

And as soon as a table cleared, we got it.

DORIS MODELL TIPOGRAPH: We had the shore dinner for about six bucks. This was what you got: a shrimp cocktail, a cup of clam chowder, the little round biscuits (which were heaven), and the hardtack like a soda cracker; then a salad of sliced tomatoes and onions, half a cold lobster, half a broiled chicken, french fries, home fries, or corn; and then the best blueberry pie or apple pie, with Breyers ice cream.

LARRY STRICKLER: The waiters all seemed to have Caribbean lilts. They were so abrupt you had to know exactly what you wanted when they came over, or else they'd be gone and you'd wait an eternity. They looked like they were moving fast, but the food never came out.

NORMAN TIPOGRAPH: They were brusque because they had to serve a lot of meals and wanted the turnover. It was hard work, and they worked for very low wages.

ELLIOT GUNTY: After they finally took your order, you'd sit there twenty minutes. The kitchen was so far away. And then it all came.

LARRY STRICKLER: You'd put some butter on the hot biscuits and it would melt. My mother would be screaming I should stop eating them. I'd be whispering to my father to ask for more.

JOE SIGLER: When a relative came to town, we'd take him to Lundy's for breakfast: clams on the half-shell. We'd bring back one of their pies, leaving a deposit for the tin plate.

But Sheepshead Bay was more than Lundy's to me. I remember watching the sun rise over the water hours before Lundy's opened. I'd go down there with Sherwood Levine, who lived in the apartment underneath me. We had this system of knocking on the radiators to wake each other up at 4:00 A.M. We'd get dressed, grab our fishing poles, and take the subway at the Parkside Avenue station. It would still be dark out, but there we'd be, fishing off the docks at Sheepshead Bay.

TERRY PERNA ARNESEN: When my father went to Sheepshead Bay, it wasn't to eat at Lundy's or Tappan's, but to buy fresh fish off the boats. He and my mother came from a small island between Rome and Naples, and fish was a staple in their diet. Every Sunday morning, he'd go down and wait for the ships that came in about noon. He'd buy eight flounder or bluefish for a dollar, bring them home, clean them, and we'd have fried fish, fish stew—you name it.

NORMAN TIPOGRAPH: A ferry used to run among all the fishing and excursion boats in Sheepshead Bay. It left the pier at Ocean and Emmons and crossed the Rockaway Inlet to Lois's Pier at Breezy Point, the western tip of the Rockaway peninsula. It cost twenty-five cents for a forty-minute ride. That's where I took Doris on our first date.

Sometimes late in the evening, after taking Doris back to her home in Manhattan Beach, I'd walk the distance to Sheepshead Bay. It would be the middle of the night, but there'd always be people fishing off the wooden bridge. I'd ask a fellow to give me a line, and I'd fish or crab until the sun came up. Then I'd grab the Ocean Avenue trolley and take it back to Flatbush, where I lived.

Everybody Knew
Everybody Else's Business

YOUR MOTHER AND MY MOTHER
WERE HANGING OUT CLOTHES,
YOUR MOTHER GAVE MY MOTHER
A PUNCH IN THE NOSE.
WHAT COLOR WAS THE BLOOD?
—Choosing rhyme

DONNA GEFFNER: Our windows of our apartment faced the court-yard. If a light was on at one o'clock in the morning, a neighbor would telephone, "Is everything OK?"

JOAN RIBAUDO: When someone was sick, the news went through the building like lightning. Within minutes, everybody knew, and people would be knocking on your door to find out if you needed something.

JOYCE SHAPIRO FEIGENBAUM: My father was an auditor for the IRS. On the way to work, people would waylay him and try to turn one of the other neighbors in. My father would take out a little pad, write something down, and say, "Thank you for letting me know." But he never did anything about it.

MIRIAM KITTRELL: Everybody knew everybody else's business: what they did for a living, who was making money and who was laid off, what was going on with the children. From their windows, the women would call to each other across the courtyard: "John—the super—was drunk last night."

"Well, he's not Jewish, so he can be an alcoholic."

MARCO CARCICH: Whenever I walked through the entrance courtyard of my grandparents' apartment house on Avenue J, I'd be aware of all these conversations going on over my head. People were shouting back and forth, from window to window: "Where are you going?" "Are you going shopping?" "Where's the game tonight?"

CAROLINE KATZ MOUNT: Notions of privacy were very differ-ent living in those apartment houses. You'd overhear another family's life: the arguments, the scraping of chairs, the creaking of furniture, the footsteps on the wooden and linoleum-covered floors, the doors slamming as people went in and out.

MAX WECHSLER: My bedroom up on the third floor faced out onto the courtyard. I could smell food cooking, hear fights, different kinds of music and ball games on the radio. And at night, if a light was on and a shade was up, I could see whatever was going on. The guy who lived in the apartment directly across from my window had married a German girl and brought her and her sister over. They were tall, blonde, and shapely—and into calisthenics, which they performed without any clothes.

What I liked best was when they lay side-by-side on the bed and did leg-lifts. Benjamin Gordon—Fidgety-Ben—would come over with the telescope he bought for stargazing; he liked the arm rotations best. Once the girls noticed us watching. But they didn't lower the shade or stop exercising. It got so that my friends were dropping by every evening for a private showing.

TOBY SCHOM GROSSMAN: Neighbors were always dropping in unannounced, but my father loved people, and having company made him very happy. I never knew my own grandmothers, but Mrs. Epstein, who lived on our floor, was like a grandmother to me. She was a tiny old lady, always beautifully dressed, with silvery tinkly jewelry and big glasses that magnified her eyes. I never had any sisters or brothers, but there were so many children in the building or children visiting family in the building that it seemed like I had a big family.

HERBY GREISSMAN: In 1948 or '49, a family named Unger purchased the first television in our building. At eight o'clock on Tuesday night, the whole apartment house went into the Unger living room. They had more people in that one room watching Milton Berle.

GAIL EISEMAN BERNSTEIN: One day when I was in the fourth grade, I came home for lunch (my mother made me a tuna-fish sandwich for lunch every day), and some men were there delivering our first television set, a Shaw Video TV. It took all day. They put our antenna up on the roof on top of the elevator shaft, so we would get the best reception.

From then on, we didn't have to go to Eleanor Schaeffer's anymore to watch TV. Everyone in our forty-two-family building used to go to Eleanor's apartment, E-1, on the fifth floor. The set was in the foyer. It was wall-to-wall chairs for the grown-ups; the children sat on the floor. No food was ever served. We were there to watch television: Milton Berle, *I Love Lucy*, *Man Against Crime*.

FREDDIE GERSHON: A couple of hundred people lived in my apartment house, and everyone socialized with everyone else. If two women had a fight over a mah-jongg game, the building lined up in two camps.

STAN GOLDBERG: Mah-jongg was the social thing for the women in the neighborhood, the status symbol. My mother's game was Class A. Class B was another game hoping to develop into Class A. You had to be sharp to be seated in my mother's game—you had to be fast, a first-rate player. Pat Meyers, the epitome of the all-American

In time, the television set replaced the radio in the honored spot of the living room.

girl, was the daughter of the number-one per-diem player in my mother's game, on call when someone backed out. That was a big deal.

Pineapple was a must. It was served at every game, sliced and spiked with fancy plastic toothpicks that looked like little swords. Sometimes my grandmother sent sponge cake up on the conveyor belt—that is, the bannister—from her apartment downstairs.

My room was about three feet from the living room where the games were played so I overheard all the conversations. Once one of the ladies said, "When my Irving wants something special, he puts his arm around me." Just then I called out, "Ma, can I have some water?" They all screamed. "Oh my God, he heard me," the lady said. "I thought he was sleeping."

The Class A mah-jongg group and spouses celebrate at a bar mitzvah.

My mother introduced me to a new player. She took a look at me and said, "This one has bedroom eyes." Later I said, "Ma, did I look that tired?" I didn't get everything right away. But as time went on, I'd realize, "Oh, that's what they meant."

The mah-jongg games were very provocative. One woman was caught planting tiles in her bosom. They were talking grand jury, but she got off. She had a good attorney.

These were bright, upbeat women who talked about world events, McCarthyism, race relations during the games. They were active in neighborhood things, formed an organization named after a local boy who was killed in the war that helped the veterans' hospital, and had

Memorial Day and Veterans Day services every year. They were well-groomed and attractive women, not yentas in housecoats with rollers in their hair.

KARL BERNSTEIN: My mother and a group of ladies on the block formed a group they called the Musicale. Each month they met at someone's home, where each woman would perform a piece on the piano, and then they would have coffee and cake. Over the years, there was less and less playing, more and more eating. After a while we started calling it the Musicalorie.

HERBY GREISSMAN: On our small block on Twenty-fourth Avenue between Sixty-fourth and Sixty-fifth streets, there were three walk-up apartment houses—about forty apartments in each building, most of them filled with families. We were war and postwar babies, kids my age, a couple of years older, a couple of years younger.

JOAN RIBAUDO: There was always a series of youngsters, like a stepladder—we grew up together. We played in the streets, and the grown-ups sat along the sidewalk and watched.

Once a father commented, "You boys don't know how to play punchball. In my day, we could have beat you." Of course, it was a challenge. This they couldn't do in the street, because it had to be properly witnessed. They went to Seth Low Park. All these men with nice upright posture walked the four blocks to the game. But coming back, they were the dregs of the earth, and in the following days we saw legs in casts, arms in slings.

HERBY GREISSMAN: The building across the street had two glass doors in front. One was always closed, and the other you opened to go in and out. The glass on the closed door broke, and for a long time it stayed that way—just the iron frame without any window pane inside. There was one kid in the building who would come down and take a running jump through the iron frame of that stationary door. He did it every day, every time he went out, every time he came in. Finally they get around to replacing the glass. Only nobody tells him. Next day, he comes down, takes a running jump, and *crash!*

He got scratched up pretty good, but we were always getting scratched and bruised from playing and fighting with each other. My mother, however, never got involved in any of her children's battles. "The children fight and make up, and the parents stay mad forever," she'd say.

JOYCE SHAPIRO FEIGENBAUM: When Carolyn Cantor got into a fight, she'd not only slap and scratch, she'd bite. One day she bit Judy Levine in the hallway outside of the Levine apartment. Judy's mother was in the shower at the time, but that didn't prevent her from hearing her daughter scream. She ran out soaking wet, with just a towel wrapped around her, grabbed Carolyn and started shaking her, yelling how she was fed up with her biting all the kids. Mrs. Cantor appeared. "Leave my daughter alone," she cried, pulling Mrs. Levine off Carolyn. The two women began wrestling on the ground. In a flash, the whole building was at the scene. My mother picked up the towel, which naturally had fallen off Mrs. Levine, and ran around the pair holding the towel over them. That was one argument that took a long time to heal.

CAROLINE KATZ MOUNT: None of the kids in our building could get into a fight when Nick, the super, was around. He'd always get in the middle, stop the battle, make us shake hands and make up. Every kid in the building loved Nick. No matter how busy he was, he always paid attention to us.

TOBY SCHOM GROSSMAN: The first time I saw Nick, I was three years old. It was a January afternoon, the day I arrived in this country. I was born in a displaced-person camp in Germany. My aunt and uncle sponsored my parents and me. They met us at the ship and brought us to their building. When we got there, it was snowing lightly and just starting to get dark. A man was standing outside, all by himself. It was Nick. I thought he was waiting for us. He took me by the hand and brought me to my aunt's apartment, which was next door to his own. I didn't understand a word he said because I spoke only Yiddish.

MARNIE BERNSTEIN: Nick was short and squat, tough-looking like a wrestler, but actually he was a very gentle and warm man who loved children. He had maybe five or six of his own, but only one son lived with him. The rest were in foster homes because his wife was unstable, in and out of hospitals. One Christmas she came home for a few days. She went into the lobby in the middle of the night, dressed in a nightgown, her hair long and wild, and rang all the bells. It was terrible. Nick's favorite child was the baby, Rosemarie. He always talked about her, showed off her picture. She stayed with him for a little while, and we all thought she was just beautiful, like a pink doll.

HERBY GREISSMAN: Nick had so much work to do. He collected the garbage from every apartment using dumbwaiters that operated through open shafts in the building. The furnace was fired by coal, so he had to stoke it every day and bring out the ash barrels.

CAROLINE KATZ MOUNT: There were so many babies in those postwar years, and the carriages for all the babies in the building were kept in the cellar. Every morning, Nick would wheel them up onto the street. They'd be standing there in a row waiting for the mothers when they came out with their babies. And in the late afternoon, he'd push them back down, making a long line of carriages, one behind the other, wheeling them around the corner, down the sloped alleyway, and into the cellar.

MARNIE BERNSTEIN: Nick had been in vaudeville with his four brothers in an act called the Shanghai Five. He let us look through his big album at the old programs, newspaper reviews, and photos of the group taken with Eddie Cantor and Jimmy Durante. They were dressed in Chinese pajamas and made up to look like Charlie Chan. The Shanghai Five played at Coney Island saloons and at theaters all over the country, even the Palace, until vaudeville ended.

Nick still had a great voice. On rainy summer nights, everyone would bring their folding chairs into the lobby, and Nick would entertain. His favorite song was the Neapolitan ballad: "Oi Marie, oi Marie, quanto notti aggio perso per te. . . ." His tenor voice was so strong, neighbors in the buildings across the street and next door heard him. They would come over, crowding into our lobby.

Nick wasn't the only singer in the building. There was also Mrs.

"There were so many babies in those postwar years."

Parker, who lived in a top-floor apartment with her husband, a cordial and elegant bookie who dressed impeccably in well-cut suits and silk shirts and ties, and their beautiful redheaded daughter. Mrs. Parker mostly kept to herself. The other women referred to her as the Nightingale, I guess because she would sit by the open window of her bedroom overlooking the courtyard, her plump arms crossed on a pillow, and sing Jerome Kern and Sigmund Romberg songs. In warm weather, when the doors to the courtyard were open into the lobby, you'd walk through and "You are the promised kiss of springtime" would be echoing through the halls.

TERRY PERNA ARNESEN: My mother sang all the Neapolitan love songs around the house while she dusted and cleaned. We always listened to records, to opera on the radio. Part of being Italian was knowing all the different Italian operas. Our neighborhood was a mixture of Italian and Jews. But when you passed by and heard the music, or saw the backyard with the tomato plants and the sweet basil and the fig tree with the little pink blossoms, you knew it was an Italian family.

ANGELO BADALAMENTI: The Italians always bought little houses, because they needed a place to have tomatoes, basil, and some flowers. That all came from the old country, along with the love of music.

When I was very young, we lived on Harway Avenue, an exclusively Italian neighborhood. Every weekend in the summer, they had shows in tents on the empty lots that were all over the area. They were mostly Italian dramas. The audience would be very quiet. Except every once in a while, you would hear somebody snore.

KARL BERNSTEIN: Mrs. Capricilli, who lived across the street from us, kept a beautiful and immaculate garden in the back and poplar trees in the front. I guess they reminded her of Italy. When Mr. Capricilli died, my mother and Aunt Sally paid a condolence call, and my cousin Billy and I went along. It was the only time I was in that house. The walls were painted purple and black. Beautiful paintings hung on the walls. She was an elegant lady, but still she used to scrub her stoop and the driveway from back to front every morning, on her hands and knees with a bucket and brush. Then she would sweep the debris in the gutter from her side to ours.

Bugsy Goldstein, who lived across the alley from us, was a hit man for the mob. He was tough. When he spoke to you, it was like hearing James Cagney. He was away a lot of the time; I guess in jail.

His daughter Joannie was my closest friend in first grade. My cousin Billy and I were invited to her birthday party, and my Aunt Sally and my mother were so excited because all the "gun molls" would be there. They wondered what they would talk about. The "gun molls" talked about what other mothers talked about: diapers, formula, babies. But at that party, Bugsy went out to get ice cream and was picked up by the police. When finally he was electrocuted, his mother and father were screaming outside in the street. Then they moved away.

MAX WECHSLER: Everyone in the neighborhood knew that Marvin's father was a big-time gangster. His family lived on Roebling Street, in a duplex apartment on the top floors of the best building in all of Williamsburg. It had a doorman, furniture in the lobby, and an elevator. Two guys dressed in dark suits always sat right outside the elevator, reading the newspapers and smoking Lucky Strike cigarettes. They were bodyguards for Marvin's father, screening all the people coming on the floor, and sometimes were runners for the numbers game.

In junior high, Marvin and I became friends. We used to play cards in his apartment after school. Once, we had finished a game of poker and were walking out to the elevator when one of the guys, a big, heavyset man, put up his fists like Rocky Marciano. "Come on, kid, let's go a round or two," he said, giving me a playful but hard slap in the face.

For the moment, I forgot where I was and lashed out at him, landing a closed fist right on his nose with all the force I could muster. He went back against the wall, and at the same instant, reached inside his suit jacket and pulled out a gun. Lucky for me, his partner jumped in front of him. "For Chrissake," he said, "he's just a kid."

The next day Marvin told me his father really gave it to the guy. Still, I stayed away from the apartment for a while. When I finally went back after a couple of weeks, the guy greeted me at the elevator. "You gotta learn to take a joke, kid," he said sheepishly. "I woulda never hurt you."

LUIS COLMENARES: Trina and Johnny Castros lived next door to us in a seven-room apartment, two of which they rented to boarders. Maybe because they had no kids of their own, they always invited us in to listen to the radio or to stories Johnny told about Puerto Rico, where he was born. Trina was very tall and thin, a Miss Brooks–type personality. Johnny was very short, with a lot of white hair; we thought he looked like Albert Einstein. He made cigars in a place on Fulton

Street, and there was always a sweet aroma in the room he kept for himself in the back of the apartment.

CHARLES HYNES: Mr. Helman spent the nice days sitting in the large open courtyard of our building, wearing very dark glasses. Once he had been an executive in the garment business, but he lost his sight when he was in his early forties. The kids used to greet him. He got to know all of us by our voices. He would say things like, "If you point one finger, three point back" and "It never hurts to talk" and "Never answer a speculative question."

AL LEWIS: We lived in four different buildings on Douglas Street, which later became Strauss Street, in Brownsville. They were tenements, six-by-eight rooms, railroad flats. People joked about putting the key in the front door and breaking the window.

DORIS MODELL TIPOGRAPH: When we moved to the brand-new Nathan Hale, on Avenue K, I thought we were so rich, because the building had an elevator and an incinerator.

DONNA GEFFNER: Our building on Twenty-third Avenue had an elevator and an incinerator, and also our very own doctor. Dr. Smilensky's office, on the ground floor right, was always filled.

The sectional couch defined the elegant apartment-house living room and was the favored spot for entertaining.

Everyone in the building used him. He knew about the head, about the ears. He knew when it was emotional; he knew when it was physical. If you were sick, he'd come up to see you in your apartment, and as soon as he walked in, you had that feeling of *refia*—that you're going to get better.

ALAN BLANKSTEIN: When I was a kid, doctors had much more of a personal relationship with the patients. They all made house calls. But even in those days, Dr. Matthew Brunner was in a class by himself. I was asthmatic, and my parents used Dr. Brunner because he was such a big specialist. His office was on Eastern Parkway, which was quite a distance from our Flatbush house, but when I had an asthma attack, he'd come to the house, and he wouldn't leave until he was sure I'd be all right. Sometimes he stayed all night. He would sit around the table talking to my parents and play the piano to keep himself occupied.

MARNIE BERNSTEIN: A blast on the outside bell announced the arrival of Dr. Kaufman. He reminded me of Groucho Marx: the bright black eyes, the wide grin, the fast, long stride. He'd storm into the apartment, examine the patient one-two-three, make a quick diagnosis, write out the prescription, get his five dollars, and be gone. The only time he hung around was during the Rosenberg trial. His brother was the judge who sentenced them to the electric chair. "Guilty, guilty, no question about it," he'd tell my father.

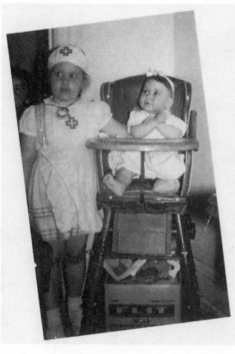

PAT COOPER: Dr. Rini's office was on First Place and Clinton, but if you were sick, he'd come to your house, sit down, have a dish of macaroni. He never got paid. I was about twelve when my father took me to Dr. Rini. "My son has an appendix," he said. "I tell you right now, you don't make the scar more than one inch and a half or I'll kill you. Because my son has to be a man. And when he takes his clothes off with a woman, I don't want my son to scare her with the scar."

I'm looking at my father. This guy's crazy. He has me taking my clothes off with three girls in the room, I'm dropping dead from the pain, and he's worrying about my scar. But if I showed you my belly now, you'd never find it.

HOWARD RAPP: For years and years we went to Dr. Grodzicker, whose office was on the ground floor of a brownstone in Williamsburg. He drove a new Oldsmobile and handled every ailment. My mother was afraid my brother was going to be short, so Dr. G. gave him a

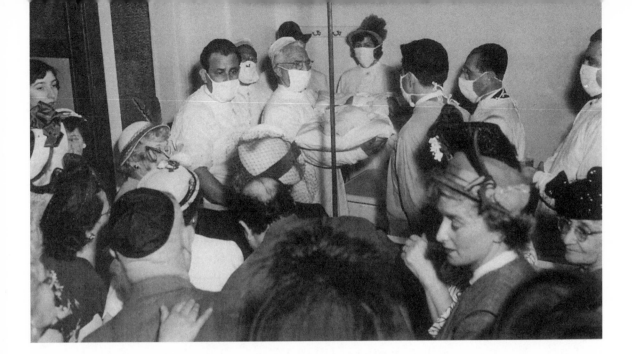

series of shots to make him grow. I got away without taking them. We both wound up the same height—on the short side.

KARL BERNSTEIN: Dr. Feller was my grandmother's and my great-grandmother's doctor. He did surgery, he delivered babies. We still have his instructions in the baby books.

His full name was A. Archibald Feller, but everyone called him Dr. Feller, except for my cousin Helene, who called him Doc Archie. She was part of the family that still lived in Williamsburg, where his office was.

POLLY BERNSTEIN: After we moved to Bensonhurst, we would go by train to visit him. Once he got sick and he said, "Polly, you'll have to get yourself another doctor." And I said, "What's another doctor? I don't know another doctor."

He was a very temperamental man. You had to watch out not to annoy him. I was in the waiting room when a religious couple came in with a little boy. All of a sudden, I heard him yelling, and when he yelled, it was really frightening. "Your child is dying, and it's all because of you. Last week you were here, and I told you to take him to the hospital. Now you're coming back here, and there's nothing I can do."

MAX WECHSLER: Cuffs on the side of the head, two meat-hook–type hands grabbing my shoulders, and a physical presence that was like a football fullback—that was Dr. Feller.

There were the times I would be pulling my pants down, and I wasn't fast enough for him. He'd help out, yanking on my belt the way somebody would pull on a window shade. Then I'd be on the table belly-down and get a needle in the behind. His famous B-12 shots. He believed in that stuff.

KARL BERNSTEIN: Dr. Feller was a massive man, six-two or six-three. He was gruff, he had a raspy voice and a bald head always covered with sweat, and he smelled of chopped liver and onions. In hot weather, he wore a cutout undershirt with his white coat over it. He came all the way to our house in Flatbush in his great big Buick. Once he had indigestion and asked my grandmother, "What do you have for heartburn?" She gave him Pepto-bismol, which he always liked.

Most of the time, though, we went to his office. During the war, when my father's car was up on blocks in the garage, we went by trolleys: the Coney Island Avenue trolley to Park Circle and the Franklin Avenue trolley to Williamsburg.

His office was the bottom level of his house, a converted brownstone on Bedford Avenue and Wilson Street. The waiting room had a fireplace and a set of children's furniture: a table with folded leaves and two little chairs. The kids would wait in line to sit on those chairs. The wait, of course, was interminable. And then you got called into an examining room, and he fluoroscoped you.

MAX WECHSLER: It had a white scale for babies that looked like it was designed for fruits and vegetables, a scale for adults with a vertical strip to measure height, about five different clocks, and glass-fronted cabinets with all kinds of bottles behind them. Everything was immaculate.

After he examined you, Dr. Feller called you into his office in the back with the huge desk and built-in bookcases. Military certificates hung on the wall along with his doctor's diplomas. They seemed like testaments to his valor. There were medals and a little statue of a soldier—memorabilia from his World War I time. The word was that he had been a major. He was always rough and ready, caring, and in perfect control of any medical and family situation. He was the kind of man that you would want to follow into battle.

MARTY ADLER: Prior to going off to battle in Cuba, Teddy Roosevelt took his troops down to Brighton, in the area that now is the very end of Ocean Parkway, and they practiced landing on the sand. A twenty-by-forty-foot area called San Juan Park marks that event. It has a plaque with part of the hull of the battleship *Maine*. For our generation, that part of Brighton was famous for its own kind of battles: the handball games.

LOUIS COHEN: I played all over Brooklyn, but especially in Brighton. I loved it. I never got tired. Every Saturday morning, every Sunday morning, no matter how cold it was, I was out there in shorts, no undershirt.

I began playing handball in the 1930s, during the Depression, when no one had money for baseball gloves and bats. All you needed for handball was a small black ball and gloves. You played anybody who came along; you needed only one or two guys to get a game going. Guys in their fifties, sixties played. I saw fellows play who were in their eighties. It was amazing how much stamina they had, but that was because they played all the time. They never stopped.

MARTIN SPITZER: Handball players were guys who worked in the shipyards and in factories; they were blue-collar workers predominantly—men used to using their hands, which were strong and callused. They showed off their strength and power on the handball court hitting that little black ball. Handball was their way of letting off steam from working all week long.

FREDDIE GERSHON: All the men were expected to play handball, and it was a rough sport. My father tore a ligament in his knee and had to wear a cast for a month. My uncle Jack Zirn got so good he went on the circuit and became a champion. He got a heart attack while playing and actually died on the handball court.

MARTIN SPITZER: The matches were very intense. You knew if you watched that you'd have to be quiet. Even if a great shot was made, there was no applause. It was not an exhibitionist era. There were no official umpires. Crowds of about two dozen people hung around at the different courts. Most were other players waiting for the next challenge. To get on the court, you had to wait for a loser.

World-class then was just the guy next door, without the big money that people make today. Even players like Jimmy Jacobs and Victor Hershkowitz would come down on Sunday in between their tournaments and play on court number one.

LOUIS COHEN: Handball was my life. My wife would say, "Lou, will you ever stop?" I said, "I'll never stop." But I got hit by a van. My back is bad. I can't bend. It kills me whenever I go out to Brighton and look at the handball courts. I want to play.

From Sweltering Stoop to Shimmering Shore

(TO THE TUNE OF ''HOME ON THE RANGE'')

WHERE THE SWEET BREEZES DESCEND,
FROM THE SHORES OF GRAVESEND,
AS WE SINK SLOWLY INTO THE BAY.

—Lafayette High School Senior Sing, 1954

CAROLINE KATZ MOUNT: In the summers, the courtyard of our building became our patio, playground, even wading pool. When it got very hot, Nick—the super—would sweep it out, run up a hose, and hang it like a shower. We would run under the water. It was a wonderful treat.

JOAN RIBAUDO: My father attached a hose to a series of connected pipes in the courtyard. He'd have the kids tell their mothers. They'd come down in their bathing suits with chairs, bring lunch, and sit out in the courtyard all afternoon, going under the spray to keep cool. It was like our own private pool club.

HERBY GREISSMAN: On Sundays, my father and his friends would set out a bridge table and chairs in the courtyard and play pinochle. The laundry hanging on the lines gave them some shade. They'd send me across the street to the candy store for sodas, and I'd get a tip.

Our living-room windows with the fire escape were right over the front entrance to the building. One summer, somebody gave me a toy bugle. When my mother said, "It's time to go to sleep," I would go out on the fire escape and blow my bugle. That became a nightly routine.

I always had an audience because on summer nights, the whole block would be lined with people sitting on bridge chairs, a row with their backs to the building, and a row facing them with their backs to the street. When Rabbi Gartenhouse, who was very Orthodox, passed by, he'd walk in the gutter because he was afraid of brushing against a woman—that's how crowded the streets were.

CAROLINE KATZ MOUNT: The sidewalk became a narrow path. When we came home with boyfriends, it was like walking a gauntlet, having to say hello to all the neighbors and knowing they were giving you and your date the once-over.

The women did their handiwork while they sat outside. They'd be knitting sweaters, crocheting blankets, embroidering tablecloths and napkins in a cross-stitch pattern. The summer of 1949, there was a craze for basket bags—crocheted drawstring pocketbooks with little straw baskets forming the base. Everyone was making them.

ALAN BLANKSTEIN: The summertime scene on East Twenty-seventh Street was like a big hotel. About a hundred people would be out sitting on the little stoops of the semidetached houses, or on beach chairs. They'd walk over, sit on our stoop for a while, then we'd go

Tar beach: the apartment-house roof was a great spot for sunbathing.

over to them. Every woman on the block I called aunt, every man uncle. It was Aunt Miriam, Aunt Evelyn, Uncle Julius, Uncle Sheldon.

JOEL BERGER: If a night Dodger game was on, you could walk down the streets, go past house after house, and hear the southern voice of Red Barber on the radio without missing a single play.

KARL BERNSTEIN: People sat outside as long as they could to avoid the oppressive heat in the apartments. They'd bring out a torch lamp with an extension cord and a bridge table and play mah-jongg or cards till eleven, twelve o'clock.

TOBY SCHOM GROSSMAN: Not only were front doors never locked, people kept them open in the summer for cross-ventilation. Sometimes on hot nights, my father slept on the roof. On Tuesday nights, we all went up there to watch the Schaeffer fireworks from Coney Island.

CHARLES HYNES: Sometimes my mother would get me up in the middle of the night and say, "It's so hot. Let's go down to Coney Island." During the war, when gasoline was difficult to get, the car ran on naphtha, and we had all these cans of naphtha in the trunk. It's a wonder we weren't blown up. But we'd make it to the beach, put our blankets on the sand, and go to sleep. How safe it was, sleeping on the beach a summer night.

MAX WECHSLER: We would wake up with sand in our ears and hair and nose. Still, it was worth it. As bad as those summers could be in Brooklyn in those years before air conditioning, there was always relief at the beach and along the water.

FREDDIE GERSHON: My parents paid around sixty dollars a month for our three-room apartment on Coney Island Avenue across the street from the Brighton Beach Baths. We used to scornfully watch "the outsiders"—those people who had to travel to the beach—get off the train at Brighton Beach Avenue, at the site of Mrs. Stahl's knishes.

We did not go to the public beach. We belonged to Brighton Beach Baths, our select private club, which cost thirty to forty dollars a season for a locker, which we shared with three or four other families. Many members were European-born and very aware that they had their picture laminated in the back of a pass that enabled them to get in

and out of the Baths. But it was their passport to a private and wonderful world.

Cooling off in the courtyard on a summer afternoon.

LARRY STRICKLER: There were no real baths at Brighton Baths, just cold showers. Still, it was a great playground, with the ocean being only one of the amenities. If you exited onto the beach, you got the back of your hand stamped so you could get back in. There were always a gang of kids waiting under the boardwalk who did not have a ticket and would beg you to blot the still-wet ink from your hand onto theirs.

Inside was a kiddy pool, a gigantic swimming pool, a diving pool, handball and paddle-tennis courts. In the early days, there were hand-tennis courts; people played with their hands. It was not until the mid-fifties that it became fashionable to play with a paddle and a dead tennis ball.

There was a big round building with a cafeteria and picnic-style benches and a beautiful bandshell where a live band with two vocalists played for nine weeks in the summer, Tuesday through Sunday, two hours a day. People would get there early to get a good seat, or they reserved one by tossing an extra bathing suit or a towel on one of the multicolored Adirondack-style chairs. We danced on the sand in the hot summer afternoons to "I'm Going to Get You on a Slow Boat to China," medleys from Broadway shows like *Oklahoma* and *South Pacific*, or mambo music like "Sweet and Gentle," "Cherry Pink and Apple Blossom White," and "Mambo Number 5."

FREDDIE GERSHON: Everyone was taking dancing lessons, learning the rumba box step, which was very big. My grandmother, Grandma Becky, loved to sing in a heavy Rumanian accent and dance to "The Miami Beach Rumba," her platform shoes and clunky jewelry adding to the rhythm. She claimed to be a gypsy, and watching her sing and dance, you could believe her.

Brighton Baths had nude sunbathing facilities, separate sections for men and women. Everyone believed the sun was healthy. The more you exposed yourself, the better. They smeared themselves with baby oil and iodine and used sun reflectors to enhance their tans. Even in the wintertime, Grandma Becky and her girlfriends would go on the tar roof of our six-story apartment house, where they'd sit with their reflectors in beach chairs and take in the sun.

RALPH GASARCH: Brighton had all these big apartment houses, and some, like the Shelbourne on Ocean Parkway that took up a complete block, were quite luxurious. They had their own lockers and saltwater as well as freshwater showers, so you wouldn't bring sand up to your apartments. The roofs had separate men's and women's solariums for nude sunbathing. There was a European feeling in Brighton that something healthful was to be gained from the beach air, the salt and minerals in the water.

We lived in the eastern part of Coney Island, but we called our neighborhood West Brighton. I guess we didn't want to be identified with Coney Island. Both Brighton and Coney had bathhouses, but those in Coney Island, like Raven Hall and Washington Baths, were less upscale. Coney Island was transient. Brighton had a sense of permanence.

POLLY BERNSTEIN: One summer we took a locker at Coney Island. I hated it like poison. My brother-in-law and his wife rented an apartment in Coney Island after they got married, and I couldn't understand it. I didn't like all the common people, the yentas, the fat ladies. I'm not exactly a snob, but I don't like schleppers.

MARTIN SPITZER: We lived in Coney Island in a house owned by my grandparents, about half a block from the beach. They fixed up the basement as an apartment for themselves. My family lived on the first floor with the porch. Upstairs were four bedrooms and a bathroom. People came from Canada to stay in the summer. It was like a boardinghouse. What a fabulous place to live in, especially during the summer.

When I went away to college in Virginia and told people where I came from, they couldn't believe it. They thought Coney Island was all rides and amusements.

BILL FEIGENBAUM: We lived in Coney Island until I was a teenager. Then my father started to do better, and we moved to more-prosperous Flatbush. But to tell the truth, I liked it better in Coney. The resident population was working-class, bright and well-read, but dissatisfied, angry, being fed that propaganda that it was paradise in Russia.

Communist party rallies used to be held at different community centers in Coney Island, and my parents, who were politically left, brought me along with them. The entertainment was great. Usually it was supplied by a local beach bum, a slim, red-headed guy with a lively sense of humor who used to sit on the beach wearing a cowboy hat, strumming his guitar. It was Woody Guthrie. He came from

"As bad as those summers could be in those years before air conditioning, living in Brooklyn, there was always relief at the beach and along the water."

Three bathing beauties
making plans.

Oklahoma or Texas, but he lived in Coney Island with his wife and two kids. His landlady, Anna Lomoff, owned a left-wing bookstore on Thirty-third near Mermaid Avenue. "That Voody, that Voody," she used to complain. He never paid his rent. But boy, he put on a terrific show. At one of the rallies, he brought a whole stack of his records along and sold them for a dollar apiece. People took them home and found they were all warped from the sun. He was on everyone's shit list.

KARL BERNSTEIN: From the heart of Coney Island, you could take the Norton's Point trolley just a short distance into another world. It started up in the air at the Stillwell Avenue subway station, crossed Stillwell Avenue on an elevated structure, dropped down to ground level on a right-of-way between Surf and Mermaid avenues, and ran to the western tip of the peninsula: Sea Gate.

PEARL GASARCH: People who lived in Sea Gate never thought of themselves as having a Coney Island address. Theirs was an exclusive enclave, only about a mile long and less than a half-a-mile wide, set off from the rest of the world by a guarded gate. It had its own garbage collection, security, and block of stores. Huge turn-of-the-century Victorian houses lined the waterfront. But by our time, they had been converted into rooming houses. When we were still living in Williamsburg, we rented an apartment in one of those old houses for the summer. It was a big dark place with varnished wood floors and stairs and bannisters. I'd climb the stairs and there would always be the smell of wood polish.

Later, my parents bought a home in Sea Gate, and we lived there year-round. Many of the people in the community were in the *shmata* business—that is, the garment trade—and during the war there was a lot of black-market money around from the goods they smuggled in from Canada. Also, for some reason a lot of bookies made their homes in Sea Gate, so there were always these big card games: pinochle for the men, canasta for the women. My father used to tell me that as the war progressed, the betting became bigger and bigger.

But to me, Sea Gate had nothing to do with playing cards. Living there felt like being in a seacoast town in Italy, far away from Brooklyn. It was a safe, gated world.

DORIS MODELL TIPOGRAPH: When we moved from Flatbush to Manhattan Beach, I thought it was like living in a resort area year-round. Our house on Dover Street had a lovely yard, and in the summertime we'd be engulfed by the aroma of honeysuckle; it was all over, so strong it was intoxicating.

I used to say that Brighton Beach, to the west, was for our grandparents; Oriental Beach, to the east (where Kingsborough Community College is today), was for the rich; but Manhattan Beach was for us.

Overchoice of summer pleasures at Manhattan Beach.

NORMAN TIPOGRAPH: Manhattan Beach was a glamorous summer place. Bands played for dancing, there were aquacades, you met lovely girls. Enclosed by Sheepshead Bay to the north and east and a magnificent beach to the south, it was a beautiful neighborhood. The streets were lined with substantial private homes. People like Judge Samuel Leibowitz, who defended the Scottsboro boys, and the wealthy Williamsburg Steel family lived there.

DORIS MODELL TIPOGRAPH: Instead of a boardwalk, Manhattan Beach had an esplanade that we walked along, trying to pick up guys. At night we'd ride our bikes along Shore Boulevard and watch the fishing boats on Sheepshead Bay.

ELIZABETH RONCKETTI: In the summers, people in Greenpoint always would go down to the East River piers. They'd sit there and dream, they'd fish. Newton Creek runs through the neighborhood. There used to be Whale's Creek also, but that was filled in. Boys have always swum in the East River. Some haven't quite made it and had to be fished out by the Fire Department.

BARRY FRANK: The thing about Brooklyn was that you always had a sense of the water. There was always that escape from the heat. But for me, it was something else as well. I was always drawn to the water. I'd get on my bike and head south, knowing I'd reach the end: the ocean or Jamaica Bay or Sheepshead Bay or Gravesend Bay. I could stand and look out at the horizon for hours.

TERRY PERNA ARNESEN: I loved to ride my bike from Borough Park down to Shore Road, to watch the ships in the Narrows coming up into New York harbor. Later on, when I taught at Curtis High School in Staten Island, I would take the ferry across the Narrows. That was before the Verrazano Bridge was built. I used to stand on the deck on foggy mornings and listen to the gulls and the foghorns. The Brooklyn docks were so busy back then. As many as twenty ships could be standing in a row, waiting their turn to get into port.

IRWIN POLISHOOK: From my home in Williamsburg, I could walk over to the Williamsburg Bridge and to the Lower East Side, in Manhattan. I would lean over the sides and look at the East River wind southward under the Manhattan Bridge and the Brooklyn Bridge till it flowed into the harbor. Or I'd look northward, follow the river along uptown Manhattan and wonder where Brooklyn ended and Queens began.

SYLVIA COLE: My first husband was a great romantic. He liked to stride along the boardwalk and the sand in Brighton, reciting Goethe. The ocean gave him that impetus to shout into the wind and the waves. That rotund German came out so big and round and dramatic.

NEIL SEDAKA: During a hurricane, I'd get dressed up in my galoshes and rain gear and walk the boardwalk. The wind would be blowing fifty miles an hour, and I'd hold onto the railing and breathe in the storm. I loved the ocean.

JUDY BERGER: Sometimes we rented horses from a stable at Bergen Beach and rode along the shore of Jamaica Bay. It gave us such a feeling of freedom and adventure. But it was also a little scary because we were so far from any kind of civilization.

Bergen Beach, Marine Park, Mill Basin, Canarsie—these were wild waterfront areas when I was a kid, so different from the crowded neighborhoods where we lived. I remember the big expanses, the fields of tall horse grass with only a lone house here and there. It seemed like the end of the world.

DAN LURIE: Our little house in Canarsie was about a quarter of a mile from Jamaica Bay. Around us were big, flat fields cut through with canals of water maybe a foot wide. We jumped across them when we played. We swam what we used to call BA (with no bathing suits) in a channel near where Starrett City is today, smearing its black mud all over our bodies. We rubbed it in good, jumped in the water, and got all cleaned off.

Some of the houses were built on stilts because the water table was so high. Most of the roads were paved with dirt. A trolley ran from the end of the BMT line on Farragut Road and Rockaway Parkway, two miles down to the water. The tracks went along a right-of-way that was a narrow path cutting through the middle of East Ninety-fifth and East Ninety-sixth streets between the backyards of the houses. It went all the way down to Seaview Avenue, crossing Avenue L, Avenue M, Avenue N. . . . At the shore was an amusement park like a miniature Coney Island, and the Golden Gate arena, where they had boxing and wrestling bouts.

When I was a little boy, I used to have the same dream over and over: I dive off the Canarsie pier and swim to the bottom of the bay. It's blue and beautiful. Then I see this big chest. I open it up, and it's filled with pearls and jewelry and money.

Once I went fishing off the pier. It was at night, so I had a little kerosene lantern with me. When I caught a fish, I got so excited, I dropped the lantern into the water, and in pulling up the rod, the fish got off the hook. I lost everything. The following year, fishing in the same area in the daytime, I threw the line in and caught the lantern. My big fish story is that the lantern was still lit.

TOM BOORAS: My grandfather's hardware store, on Atlantic Avenue just below Hicks Street, was close by the waterfront. There were berths from the foot of the Brooklyn Bridge to Thirtieth Street and the Bush Terminal area. The Navy Yard came around the other end. Right under the Brooklyn Bridge was where Brillo manufactured the soap pads. All the raw materials came in on ocean vessels and were loaded into what they called boat warehouses.

My grandfather serviced pretty much that whole waterfront area in the lower end of Brooklyn. All these big, hulking longshoremen would buy their grappling hooks from him. They would either lose them or misplace them or get drunk and leave them behind. So they'd always need new ones. My grandfather sold them by the thousands.

LONNY IRGENS: My grandfather came to Bay Ridge from Norway and worked as a shipping master. Only recently did I learn what that job entails: a shipping master finds drunkards or tramps, knocks them out, picks them up, and shanghais them. When they wake up, they're out at sea. My grandfather accomplished this with the use of one arm. The other arm he lost when a train ran over it. He was one tough guy.

BOB ARNESEN: From Sixty-ninth Street up, the Brooklyn waterfront was lined with docks, which probably is why so many Scandinavians settled in Bay Ridge. They were seafaring people, and many worked on the ships.

Crossing the Narrows from Brooklyn to Staten Island, ferry-goers never tired of gazing at Lady Liberty.

TOM BOORAS: From the time I was a kid, I was fascinated by the docks, the ships, and the water. Our house in Brooklyn Heights was right near the East River. When we were dating, my wife and I had this routine, it was like a ritual: I'd walk from my house on Sydney Place to her house on Hoyt and Warren. Then we would walk back on the Promenade, looking at that magnificent view of the New York City skyline across the river. Before the Promenade was built, around 1954, we used to walk across what they called the Penny Bridge that went from the end of Montague Street across to the St. George Hotel. We'd go up to the balcony above the hotel's saltwater pool and watch the swimmers below.

LUIS COLMENARES: The St. George had the only saltwater pool in Brooklyn. It was enormous and had a waterfall at one end. The

walls, the ceiling, and the hallways leading to the pool were of a kind of golden, bluish glass carved with mermaids, mermen, and beautiful fish. If you sprang up off the high diving board, you could almost touch the glass ceiling.

TOM BOORAS: As I was a water rat, I could watch the swimmers at the St. George for hours. My father was the swimming coach at St. Francis Prep, and I had been swimming there from the time I was eight. From my earliest days, I've had this connection to the water. That's my connection to Brooklyn.

MARCO CARCICH: Out in Gravesend Bay you can see small lobsters, abundant fish. The whole coast along Coney Island is still one of the clearest sections for diving in the region. At every tide change, there's a complete change of water. The sweep of the Atlantic current drains the East River, the Hudson River, all the inlets. And that makes Brooklyn's shorefront the cleanest water in the New York area.

ELI WALLACH: Wherever you are in Brooklyn, you have a sense of the sea. From Coney Island, to the shorefront communities of Sea Gate and Manhattan Beach, to all the bridges that link the borough to other shores, to the boats coming into port, to the avenues and parkways named after the ocean and shore—there's water, water everywhere.

CHAPTER 8

Coney Island

THERE STANDS ME WIFE,
THE IDOL OF ME LIFE,
SINGING ROLL OR BOWL A BALL,
A PENNY A PITCH.
—Barker's song

HENRY GERSHON: The subway doors opened up at the Stillwell Avenue station of the BMT, and I stepped out onto the elevated platform. There was brilliant sunshine, a breeze coming off the ocean, a taste of salt air. The masses of people swept me along onto Surf Avenue. I had only been in this country for a year, and I didn't know where to look first. I heard the organ-grinding music from the carousels, and that reminded me of the fairs in Europe. But they were nothing like Coney Island.

ELI WALLACH: I was entranced by the life-sized puppets enacting battle scenes. There were the freak shows, the bearded lady, the fat lady, the barkers, the whole carnival atmosphere of Coney Island. They influenced my decision to become a performer.

MARTIN SPITZER: Aromas came from all the little shops on the boardwalk: the melted butter on popcorn and hot corn on the cob, the sharp mustard, the burnt sugar from spinning swirls of cotton candy.

BILL FEIGENBAUM: You looked up and saw little wonder-wheel cars swaying in the blue sky, the parachutes opening up like big clouds before they dropped to the boardwalk. You heard the cries of barkers over loudspeakers, trying to lure the crowds, the roar of the roller coaster plunging down the wooden tracks and the screams of the riders.

NEIL SEDAKA: I knew every roller coaster in Coney Island. The Cyclone was the biggest; second was the Thunderbolt, across from Steeplechase. Down was the Tornado, the LA Thompson, the Bobsled, then the Virginia Reel, which was a round car that went up and down hills. Once in the wintertime, I had to walk up and down the tracks of the LA Thompson when it was closed. I don't know what it was about roller coasters; I was a bit freaky about that.

MARCO CARCICH: My first time on the parachute ride was a beautiful clear day. Before me was all of Coney Island, the whole beach crowded with people, the sparkling sea. I had never been up so high before. In those few seconds before the canopy of the parachute opened, sitting there with the straps dangling, I was as frightened as I've ever been.

KARL BERNSTEIN: We were on the Whip on a Friday night, all the guys from APO, the service fraternity at Brooklyn College. You sat two in a car and it went along smoothly till you turned the corner where it would whip around. We kept staying on. A crowd was waiting. They kept screaming, "Get off, get off." When we finally did, we pooled all our money, maybe twenty dollars and told the operator to keep the crowd that got on going till the money ran out. Those guys were screaming. When they finally got off, they were limp, wet rags.

Our favorite ride was the Tornado, because just as you got to the top, you overlooked one of the ladies' bathhouses, and it was always filled with nude women. But just as you got a good look, *whoosh!* you went down.

MARCO CARCICH: The people who worked in Coney Island formed a clique. Any kid of a member of the clique could go on all the rides for free. Since my grandfather worked at Bushman's Baths, when I'd come up to a ride, they'd say, "That's Matty's kid. Let him on."

Bushman's Baths was right on the boardwalk next to Manny's Knishes, which my grandfather's friend owned. Sometimes I'd go into the steambath. What struck me most about it was the strong odor of soap. I'd inhale and feel that the whole inside as well as the outside of my body was clean, 100 percent clean. The first time I went in there, I had a towel wrapped around my waist, but my grandfather pulled it off. "There's nothing to be ashamed of. The human body is something beautiful," he said.

Most of the time, though, I just liked to wander around on the boardwalk, which went on for miles. It was made of beveled planks, cut at probably a 30-degree angle, which gave it a herringbone effect and made it look wider than it actually was. All over the boardwalk were food concessions; penny arcades; rides and games like the poker game Fascination and the guessing games Guess Your Weight and Guess Your Age; shooting and throwing arcades; scooter ball, where you tossed a ball into a series of concentric rings and if you won, you got these coupons that you collected and saved in a big bag. At the end of the summer, I'd trade in five pounds of coupons and walk away with a whistle or a key ring. The most common prize was the Kewpie doll, which was made of hollow plaster, painted with gaudy colors, and decorated with gilt or sequins that got all over your hands and clothes. The Kewpie dolls were made by one manufacturer, so they all looked the same, although some had feathers stuck on their heads or were attached to long sticks. There were also piggy banks, teddy bears, and big cuddly dolls up on the shelves behind the games. But you didn't have a choice. They gave you what they wanted, usually the key rings or the Kewpie dolls.

The whole place was so confusing. You'd go off the boardwalk down one block, and there'd be rides and a new area to explore. For years, I couldn't map out in my mind where I was, where all the rides, the concession stands were. I would try to look for a focal point to get back to the boardwalk: a billboard, a flagpole.

I guess I never got over that early childhood experience of getting lost at Coney Island. I was about four or five, and my father and I had walked from the beach down to Nathan's for hot dogs. On the way back, we got separated in the huge crowd. I watched my father disappearing into the mob of people that was moving toward the boardwalk. He was holding up five franks in each hand and calling out my name. Soon all I could see were two plates of franks above the crowd. There was so much noise, I couldn't yell loud enough for him to hear me. I panicked. My next recollection is being held up in the air by some cop blowing a whistle and crying, "Whose kid is this?"

But by the time I was a teenager, I had developed a pretty good sense of the area. By then, one of my favorite occupations was sitting with a friend under the boardwalk and sifting through the sand for change. Also, we'd look up through the cracks and air spaces and watch people walking overhead. We could spend hours looking up the ladies' dresses. I'd catch a glimpse of something, and my imagination would run wild.

ROBERT MERRILL: I liked to sit under the boardwalk, strum on my ukulele, and sing along, imitating Bing Crosby. I didn't bother taking the train, I would walk to Coney Island all the way from Bensonhurst.

IRVING FIELDS: I played the piano in dozens of saloons on the Bowery, the pedestrian street running parallel to the boardwalk. I was about twelve or thirteen at the time, and I used to get paid off in hot dogs and sodas.

SHELLY STRICKLER: Late at night, people gathered in the little open-air gazebos on the boardwalk and made their own music, singing along to accordions, concertinas, balalaikas.

RALPH GASARCH: There was an entire week of big parades down Surf Avenue. The firemen from all over the city came on Fireman's Night, their red fire trucks polished and shining. There was Policeman's Night, baby parades on Saturday afternoons, floats and clowns and music.

MARTIN SPITZER: The Mardi Gras was on Labor Day. It was like New Orleans, with all the floats on Surf Avenue. I helped my uncles make confetti in the basement of my grandmother's house and sell little bags full for five cents apiece.

MURRAY HANDWERKER: One time, we had the Brooklyn Dodgers in the Mardi Gras parade. I remember Jackie Robinson sitting on the back of a car, waving to the people. The year the Brooklyn Dodgers won their only world championship, they came through Coney Island in a car caravan.

PAT AULETTA: I had a sporting-goods store on Stillwell Avenue, but I also sold a lot of beach stuff: Coppertone, bathing suits and caps, pails and shovels, sun reflectors. Did I sell them? I had a waiting line. There weren't many amusement parks, unlike today. Coney Island was a poor man's paradise.

MURRAY HANDWERKER: Coney Island was open twenty-four hours a day, and there was always a police presence. From Decoration Day to Labor Day, each precinct had to give up a certain number of officers to work in Coney Island. There were millions of people and very little crime.

Nelson Rockefeller (second from right) enjoying a Nathan's hot dog.

Steeplechase was in its heyday. There was no more Luna Park; it had burned down. Feltman's still had its shore dinner crowd and the oompah band used to play where Astroland is now. The rolling-strolling chairs would go up and down the boardwalk. And in the midst of it all was Nathan's.

Back in 1916, Eddie Cantor and Jimmy Durante talked my father into opening up his own frankfurter stand to compete with Feltman's.

They told him to sell his franks for a nickel, as Feltman's charged a dime. He started with a corner stand on property he rented (and later bought) from George Tilyou, the owner of Steeplechase. And then the subway opened up—the terminal at Stillwell Avenue—pouring the people out to the beach. That made Coney Island and Nathan's.

He was there, but without a name. People used to say, "Nathan, why don't you put up a name? I tell people to go down there, and I can't tell them what name." So in 1925, he incorporated. The word *famous* was being used a lot then. He put the sign up: Nathan's Famous.

BILL HANDWERKER: As a kid, I had no concept of what Nathan's meant. I just knew my father and my grandfather worked together in this big restaurant. As I got older, I began to realize the importance of it—how much people enjoyed eating at Nathan's and Coney Island amusements in general.

DOROTHY HANDWERKER: Sundays at Nathan's, there was such excitement. Murray was so enthusiastic, always full of ideas. He had lobster in New England and got the idea to bring lobster roll to Nathan's.

MURRAY HANDWERKER: On a Sunday morning, I'd get to Nathan's at 6:30. We had to blanch the potatoes. That means we half-cooked them and stored them in hundreds of wire baskets. When you had 90, 100 degrees before there was air conditioning, people who lived in New York streamed out of that subway terminal—great masses, crowds of people. On the way to the beach, people would stop for a drink or a hot dog. Then by two, three o'clock in the afternoon, it was the peak period, and it was crazy. The interesting thing, though, was the hotter it was, the less business we did. It was too hot to eat. Not that we didn't make money on the soft drinks— they ran off the beach to get sodas, sodas, sodas.

BILL HANDWERKER: If it was hot and the weather changed to rain in the late afternoon, the number of people coming off the beaches would be so astronomical that I could not raise my head from serving the french fries and collecting the money for, like, an hour straight. Everyone had to pass us on the way to the subway.

MURRAY HANDWERKER: When I first started working, Danny Fariello used to deliver the blocks of ice. One day we were short, and my father hired him to help out. That was it: Danny became our fastest handler. People came around just to watch him. You'd say, "Give me five franks," reach for your money, and when you looked up, the five franks were there. He served a frank a second.

My job was to see that everything was being run properly. Everyone handled cash. To ring up money held up service. So I designed a box with a chute and a fan to suck the money down. At the end of the day, we smoothed out the salty, greasy bills and counted them by hand.

During the summer, managers worked seven days. I told my father, "You gotta give them a day off." The first week that I gave these old-timers a day off, every one of them got burned to a crisp after hitting the beach. They couldn't come to work the next day. My father gave me hell. As for myself, I never went on the beach in the summertime. I was too busy. If I had a day or half-a-day off, we'd walk on the boardwalk, go to Steeplechase, the Aquarium.

The winter of 1947 there was the big blizzard. I walked to work all the way from East Twenty-third and Avenue M. The plow had

Steeplechase Park: "It didn't have the technology of a Disneyland, but it had an innocence that was so appealing."

pushed the snow against the store. The shutters were closed because it was so cold. But the workers were there from the night before; they had been snowed in and slept in the warehouse. So we opened for business. That day we sold twelve hundred franks. People drove up on the sidewalk to the opened windows and bought their franks and french fries. My father called from Florida. "What are you doing there? The place is closed, isn't it?" I said, "Dad, the place is open."

In 1954, Feltman's closed down. That summer we sold fifty-five thousand frankfurters in one day. But another year in the early fifties, we didn't do business. It was a magnificent summer. Beautiful weather—I don't think it rained one Sunday. But it was the year of the polio scare. The beach was empty. People wouldn't sit near each other, wouldn't go to crowded places. It was a rough season.

We were the original fast-food operation. We called it finger food; you didn't need a knife and fork. But it was always quality. My father insisted on that. Our potatoes came mostly from Maine. My father would go there to buy them. Originally, the french fries were put in a glassine bag—waxed paper. You had to open them up and put the scoop in the bag. Then we designed the cone, because you didn't have to open it. Corn was always a favorite. It came from Idaho, and we stored it in a freezer. The hot dogs were my mother's recipe, her spice formula, but they were made by Hygrade, which used to be a half-a-block away from Peter Luger's. We supplied the spices. All beef, less fat than the government allowed. I took over an old bathhouse to store all the food.

BILL HANDWERKER: I grew up in Lawrence, Long Island, where a typical birthday party was going bowling or roller skating. But every one of my birthdays for the basic years of my childhood were spent at Coney Island. My mother would bring me and about six of my friends to Nathan's. We could order whatever we wanted. The hot dogs were the favorite, of course, and then the lobster rolls. We'd go on the rides, walk along the Bowery, and from there enter Steeplechase Amusement Park. I loved their horse ride. I was less than thin, and the principle of the Steeplechase ride was the heavier you are, the faster you go. I won every time.

BILL FEIGENBAUM: It's amazing that nobody got hurt on those Steeplechase horses. Nobody got strapped in. Two people sat on a horse one behind the other. The ride went on sheer gravity. It was great for the boy-girl stuff; you'd go on with a girl, she'd be in the front, and you'd have to hug her tight to hold on.

The whole idea of Steeplechase was fun and sex. Everything was based on guys and girls making close contact. When you came in the main entrance on Stillwell Avenue, you had to go through a huge revolving barrel. Everybody would fall down and turn over, bump into each other trying to get up, fall down again, one on top of another. The Steeplechase horse ride exited onto a stage where wind tunnels blew up the girls' skirts, and clowns ran around giving people little electric shocks. When I worked at Steeplechase, I used to spend my whole lunch hour sitting in the audience watching the parade of people coming off the horse ride. And I was surprised to discover so many girls didn't wear panties. I remember one woman—she must have been 250 pounds—who did a little belly dance and had nothing on under her skirt.

MARCO CARCICH: You went down this enormous slide that landed you on one of maybe ten or fifteen large metal discs spinning in different directions. You'd slide onto one and spin left, then roll onto another one and spin right. You couldn't stand up on the discs. They kept you rolling over and spinning you around.

BARRY FRANK: My uncle, who was on the police force and looked as Irish as could be, would always get passes to Steeplechase. My favorite thing was sliding down into the pool, even though I always got an elbow burn or a knee burn because I couldn't land right.

"Most of the time, though, I just liked to wander around on the boardwalk, which went on for miles."

Going through the barrel and posing by the pool. "The whole idea of Steeplechase was fun and sex."

BILL FEIGENBAUM: The summers of 1956 and 1957, after my junior and senior years in high school, I was a Steeplechase scooter boy. I got the job through my friend Jerry Pellegrino, whose Uncle Jimmy was the manager. George Tilyou, the owner, wasn't Italian, but Jimmy was. And everyone who worked there was Italian except for me and two other Jewish guys.

As a scooter boy, my job was to bust up jams. I didn't wear a uniform like Jimmy, who worked the barrel, because the scooter work was so dirty. And there was always that smell of grease combined with the cotton candy and the salt of the ocean. But I loved every minute of it.

On Saturday night, the ride was jam-packed. Each scooter held only two people. People waited for as long as an hour and a half on a line that went all around the ride. There were a lot of single girls waiting, and you could attract their attention by showing off your athletic prowess, like flipping over the carts or running in between them to bust up the jams. I practiced a lot and could go from one end of the ride to the other without touching the floor, just by car-hopping on the little running boards around the cars. While the cars were emptying out and other people were getting in, I had the chance to pick up a lot of girls.

Once there was this southern guy waiting on the line who was bragging he was Elvis Presley's cousin. I bet him ten dollars to prove it. He takes out his wallet, and he's got this long series of pictures of him and the King hugging. He *was* Elvis Presley's cousin. The money this guy made doing that!

A camaraderie existed among Coney Island scooter boys. We all knew one another. We had our special heroes. One was a guy called the Cockaroach. He would spend every summer going cross-country from California to New York, from scooter ride to scooter ride, doing cartwheels and acrobatics across the ride. All summer the rumor kept going: "The Cockaroach is gonna be here by Labor Day." I thought they were making this up, like it was some kind of joke. But sure enough, Labor Day, the Cockaroach showed up. He must have been about thirty-five years old and looked like an aging Hell's Angel. And he did unbelievable acrobatics across the whole scooter ride, busting up these jams. He only got paid the standard seventy-five cents an hour, the same we all made. He did it because it was his thing.

Steeplechase was my thing. Everything was based on having a good time, on innocent sex. There was all that touching, hugging, falling down, bumping into each other, air ducts everywhere, stupid jokes everywhere. Music blared over loudspeakers: "Bye-Bye Love" or "Sha-boom by ay, ya-da-da-da-da. . . ." The art direction was great. It was such a beautifully designed place: blazing hot carnival colors, art deco motifs, the logo of the smiling man with all the teeth, the gorgeous imported merry-go-round. It didn't have the technology of a Disneyland, but it had an innocence that was so appealing. It was the best thing in Coney Island.

MARCO CARCICH: Almost every day of every summer I spent with my grandparents in Brooklyn, I would go to Coney Island. I had such a great time. I never wanted the summer to end.

But one day I was taking the trolley back to my grandparents' apartment when it suddenly came to a halt. All the passengers were surprised. It wasn't a regular stop. Nobody was waiting to get on, nobody was getting off. Then the conductor got up. He walked down the length of the trolley car and solemnly shook everybody's hand. "This is our last trip," he said. "The trolley won't be running to Coney Island anymore."

CHAPTER 9

One Nation—Under God

FIRST COMES THE CHURCH,
THEN COMES THE STEEPLE,
OPEN THE DOORS,
AND OUT COME THE PEOPLE.

—Finger game

CLIFF HESSE: We belonged to a Lutheran church. A block away was the Russian Orthodox. Down the block was a synagogue and a small Catholic church. Nearby was an Episcopalian church and some Baptist churches and another kind of Lutheran church. They don't call Brooklyn the borough of churches for nothing.

BOB ARNESEN: My mother belonged to the Norwegian Methodist Church in Bay Ridge. I joined the Scotch Presbyterian on Seventy-fifth and Sixth. The parishioners spoke with burrs, and the minister was named Ian Scott, but the organist was Norwegian. Bay Ridge was filled with churches.

CHARLES HYNES: It was one of the wealthiest parishes in Brooklyn. For midnight mass, people like the Trumps, the McAllisters drove up to Holy Innocents on Fort Hamilton Parkway in horsedrawn carriages.

PAT COOPER: Sacred Heart in Red Hook was one of the poorer parishes in Brooklyn. In the winter, the priests would collect coal from between the tracks in the train yards and bring it to families who didn't have enough fuel to heat their houses. The younger priests would go around and bang on the doors: "Mrs. Esposito down the street, her husband lost his job. We have an obligation here." And people would give twenty cents, send a piece of meat, some vegetables over.

TERRY PERNA ARNESEN: The church on Fourteenth Avenue and Sixty-fourth Street was referred to as the Italian church. We lived closer to the one on Seventeenth Avenue and Forty-sixth Street that had mainly Irish parishioners. But they acted as if we were invading their territory. "This isn't your church. You really belong to the one on Fourteenth Avenue," they said. This enraged my father. Like many of the Italian immigrants, he was anticlerical, always angry at the Church. But the children reversed, became ardent Catholics.

TOM BOORAS: There was so much ritual in Catholic life, it spilled over into your social life. When I was a kid, Catholics weren't allowed to eat meat on Friday, and so we developed a ritual for Friday night, which was our date night: a whole crowd of guys and gals would jump into cars and drive from downtown Brooklyn to Coney Island. We had it timed so that we got there as close to midnight as possible. At the stroke of midnight, we'd be standing at Nathan's hot dog counter. A minute later, meatless Friday was over, and we'd be devouring franks.

In order to receive holy communion, you had to fast from midnight Saturday until you went to mass Sunday morning. We found a church that had mass at 1:15 A.M.: St. James Procathedral, on Jay Street. That made for another ritual: Saturday night, my buddies and I would hang out at a corner tavern on Jay Street, drinking beer till midnight. A quarter to one Sunday morning, we'd cross over into St. James Pro and sit down like the little holy boys that we were. A half-hour later, we'd get up and walk down the aisle for communion. We'd be kneeling at the rail, and the priest passing before us would always stiffen as the smell of the beer hit him.

RICHARD KEHOE: A Roman Catholic population surrounded St. John the Baptist Church in Bedford-Stuyvesant. You could go from kindergarten to university without leaving the area. The grammar school was for boys and girls from the parish; but St. John's Prep, the high school, drew from the whole city and was all boys. The buildings were clustered around Lewis Avenue between Willoughby and Park. On one side you had the old brownish-stone college building, the seminary, the residence for the priests. The prep was across the street from these buildings; next to it was the grammar school. The church, a large neo-Gothic structure built some time around the first decade of the twentieth century, was behind the college building. Beyond it was the athletic field, which didn't have a blade of grass. We called it the dust bowl.

A familiar scene in the borough of churches: receiving communion — here at the Holy Trinity Episcopal Church.

ROGER GREEN: St. John's, Concord Baptist, and Cornerstone Baptist were anchors in the Bedford-Stuyvesant community. The pastors of both Concord and Cornerstone graduated from Morehouse College in Atlanta, the same school Martin Luther King, Jr., attended. Everybody who goes to Morehouse comes away with the same kind of preaching style. The Baptist religion was very strong in central Brooklyn, and these two churches were the most renowned.

Concord Baptist, the largest African-American Baptist church in Brooklyn, had originally been in the Fort Greene area. When it burned down, there was a major fund-raising effort to build the new church in Bed-Stuy, a project in which my grandmother Alice Dedham was very involved.

Every Friday, my father would pick up my two girl cousins from Brownsville and bring them to Madison Street to stay with us. Early Sunday mornings, my grandmother would cook breakfast for us, and then we'd all go to church.

Our family had come to New York to escape the racial conditions that existed in the South. But nonetheless, we were definitely rooted in the southern traditions. Our church had various clubs reflecting the different places people came from: a North Carolina club, a South Carolina club, a Virginia club. My grandmother was head of the North Carolina club. She was also the head of a group called the Dixie Belles and the Gospel Chorus. Furthermore, she was part of the building committee and deaconess at the church. With all those activities, there was always an event. Sundays I was not at home.

HOWARD JONES: I began playing basketball at Concord. My brother was a Boy Scout and I was a Cub Scout there. All the churches in Bed-Stuy had Boy Scout troops.

ALBERT VANN: Our troop, Number 199, met at Brown's Memorial Baptist Church. On Brooklyn Day, when entire congregations from the Baptist and Methodist churches would turn out in all their finery, they were always led by the Boy Scouts. Those were magnificent days.

CLIFF HESSE: There was a special route we'd follow for the Brooklyn Day Parade. All the churches took part. There were so many different sects, and you got to know all of them.

JOAN MAYNARD: Brooklyn Day was originally a Protestant holiday. As a Catholic child, I couldn't participate. I was going to Holy Rosary School, and the nuns would

never let us out of school early. So I'd run like heck to get home, get out my clothes, and go out on Stuyvesant Avenue to watch my friends marching in the parade. After, they all went to their individual churches for ice cream and cake. Today, all the public schools are closed for Brooklyn Day. But I can still remember how it felt to see that wonderful parade, with all the varieties of Protestant observance, from the sidelines and be excluded from the celebrations.

SOLOMON AIDELSON: Every shape and form of Jewish life I knew in Europe before the war existed in Brooklyn in the 1950s: the Bund, the leftists, the nonaligned, the observant, the Hasidic. Brooklyn was an area rich in Jewish cultures.

DICK KITTRELL: My family was what one might call sentimental Orthodox. Neither my grandparents nor my mother were particularly learned or observant. But there was the celebration of the Jewish holidays and the support for Jewish causes. My grandmother was always shipping clothes to Palestine. And we were always putting coins in the blue *keren ami* box that stood on a shelf in our kitchen. I actually collected more money two years in a row in my box than any other kid in my Hebrew school. I would sneak onto the subway at the Brighton Beach station and go back and forth to Times Square, going among the passengers and getting contributions.

Grandpa reading the Haggadah at a Passover seder.

On Friday afternoons, I would come home from school and find Grandma preparing for Shabbos. The floors were scrubbed and shining and covered with the previous Sunday's Jewish newspaper. On a white tablecloth on the kitchen table, she'd be making a strudel, the dessert for our Shabbos dinner. After preparing the dough, she'd roll it out and stretch it paper-thin until it covered the entire table. Then she'd add the filling of apples, raisins, and nuts and roll the strudel into its traditional shape.

Grandma was also a moonshiner. Before Passover, she'd prepare raisin wine. It was sweet, felt good going down, and packed a terrific kick. Passover was the one time Grandma allowed me to have coffee. For breakfast I'd get a tall glass filled half with coffee and half with milk. I'd stir in four spoonfuls of sugar and place some pieces of matzoh in the glass. I'd spoon it out and eat the soft, sweet pieces.

DONNA GEFFNER: Around the time of the Jewish holidays, our apartment house would have an aroma, a *shmeck*. You'd walk through the halls and smell the soup simmering and the breads baking. Goldie on the third floor, God bless her, would bake the honey cake, Mrs. Levine in the apartment beneath ours would make the challah, and my mother would make the stuffed cabbage. My job was to bring Goldie and Mrs. Levine the stuffed cabbage and get the cake and the challah from them.

IRWIN POLISHOOK: In the fall of the year, Brooklyn always has a particular smell of damp leaves, of something smoky in the air. The leaves fall from the trees. Acorns litter the ground. And I am always reminded of going to shul on the High Holy Days.

DONNA GEFFNER: All the people would come out. And they'd be well-dressed. You'd stand on the corner, walk on Bay Parkway, Ocean Parkway. It was the time to see people, flirt with the boy you had a crush on. Maybe he'd show up at Temple. It was the time to wear your new outfit: the gray felt skirt with the white poodle and the chain, the cardigan sweater and the bobby sox.

MORRIS FRIEDMAN: Before the High Holy Days, we would be outfitted with new suits. As my mother was ill, my father did most of the shopping. Often he would buy things without our being present. Sometimes the shoes were a little too big or a little too small, but we managed. During the rest of the year, we could go for months without him buying us clothes, but come the holiday, everything had to be new.

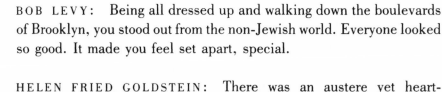

BOB LEVY: Being all dressed up and walking down the boulevards of Brooklyn, you stood out from the non-Jewish world. Everyone looked so good. It made you feel set apart, special.

HELEN FRIED GOLDSTEIN: There was an austere yet heart-warming atmosphere at B'nai Israel of Bay Ridge during the High Holy Days that made me want to sit with my family rather than run around outside with my friends. Everyone was orderly and composed. It was a serious occasion. My grandfather Isaac Boehm, who was an important man in the synagogue, would be up there on the *bima*—the platform. The silver threads on the neck of his *tallit* glittered as he stood before the Torah scrolls that were enclosed in gleaming silver cases. When they were lifted, the little ornaments on top would tinkle. It was like a fantasy world to me.

MARTY ADLER: For Simchath Torah, we got a little flag with an apple stuck into the tip of the flagpole and a candle stuck into the apple. All the kids would march around the neighborhood with their flags. We belonged to an Orthodox shul. It seemed to me that everybody was Orthodox then.

MORRIS FRIEDMAN: Many people who attended Orthodox synagogues were not Sabbath observers. They came from European backgrounds. They were more comfortable with Orthodox ritual, to men and women being separated. A Conservative synagogue would be foreign to them.

HERBY GREISSMAN: My father wanted me to go to the little shul he belonged to. It was one long room with a doorway in the front and the back, no windows on the sides, and a long aisle down the middle with wooden benches on each side. I told him, "I don't understand Yiddish. If you want me to go, you gotta send me where I can understand it." So we shifted to the newer, more modern synagogue on Twenty-third Avenue. But my father never forgot Rabbi Gartenhaus and the little shul. On Succoth, when they needed fruits to decorate the succus, or on Simchath Torah, when they needed apples, he kept him supplied.

DICK KITTRELL: My grandfather was an itinerant shul-mensch. Each year he went someplace else. Once he found a storefront synagogue on the boardwalk in Brighton.

MORRIS FRIEDMAN: Most of Brooklyn's big synagogues were built in the 1920s. They were regal, impressive structures with the Ark as the focal point and a balcony area for the women. The Brooklyn Jewish Center on Eastern Parkway, which today is a Lubavitcher facility, was once a cathedral of Conservative Judaism. People would walk miles to listen to Rabbi Israel Levanthal, one of the giants of that period.

Borough Park was more upscale than Crown Heights or Williamsburg, which also had big Jewish communities. It had a number of distinguished Orthodox congregations, such as Temple Beth El, on Forty-eighth Street and Fifteenth Avenue, and one major Conservative synagogue: Temple Emanuel, on Forty-ninth Street and Fourteenth Avenue. Kuzavitsky, the greatest of all the cantors, was in that congregation.

When you saw a Jew walking down a Borough Park street on a Saturday morning, you never knew which synagogue he was going to. It had nothing to do with membership. It had to do with where a particular guest cantor was dovaning. The great cantors went around to different synagogues, and people would go to hear them. It was the golden age of cantors.

SOLOMON AIDELSON: When I came to this country in 1953 and saw the remnants of the great Hasidic dynasties in Brooklyn, it made me feel like nothing had changed. The Hasidic communities grew and flourished in Brooklyn in the years after the war. Very few rebbes had survived the Holocaust. But those that did developed a following, because people wanted to hang onto something that was familiar to them.

PRECEDING PAGE
The High Holy Days and
simchas (celebrations) were
times to dress up in your
very best.

For a while I lived with my great-uncle Sholem Kalish, the Amshinover rebbe—a group named for a city in Poland where this Hasidic dynasty originated. He spent the years of the war in Japan, where he and other Jews were treated very civilly. By this time, he was in his seventies and living in an old-fashioned three-story stucco house in Borough Park. It was an open house. Anyone could come in for a meal or for a place to sleep—and of course, for advice. He was the most generous man I ever knew. Someone would give him a donation. The money would be lying on the table. If the next person to come in was in need, he'd give the money to him.

ISAAC ABRAHAM: My parents were survivors of Auschwitz. After the war, they came to Williamsburg, and my father became a Satmar—a Hasidic group named after an old town in Russia. It is basically a congregation and a school system with a rebbe at the hub of the wheel. We lived just a block and a half away from the old grand rebbe Joel Teitelbaum. I used to walk over with my father and brothers to see him. In my younger years we lived in a two-bedroom, top-floor

The whole *mishpachah* (extended family) assembled for a Brooklyn bar mitzvah.

unit on Taylor Street next to a chicken market. We learned how the kosher slaughtering and salting of chickens was done.

BOB LIFF: Every year around Succoth, people in black coats and hats would go walking down the street carrying a *lulav* and an *esrog*: the palm leaves and a citron, which is a lemonlike fruit. They'd come up to you and say, "You Jewish?" You'd say, "Yeah." They'd interrupt the punchball game, stick a yarmulke on your head, stick those things in your hands, and make you say the *broche*—the blessing. Years later, as a reporter covering the Lubavitch, I realized that's who those guys were.

CLARENCE NORMAN, SR.: My friends and I were hanging out on the stoop one Friday night in August when this very simple couple walked by and said, "Come and be with us." We had nothing better to do, so we ambled over to this little storefront church on Flushing Avenue.

Mr. Kendrick, a former nightclub performer, was the self-ordained

CONFIRMATION DINNER & RECEPTION
TENDERED BY
MR. & MRS. NAT KOEPPEL
IN HONOR OF THEIR SON
JEROME

minister. Mother Kendrick was a gray-haired grandmotherly type, wearing the long black dress typical of the Pentecostal church. Their whole thing was to save souls, and I was a lost soul. At that time, I did not know where I was going, but they told me, "This is what the Lord wants you to do."

I started going to Bible classes and revival meetings where you shout and have a good time, singing along to the piano and tambourine. I'd stay till two or three o'clock in the morning and walk home, never fearing anyone. I began teaching Bible class and became a deacon in this small church. After a while, I decided I wanted to become a minister and enrolled in Howard University.

When I came home for Christmas, my wife and I went over to the Little Zion Baptist Church in Williamsburg. They were in the midst of a controversy. Since I was a young man home from college, I was asked to help organize a church. We started with ten men and their families in a storefront at 122 Throop Avenue. They ordained me minister of that church, and I organized them into a Baptist mission. I intended to stay for a year and then go back to college. I stayed two years. I stayed three years. In 1962, we moved out of Williamsburg and bought a Presbyterian church on Monroe Street. In 1967, we moved into a former catering hall in Crown Heights.

During the fifties and early sixties, the emphasis was placed on living, dying, going to heaven—not the social ills of the community. Most of us in the clergy supported the civil-rights protests morally and financially, but we did not get personally involved. But after the march on Washington in 1963, as we moved through the black power era, the black theology period, I became conscious of the fact that the church had a role to play socially. It was then that I became involved in the struggle. Today I am pastor of the largest Baptist congregation in Crown Heights. That little storefront church on Flushing Avenue was the doorway to my salvation.

A Brooklyn Heights family in their Easter Sunday finery.

Americans All

IF YOU PLEASE AND THANK YOU,
SAYS THE AMERICAN CHILD.
AND EVERY TIME SHE SAYS IT,
SHE SMILES AND SMILES AND SMILES.
—Kindergarten song, P.S. 177

FRANK BARBARO: When I was growing up, you had an ethnic mix across the borough. You had Jews, you had Italians, you had Poles, you had Irish, you had blacks. Predominantly it was working class, and people were struggling. I'm not suggesting racism, anti-Semitism didn't exist. But people more or less stayed in their neighborhoods, and if someone ventured out, he was looked upon as an oddity, not someone to be attacked.

ALAN LELCHUK: At the handball and basketball courts at Lincoln Terrace Park, I saw camaraderie and rivalry, but never violence. That was remarkable because of the mixtures, the rivalry of neighborhoods. When you played teams from another area, you were playing against that different culture. But it was always within strong boundaries of gamesmanship and decent behavior.

BOB ARNESEN: For the longest time, Bay Ridge had the largest Scandinavian community in the United States outside of Minnesota. On my block, though, we were the only ones. Salami, a Syrian boy who ate the big flat breads, was a good friend of mine, along with Jackie Woods, who was Irish, and Arnold Kahn, who was Jewish. My father's friends were the men in his poker game: Italians, Jews, Irish. We associated freely, did not divide up into ethnic enclaves. It seemed most immigrants then did not dwell on their ethnicity. They tried to become fully assimilated Americans.

TOBY SCHOM GROSSMAN: I helped my mother study to become a citizen, tested her on the questions in the book—who was president, etc. She came home from the test with a big smile. "I think everything's OK."
    "How do you know?"
    "I told the judge I love the United States of America."

POLLY BERNSTEIN: How much I wanted to become a citizen! When my family emigrated, we couldn't come into the United States, so we settled in Canada. In 1940, I married an American, crossed the border illegally, and moved here. Lots of people did that then. A man on our block worked for the Immigration Department. I knew if he went through my papers, he could get me deported. Every time I saw him, I would take a walk somewheres. Years later, after I became a citizen, I told him. He said, "For crying out loud, you should have let me know. You could have been a citizen in three months."

TERRY PERNA ARNESEN: My sister began P.S. 180 speaking Italian, which was her first language. After a few days, she told my father that she never wanted to speak Italian again. He agreed: "We speak English, we speak English in the house." He went with my mother to the local junior high school two nights a week to take English for foreigners. My mother used to sit around the dining-room table with us and follow our homework in English. She was reading *The New York Times* and *The Wall Street Journal*.

My father wanted us to be part of everything in his new country. When the priest paid us a call to find out why we weren't going to parochial school, my father said, "I didn't come to this country so that my children can go to Catholic school." Everyone wanted to be American. Typically, the Italian boys of my age would marry Irish girls, to make sure they melted into the English-speaking scene.

KARL BERNSTEIN: Mrs. Montana, who lived down the block, was very Americanized and only spoke English—until her daughter had a big fight with her husband, and it spilled into the street. Then I heard Mrs. Montana yell in Italian. She was too much of a lady to say what she had to say in English in front of the neighbors.

DONNA GEFFNER: We were tested for speech in my English class at Lafayette High School. As I was in the drama club and very enthusiastic over speech, I probably gave an affected reading, which the teacher interpreted as a foreign accent. She gave me a letter to take home to my parents stating that I was going into a special speech class.

My father, who had come to this country as a small boy and was very proud of being an American, took great offense. "What does this letter mean?" he shouted. "They think you come from European parents? You're an American!" The next day he went into school and stormed into the speech chairman's office. "My daughter is not going into speech class," he told Miss Curran. "She is not foreign-born. I'll have you know my grandfather fought in the Civil War."

FRANCES BLUM: Growing up in Bensonhurst, I knew Jews and Italians. That's how the world was divided up for me. Until one day, a friend and I went for a long walk and ended up in Sunset Park. I couldn't believe what I saw. Here there were all these Scandinavians, so many handsome blondes. It was like going into another world in Brooklyn.

BOB ARNESEN: Among the people I knew, there was a great deal of intermarriage. My mother was the only one from her family who

I pledge allegiance to the flag of the United States of America and to the Republic for which it stands, one nation indivisible, with liberty and justice for all.

married a Norwegian. My wife is Italian; my children are married to people from different backgrounds.

TERRY PERNA ARNESEN: Marrying Bob gave me the chance to learn about a whole different culture. I would go out to watch the big parade and join the festivities at Leif Erikson Park every May 17 to commemorate Norwegian independence from Sweden. Many Scandinavians were in the home construction field, and one of the customs I found so appealing was the way they placed a branch from a tree on the top of a house before putting on the roof. I was told that was their way of saying we're almost finished. But to me, it was also a symbol of something God has made, a reaching to the top.

BOB ARNESEN: We are living proof of the melting pot that Brooklyn used to be. We combined our heritages. Christmastime, we'd have a Scandinavian kind of rice pudding, crepes filled with jelly and dried fruit with cinnamon thickened with tapioca, and all kinds of Italian fish dishes.

MATT KENNEDY: If the lady next door cooked gefilte fish, she'd pass it over the back fence; if my mother made corned beef and cabbage, she'd give to her. We used to boast and brag about the variety of ethnic groups who lived together in Coney Island. I wish I had a nickel for every time I was in the shul. If the Catholics had a bazaar, it was patronized by the shul, the Lutheran church, the whole community.

ELLIOT GUNTY: My grandfather lived with us in our one-family house in a mixed Flatbush neighborhood. He was a little man who came from Austria, very Orthodox. On Saturdays, he would walk down the street on his way to Temple, and all the gentile neighbors would clear a path for him. "Mr. Harris, good morning." "Mr. Harris, how are you?" They showed him the highest respect.

MORRIS FRIEDMAN: When my father was out in the backyard of our Borough Park house doing carpentry work, our Italian neighbor would come over. On Friday nights, he would come in to turn out the lights for us. It was that kind of a relationship. We could ask one another for things. Our neighbors became very familiar with Jewish customs. We'd put up the succus, and they'd come in, have a drink, something to eat.

ANGELO BADALAMENTI: Since my family was the only goyisha one on the block, I became the Shabbos goy at the synagogue on West Seventh Street and Avenue P. After I shut the lights, the rabbi would show me the bowl filled with change—he couldn't touch the money

"Our neighbors became very familiar with Jewish customs." Manischewitz Wine owner Meyer Robinson (far right) treats the Dodgers to dinner and ample samples of his kosher wine.

because it was the Sabbath. I would go in whole hog. "Wait, Angelo," he would say. "Take one." I would dip in and hope it was a quarter.

CHARLES HYNES: I lived at 224 Hinckley Place, in an eighty-four-family apartment house with two goyisha families: the super's and mine. I learned a lot of Yiddish expressions living there.

TERRY PERNA ARNESEN: On Sundays, all my brother's Jewish friends went to the Workmen's Circle for Yiddish lessons. He was left with nothing to do. My mother gave him the fifty cents so he could go along. Later on, when he was delivering groceries, the old Jewish ladies just loved this little Italian kid who talked to them in Yiddish.

FRANK BARBARO: My aunt lived at 1926 Seventy-second Street. She was from Italy and could not speak one word of English. Her neighbor in number 1924 was a Jewish lady who also did not speak one word of English. They sat on the bench in front of their houses and talked for hours. Nobody could ever figure out how they communicated.

JOEL MARTIN: The neighborhood I grew up in, on the border of Flatbush and Borough Park, was largely Jewish and Italian. We didn't know of things like racism and prejudice. But one day, I overheard the adults talking: "The neighborhood is becoming mixed." What happened? An Irish family had moved onto the block. You could be Jewish, you could be Italian. There was kreplach, there was ravioli. But from Irish, they didn't know.

We spent days walking our way up the cellar doors in back of their house and peeking in the windows. We wanted to discover what made that family different. They were blonde, fair-skinned—but other than that, they seemed like us. We couldn't figure out what the big commotion was all about.

In some ways Brooklyn seemed to be more of a beef stew than a melting pot. The carrots and the celery were all in the same pot, but they never got to really know each other.

HERB BERNSTEIN: When I was twenty-two, I began teaching in a junior high in Ridgewood, on the Brooklyn-Queens borderline. It was a blue-collar, Polish-Irish-Italian-German neighborhood, the type of place that if you hit a kid, the parents said, "You're right."

Once two girls had a fight, and one said to the other, "You no-good Jew bitch!"

I said, "Elizabeth, why did you say that? Rosemary isn't even Jewish."

She said, "I know, but my father always says that when he gets mad at somebody."

I said, "Do you know that I'm Jewish?"

She started to cry. "You have blue eyes, you're handsome and nice."

The word got out. The kids said, "We thought you were German, we thought you were Polish."

I said, "Does it have any effect, does it make a difference?"

They said, "No, but we didn't expect."

MARNIE BERNSTEIN: At some point I learned that Jesus was Jewish. I passed that along to my Italian friend, Mary Quintero. "He may have been once," she said, "but he isn't anymore."

JOE SIGLER: We knew the Knickerbocker Club on Tennis Court was restricted, but we didn't care. Our neighborhood was predominantly Jewish, but I had Irish friends, Italian friends, a Greek friend, a black friend who lived down Ocean Avenue. There was no black-white-Hispanic issue.

DICK KITTRELL: As a teenager, I was involved in the B'nai B'rith Youth Project, collecting canned food for Brooklyn Jewish Hospital. We divided up Crown Heights and Brownsville, and I got the blocks around Carroll Street and New York Avenue, an area with a lot of brownstones. It turned out to be a black neighborhood right in the midst of a white neighborhood. People were very nice and gave me lots of canned food. It was my first contact with a black community, but they had been there for years.

WILLIAM THOMPSON: Brooklyn started with a small black population, just Bed-Stuy and the poor who lived in Brownsville. Harlem had the name—the action was in Harlem. But after a while, in terms of numbers, we ate them up.

HOWARD JONES: When I was a kid, Bedford-Stuyvesant was an integrated neighborhood, and I was oblivious to prejudice. I knew I was a different color than white kids, but there never was a question of race. Maybe that's because I lived in a vacuum of sports. We all played ball together.

ROGER GREEN: My parents were part of the in-migration of African-Americans from the South just before the war. We lived in Bedford-Stuyvesant, which was essentially a working-poor and working-class neighborhood during the 1950s and 1960s. We did have some families from the West Indies, though, and they tended to come here with some disposable income, so they could purchase property.

WILLIAM THOMPSON: When the West Indians hit Brooklyn, property was their thing. They're the ones who bought the brownstones. Relatives would come into our house. My mother would get them a job working in service, as they called it—as a domestic, a cook—until they saved enough money. My father would find them a house. Boom! They'd start.

ROGER GREEN: We were first-generation New Yorkers, and we were mindful of that. I had a healthy childhood. Still, it was inevitable there'd be times when I'd be confronted with racism. When we moved from Bed-Stuy to Carroll Street in Crown Heights, we were one of the first black families in that neighborhood. Everybody was very civil. The only incident I recall happened at P.S. 222, where a white student once called my friend and me "nigger," and nobody said anything.

Children of immigrants and in-migrants on the steps of Brooklyn College.

But when we were bused into Winthrop Junior High, which was near the Rugby section of Brooklyn, we made sure not to wear our better clothes on Fridays, because we knew we would have to fight our way home. The white kids from Pigtown, as they used to call it—because people used to raise pigs in their backyards—would waylay us.

JOAN MAYNARD: Of about thirty-two kids in my graduating class at Holy Rosary High School in 1946, there were six blacks—one boy and five girls. Rita, an Irish girl, had a graduation party. She invited the black boy because the white boys told her if she didn't, they weren't coming. But she didn't invite any of the black girls. I had no illusions.

JOYCE SHAPIRO FEIGENBAUM: The granddaughter of the black janitor in our building came to live with him, and Helen and I became friends. This caused a controversy in my home. My mother was afraid for me to play with her. This one time, my father, who was always a kind of retiring figure in my upbringing, came forward. "Leave her alone, let her play with the child." Imagine, we deigned to do

Two heroes of the time of growing social consciousness: Jackie Robinson and Dr. Martin Luther King, Jr.

this child a big favor. Helen and I were good friends until the sixth grade, when she made the SP, a class where you skipped a grade, and dumped me for Lila Dansky.

ROGER GREEN: My father came here from North Carolina when he was thirteen years old because of a racial incident. He was always a fighter. His greatest hero was Paul Robeson.

WADE SILER: I came to Brooklyn from North Carolina. I had been a Yankee fan, a DiMaggio fan. But being in Brooklyn when Jackie Robinson came up, I was transformed into a Dodger fan. As a black man, it was so exciting for me to see him.

RACHEL ROBINSON: The one thing that concerned Jack was the possibility of an overenthusiastic black response. We saw it more in the South than in Brooklyn, but every time he came up to bat early on, even if he hit a pop-up, there would be a tremendous reaction. We worried this overresponse would lead to fights in the ballpark, but it didn't happen.

BILL FEIGENBAUM: We used to go to Ebbets Field—local synagogue groups, left-wing groups. All the left-wingers, who were mostly Jews, were great champions of liberal causes at that time. It was a big victory for them when Robinson got into the major leagues. We'd sit in the bleachers and watch Jackie Robinson and cheer more for him than anyone else. He was red hot.

JOEL BERGER: There was a social consciousness among many people. There were teachers who were committed to civil rights, and they passed it along to their students. Some belonged to world peace movements. At Lincoln High School, one teacher brought in Earl Robinson's "Ballad of Americans" to study and sing; another had us read Richard Wright. More than a few ended up being named communists or sympathizers, railroaded by an investigation, and made to retire or resign. Their civil rights were violated—they did not have due process. It was part of the climate of the time.

LARRY STRICKLER: Morris Lipshutz was my friend's teacher in P.S. 253. One day in 1952, he disappeared. There was no explanation; it was as if the earth opened up, and he was gone. Parents were up in arms. This was a great teacher, a man of principles. They staged a rally for his reinstatement. But he was branded a communist and became a victim of the McCarthy witch-hunt.

Henry Modell gets Jackie Robinson's autograph. Jackie was "red hot."

"My universe was opening up. . . . I was meeting kids from all kinds of backgrounds."

FRANK BARBARO: The Red hunts, the witch-hunts were part of the attempt to kill the militant, progressive trade-union movement. The ruling financial circles of our society were very frightened of that movement and had to stifle it. The Communist party never was a big party in this country. At its highest point, it had twenty thousand members, most of whom were in New York City. Nevertheless, unions in the fifties made tremendous advances because the economy was growing.

JUDY BERGER: There were reactionary forces around that tried to link the civil-rights movement to communism. But there were teachers, community leaders, rabbis, priests, and ministers all over Brooklyn who worked hard to promote ideals of brotherhood and integration. If you were active in student government, you got caught up in it.

CAROLINE KATZ MOUNT: The National Conference of Christians and Jews began working with high schools, promoting interfaith activities, civil rights. They had summer camps in upstate New York, and all the high schools sent delegates. This was the time the boycotts and sit-ins were starting in the South. I came back all fired up, full of youthful self-righteousness. When my father asked me how many black girls were in my bunk, I said, "I don't know. I didn't notice."
  He became exasperated. "How could you not notice such a thing?"

I ran into the bathroom crying at the intolerance I was experiencing in my own home and reminding myself what they told us at camp: when we came home we wouldn't find as perfect a world as there was at NCCJ.

But my universe was opening up. For the first time, I was meeting kids from all kinds of backgrounds, from all over the city, who were interested in broader social issues. I started attending meetings in downtown Brooklyn, which for me was a big trip. "Black and white together, we shall not be moved"—that was our credo.

ROGER GREEN: I was always aware that there were white folks who were supportive of the movement, because of the way my father presented things to me. He was active in the NAACP and CORE. He was on the front lines, marching, picketing. On Fridays, he'd come home with oak tag and have us write up slogans. Saturdays we'd go out and boycott Woolworth's, because it was segregated in the South. The demonstrations were educational experiences. My vocabulary started building. I learned words like *discrimination* and *segregation*. My father would take me when Dr. King was in town, and hearing him speak was so moving. Those kinds of experiences saved me. I started believing in something.

CAROLINE KATZ MOUNT: By the late 1950s, we were starting to get a sense of changing times. We knew about *Brown* v. *Board of Education*, and many of us were imbued with idealism and a desire to make things fairer for everyone. It seemed so right and also so easy, so within reach. There was this poster you'd see on billboards, in buses, and on trains. It showed a frowning white woman, a couple of white kids with baseball equipment, and a black kid on the sidelines. And one of the white boys is saying to the woman, "What's his race or religion got to do with it? He can pitch."

PART THREE

The Days of Our Glory

WHAT HIGH SCHOOL DID YOU GO TO?

HANGING OUT AND MAKING IT

CHAPTER 11

What High School Did You Go To?

OH, TALK NOT TO ME OF A
NAME GREAT IN STORY;
THE DAYS OF OUR YOUTH ARE THE
DAYS OF OUR GLORY.
—GEORGE GORDON, LORD BYRON
—Epigraph in the 1960 Lafayette High School Yearbook

JOEL BERGER: Even now after all these years, whenever I meet somebody and it comes out he came from Brooklyn, I ask, "What high school did you go to?" If a person of a certain age tells me he went to Brooklyn Tech, I know he had to have done well scholastically. If he went to Lincoln or Midwood, Madison or Erasmus, Lafayette or New Utrecht, we were similar: middle-class kids with aspirations of upward mobility. We grew up in the same kind of neighborhoods, we were part of the rivalry between the schools, we attended the same basketball and football games. If he went to Boys High or Eastern District, we were different. He was tougher, hustled a buck more, had a special lingo.

There was a high school with thousands of students in every Brooklyn neighborhood. In some ways they were alike, yet each had its own identity. It was like all the Brooklyn high schools were part of a league, and yours was the best.

HOWARD JONES: You had so much school spirit. You knew the words to the school songs, which were often original compositions written by the music teachers. You would sing, and you would cheer, and you would cry. You went to the games, took part in school activities. White and black, there was a spirit of support.

When I was at Boys High, from '44 to '48, our rivals were Brooklyn Tech, Manual Training, and Thomas Jefferson. When we lost a football or basketball game to them, we couldn't go back into the neighborhood.

BOB ERTEL: Everyone at Midwood seemed to be on some kind of team or a cheerleader, even though we hardly won any games. For three or four years, Midwood lost every football game. When they tied Manual Training at last, it set off a tremendous celebration.

ALAN LELCHUK: In 1955 the Jefferson basketball team won the city championship, a feat tantamount to being one of the top thirty college teams in America. Bernie Tiebout, my best friend and a great black player, was on that team. That was the year the Dodgers won the World Series, and there was a feeling in Brooklyn that we could conquer the world.

HOWARD RAPP: The kids who lived on my side of Rockaway Parkway went to Jefferson; the kids who lived on the other side went to Tilden. All of us had played on the street together, had gone to elementary school and junior high together. Now we were the biggest rivals because our loyalty was to our high school. We faced off at what became the major event of the year: the Thanksgiving morning football game at the Boys High field.

EVERETT KERNER: The kids at Tilden had such a love and feeling for the school, you couldn't get them out of the building. It was the focus of their lives, just like in a small town.

ABE LASS: The high school years are the flowering of adolescence. There is never again the same sense of awakening to the world. And here you had first- and second-generation American adolescents, sent to school by parents highly motivated for their kids to succeed, meeting up with great, dedicated teachers. It was a school system you will never see again.

We called it the Fertile Crescent. It started along the shoreline with Lafayette. Then came Lincoln, backed up against the ocean. Then inland was Madison, then Midwood, then Erasmus—a really great school of its time. Tilden was further inland, a good school also. There was a strong intellectual current in the schools and an informed, highly liberal faculty. Everything the school did was right to the parents. They didn't demonstrate against it. The teachers were unquestioned authorities. My friend Sam Levinson, who at one time taught Spanish at Tilden High School, told this story, which was probably apocryphal: "I got a note home from school which I gave to my father. 'Dear Mr. Levinson, your son Samuel shows signs of astigmatism.' My father read it and gave me a smack, crying, 'To a teacher, you show signs of astigmatism?'"

During my tenure as principal, from 1955 to 1971, Lincoln was, in my book, the best academic high school in the city without any specialized examinations. I was there for the glory days. Lincoln drew from a middle- and lower-middle-class neighborhood. A small number of kids came from Manhattan Beach, but mostly they were from Brighton and Coney Island. And there is a very close relationship between what we call socioeconomic standing and intellectual achievement, no question about it. So what was it that made Lincoln so special?

Out of the five thousand students, 80 to 85 percent were Jewish, with what that means in terms of orientation to education, to family, to respect for learning. The whole thing comes into the school. Lincoln, though, had something more. Fully 50 percent of the kids were either children or nieces or nephews of Lincoln graduates. There was that continuity to the 1930s, when it opened. The neighborhood was stable; people stayed. So the students were not just going to high school, they were going where their mother or father, their uncle or aunt had gone.

IRVING FIELDS: Lincoln was white and brand-new when I attended. In the springtime, the cherry trees blossomed on the front lawn. It was so beautiful. Because we were near the ocean, there was always the smell and taste of the sea in the air. I'd come down the broad front staircase, cross over to the pedestrian path along Ocean Parkway, and walk all the way home to Twentieth Avenue and Sixty-second Street.

JOEL BERGER: We had the feeling we were lucky to be going to Lincoln. It was customary to throw pennies, which have Lincoln's head on them, to wish someone good luck or pay him a compliment. In required music, we threw pennies at our teacher, Mr. Goldman, to show our appreciation. Before a big game against Madison, we'd shower the statue of Lincoln with pennies.

ABE LASS: I'd come into Lincoln early in the morning, throw my hat and coat in the office, and start my rounds of the building. I observed a class every day. I didn't come to see a teacher who wasn't doing a job. I just wanted to see what was going on.

Within the first couple of days of my being principal, I was walking around, appraising my real estate, strolling through the halls, and I see a kid standing there. "Do you have a problem?" I asked.

He said, "No, I don't have a problem."

I said, "Who are you?"

He said, "Who are you?"

"I'm the new principal, Abe Lass."

He reached out and shook my hand. "I'm the new student," he said, "Harvey Keitel."

Abe Lass strides across part of his "real estate": the Lincoln High School football field.

RALPH GASARCH: Lincoln had the best cafeteria anywhere. It was run by Florence Green, a plump and happy nurturer, a woman way ahead of her time. She introduced gourmet food. She had a pizza maker come in for the kids before pizza was a household word. She baked rugelas out of the excess butter and sold them on Fridays. People lined up to take home weekend packages.

ABE LASS: Lincoln is the only school in the country that has produced three Nobel Prize winners. An elderly lab assistant named Sophie Wolf, a clucking-hen kind of woman with a maternal interest in the kids, was responsible for that.

JOEL BERGER: Thomas Lawrence, a biology teacher at Erasmus, had the most Westinghouse semifinalists of any school in the country. Ten, twelve, fourteen a year in the late fifties, early sixties. Erasmus Hall was, at one time, the premier of all the schools. The principal, John McNeil, was an English educator of some note and a colonel in the Air Force during World War II. He ran the school like a squadron.

GAIL EISEMAN BERNSTEIN: Dr. McNeil was very strait-laced, unapproachable. He wore white shirts with pointed collars, ties, and vests.

KARL BERNSTEIN: His administrative assistant was Miss Grace L. Corey, who would dock teachers for being a minute late. That's the kind of school they ran. Nobody stepped out of line.

Erasmus was the only high school in Brooklyn that didn't have girl cheerleaders. But these guys got the crowd going.

GAIL EISEMAN BERNSTEIN: Erasmus was the only school in the city that taught classical Greek. They catered to the elite, to the very bright students. But if you were a middle-of-the-road student, it was not the place for you.

JOEL BERGER: Erasmus was the first public high school in the State of New York, with origins in the 1600s, and it retained this sort of English-preparatory-school atmosphere. In every other high school, the kids went to study hall. In Erasmus, they went to "chapel"— which was the auditorium, but it had stained-glass windows. The Erasmus kids who were in student government wore shirts and ties. They were college-bound.

GAIL EISEMAN BERNSTEIN: It was the only high school in Brooklyn that did not have girl cheerleaders. That went back to the olden days, when it wasn't proper for young ladies to show themselves.

JOEL MARTIN: All through junior high, I heard horror stories that Erasmus Hall High School had a tough principal, that you had to take things like math, that you had to study. My friends went to Erasmus, my girlfriend went there. But thank God, I could draw. That's how I escaped. By going to the High School of Art and Design, I avoided Erasmus and was able to major in cartooning—that meant I could legally read comic books all through high school.

BOB LEVY: Erasmus was like a castle. You couldn't find your way around it. I had to come in at six in the morning for detention. There was no elevator, and it was a long, long walk up the stairways to the bell tower.

STEWIE STONE: I never knew how big Erasmus was. I never realized it had seven thousand students. I just walked in a door and stayed inside, going from classroom to classroom. I was a senior before I found out about the quad in the middle of the building, with the original schoolhouse and the statue.

JACK EAGLE: I was a senior before I found out there were streets in the Erasmus district like Tennis Court and Argyle Road. There was a dichotomy at Erasmus between the kids from the poor part of Flatbush, where I lived, and the ones from the rich part.

GAIL EISEMAN BERNSTEIN: The girls who had the clothes lived on Albemarle Road, Rugby Road, Ocean Avenue. They were the wealthier but not necessarily the smarter kids, and they formed a clique. The poorer kids lived on Rogers Avenue, Linden Boulevard, near Holy Cross Cemetery. The Erasmus district went up all the way to Eastern Parkway and Crown Heights. It drew from such a wide variety of neighborhoods.

BOB ERTEL: Midwood was in one of the richest neighborhoods in Brooklyn, on Bedford Avenue, right next door to Brooklyn College. When you went to Midwood, you had the feeling you were on a campus. I came there from Montauk Junior High in Borough Park, which was famous for an enormous amount of lunchtime fights. The whole school came out to watch them. From Montauk, kids fed into Erasmus, New Utrecht, or Midwood. When I arrived at Midwood, when I saw those big pillars out front and the domed roof on top, I thought I was in heaven. Also, I had never seen so many beautiful girls.

There was a distinction at Midwood between the tough kids—guys who wore the DA haircuts and motorcycle jackets and gals who wore the tight skirts with the slingback shoes—and the Ivy League–looking kids who were college-bound. But overall, the school was scholastically elite. Kids from out of the district went there if they had pull—like their father was a judge, their uncle knew somebody. That's how desirable it was.

KARL BERNSTEIN: I lied about my address to go to James Madison High School, a few miles south of Midwood High, along Bedford Avenue near Kings Highway, and a similar kind of school. The kids were mostly children of doctors, teachers, lawyers. Over the front doors was the inscription: "Education is the true foundation of civil liberty." James Madison said that.

RICHARD GOLDSTEIN: The inscription at the front entrance of Thomas Jefferson High School, in Brownsville, was "Let reverence for the laws be the political religion of the land.—Abraham Lincoln." The inscription in the auditorium was "A thing of beauty is a joy forever.—John Keats." Thomas Jefferson didn't make it on the walls, anywhere.

HOWARD RAPP: Jefferson was an integrated school, but there was no black-and-white situation. And God forbid if anyone went after a kid from my school. We always protected our Jeffersonians.

EVERETT KERNER: At Tilden, there was a contrast between the Jewish kids from the private homes in East Flatbush and the less

Fifty-first
Commencement
Exercises

James Madison High School
Brooklyn, New York

June 27th
Nineteen hundred fifty-one

Program

1. PROCESSIONAL—'March of the Peers' from 'Iolanthe' . . . . Sullivan
2. 'STAR-SPANGLED BANNER'
3. SALUTE TO THE FLAG
4. CHORAL SPEAKING FROM 'ECCLESIASTES' VOICE CHOIR OF SENIOR ENGLISH CLASS
5. SCHOOL HYMN—'Deo Gratias'
6. GREETING—MR. MURRAY DAVIS SENIOR CLASS ADVISER
7. HONOR FORUM Graduates: DORIS GELLER, JAY HOFFMAN, MARTIN HYMAN, AGNES LEIBOWITZ, EDWARD ORSHAN, ALAN RICHTER, ROBERTA RUBIN
8. OVERTURE—'Egmont' . . . . . . Beethoven JAMES MADISON HIGH SCHOOL BAND UNDER THE DIRECTION OF MR. AARON RAPHAEL
9. ADDRESS—MR. MAX NEWFIELD PRINCIPAL
10. 'THE GREAT GATE AT KIEV' · Moussorgsky BAND
11. PRESENTATION OF AWARDS MR. GEORGE B. DOWNING
12. CLASS GIFT TO THE SCHOOL JEFFREY BROIDO PRESIDENT OF SENIOR CLASS
13. CONFERRING OF DIPLOMAS MR. MAX NEWFIELD, PRINCIPAL
14. SONG—'GOING BACK TO MADISON'
15. RECESSIONAL 'Madison Forever' . . . . . . Hadley

Audience will kindly remain seated until after Recessional

affluent Italian youngsters from the Canarsie area. But I don't remember a fight or conflagration between them. Scholastically, it may not have had the reputation of Midwood or Erasmus, but it was an excellent and beautiful school in a lovely residential neighborhood.

A school bus en route to Lafayette. On rainy days, your bus always got stuck in the mud.

FRANCES BLUM: New Utrecht, in Borough Park, was old even when I went there in the early fifties. I think it was built sometime in the 1920s. There was nothing fancy or very pretty about the school or about the West End elevated line it overlooked. There was a rumor that the Mafia had a hand in building it, and that was why everything was so topsy-turvy. The back of the building should have been the front. The gym was behind the stage of the auditorium, separated by a wall that went up and down. When it was down, you had the stage. When you picked it up, you had the gym.

The students were mostly working class but with a middle-class ethic. Many of the girls took a commercial or co-op course, where they worked one week and went to school the next week. We were brought up to finish high school, go to work, get married, and have children. Many of the Jewish boys were going to college, and it seemed to me most of the Italian boys were going into blue-collar work. But we liked them better; they were the heartthrobs, with the black pompadour hair. The Jewish boys were the shorter, pudgier types.

CAROLINE KATZ MOUNT: Lafayette was built in 1939 in a deserted area of Bath Beach. There were rumors that the empty lots

Lafayette High School: "The building looked . . . more like an orange-colored factory than a school."

around the school contained the bodies of Murder, Inc., victims. The building looked like a WPA project—very simple and spare, more like an orange-colored factory than a school. Parts of Benson Avenue were still dirt roads through the 1950s, and on rainy days the school buses always got stuck in the mud.

The district was Bath Beach, Bensonhurst, and parts of Flatbush—a wide range of neighborhoods, from working class to upper middle class. The population was pretty evenly divided between Jewish and Italian kids.

ANGELO BADALAMENTI: There were so many talented people at Lafayette, so many kids interested in classical as well as popular music, theater, art. You were encouraged to be creative. In the afternoon after classes, I could go into the empty auditorium, sit down at the piano, and improvise. I liked to fool around with tunes of the forties and fifties, songs like "These Foolish Things Remind Me of You." At that age, you like to indulge in that kind of reflective mood.

Vito Farinola, who later became Vic Damone, went to Lafayette with my brother. The Italian teacher loved him. She'd say, "Vito, come up here with your beautiful voice and sing something." Vito was happy to oblige. He would get up and sing: "Come back to Sorrento. . . ." All the guys couldn't control themselves. They would roll off their chairs, go *"Uggggh."*

JOYCE SHAPIRO FEIGENBAUM: The most popular boys were
the guys on the football team, especially after Lafayette won the public
league championship in '54. Several of them had been left back, but
that didn't matter. There was this anti-intellectual strain; if you wanted
to be popular, you didn't let it get around that you were an A student.
So these Super Seniors, as we used to call them, suffered no loss of
prestige for being in high school an extra term. They took things like
home economics—imagine tough, big football players in aprons! The
whole bunch of them were so crazy, so wild. One went on to become
a bouncer in the Peppermint Lounge. They represented adventure.
You had to fight them off a little harder.

MARTY ADLER: Ft. Hamilton High School didn't have a football
team. It was younger than most of the other high schools, and it didn't
have the characters or the history. The kids were good students and
good citizens, but maybe they had a little less flair than other Brooklyn
kids. Still, it was a handsome Greek-style building set on a bluff
overlooking the Narrows in an upper-middle-class, safe and beautiful
neighborhood.

Since I lived in Borough Park, I expected to go to New Utrecht   **Lafayette's football heroes:**
High School, but my whole graduating class from Pershing Junior High   **"You had to fight them off a**
went to Ft. Hamilton. Either New Utrecht was too crowded or they   **little harder."**

wanted to get more Jewish kids into Ft. Hamilton. The school's population was about 2 percent Jewish, 30 percent Greek and Syrian, and the rest Scandinavian.

When I was in high school, they were driving in the piles to build the Verrazano Bridge. We were allowed out for lunch, and we sat on Shore Road and watched.

BOB GERARDI: When I entered Brooklyn Tech, in the early fifties, the enrollment was five thousand boys, from all boroughs. It was a competitive school; you had to score high enough on a test to get in. It was one of the finest high schools anywhere.

The school was built as a WPA project. It had its own radio station. It offered a course in architecture, and every semester a frame of a one-story house would be built in a classroom. There was a power lab that looked like a movie set, with dynamos and pipes running all over—huge pumps, things that you might see in a city power station. There were forges where metal could be bent and changed, wood shops where castings for engine parts were made. Kids learned to handle powerful machinery.

MAX WECHSLER: Boys High looked like a jail out of the Middle Ages. Which is not to deny its magnificence: the ornate towers, the Tiffany glass windows, a massive pipe organ in the auditorium. The building itself took up a whole city block in the heart of Bedford-Stuyvesant, and the little brownstones and small apartment houses that surrounded the school seemed like small pieces on a chess board. Boys High was what controlled the board.

Since the school was unzoned, the students came from everywhere—a mix of black and white, Jewish and Christian. Since it was an all-boys school, there was a rowdiness and roughness that was kept under control by tough teachers and even tougher deans. We were all aware we were at a place of great tradition and history, with many famous and distinguished alumni, some of whom came back to speak at assemblies. The serious athletes and the serious students got what they wanted at Boys High because in the postwar decades, Boys had great teams and wonderful teachers.

TERRY PERNA ARNESEN: Bay Ridge High was an all-girls school that was run like a finishing school. The building was a beautiful Victorian structure with turrets and towers overlooking the park. Inside was a lobby filled with antiques. The young ladies were always properly dressed and very proud to be there. They studied a combined academic and commercial course because the belief was they would have to work and go to school at night. Bay Ridge prepared them for both.

It was the only high school in New York that taught Norwegian. The students were mostly Scandinavian and Irish, although some were Italian. Many had gone to parochial elementary schools, and the parents felt comfortable sending their daughters there.

Three Irish women were principals: McGinniss, Fitzpatrick, Ryan. Miss Fitzpatrick was about five-six, a dignified, handsome woman, subdued in dress and coiffure. She'd walk down the hall with that elegant carriage, and everyone would take notice. But she was also a martinet, very antiunion. She handpicked her faculty, although Charles Cogan, who was president of the UFT—the teachers' union—taught there. Him, she didn't handpick.

RALPH GASARCH: Lincoln's original principal, Gabriel Mason, was the first to handpick the chairmen and faculty. Then he retired to his office to play chess and rehearse his lines (which he would always forget) for the Varsity Show. Since he had to have a starring role every year, all the plays had to have an older man as a lead.

But he trusted the people he brought in. Most of them were inbred, married to teachers or supervisors. They lived in those enormous houses in the fancy areas of Flatbush and owned pieces of summer camps. Overall, though, they had a Depression mentality.

ABE LASS: Coming out of the Depression, teaching was a coveted job. As Sam Levinson used to say, teachers weren't making much, but they were getting salaries when other people were selling apples. Teaching in the city was a pleasure; because it was secure, gifted college students, often the top drawer of their class, became teachers. They lasted through the postwar decades. This was a phenomenon.

JOEL BERGER: High school teachers had to pass very rigorous and competitive exams and earned a higher salary. They were masters.

Hermine Bernstein, who taught art, helped me learn the ropes my first year of teaching at Erasmus. She was striking-looking, with jet-black hair pulled back into a chignon, dark lively eyes, and a bright Ipana-toothpaste smile. Hermine was like a certain type of woman teacher of that time who dressed in bohemian-style clothes and dramatic jewelry. On weekends, I would see them in museums, at concerts and the theater.

GAIL EISEMAN BERNSTEIN: There were also these mean old bitty women at Erasmus: Miss Corey, who had white hair and scrunched up glasses; Miss Carpenter; Miss Genung; Miss Brenner, who spit when she talked and made you stand up to recite your Spanish conjugations; Miss Alberta Crespi, who taught math and gave me a zero when I tried to copy a test and the girl in front covered up her paper with her arm. There was a man who taught biology who was still wearing spats in the late 1950s.

ABE LASS: Typical of the staff at Lincoln was Leon Friend, art chairman and the greatest single art teacher in the whole city. Leon had insomnia. He arrived at school at 6:00 A.M. The gates were locked, but he had the key. Leon had a group of devoted followers: the art squad, kids who scaled the spiked fences at that hour to be with their maestro. They were crazy about him, and for a very good reason: he was crazy about the kids. I can't tell you how many of Leon's students walked from Lincoln right into a job at any one of the big advertising companies.

Lou Gossett was one of the very few blacks in Lincoln when I was principal. His mother was vice-president of the Parents' Association, and Louie was a basketball player with the special condensed programs for athletes: no gym, four or five periods of classes, lunch, and out by 11:00 A.M.

"Hermine Bernstein, who taught art, . . . was like a certain type of woman teacher of that time who dressed in bohemian-style clothes and dramatic jewelry."

"Mickey Fisher was teacher, coach, friend, and parent to every kid who played basketball for him at Boys High."

During his last year, Louie broke an ankle and was transferred into Gus Blum's class. Gus had wanted to be an actor and a director. But times were bad, so he sublimated his feelings about the stage by teaching drama and directing two student productions a year. Louie had never been in any dramatic class or play before, but Gus spotted his acting potential. Louie bloomed under Blum. Had he not broken his ankle, he might never have become an actor.

LARRY STRICKLER: Gustav Blum was a short, rotund man with a warm heart and great sensitivity. In my senior year he had a heart attack and was rushed to the hospital. After that he couldn't come back. He wasn't a young man. Today you hear you need young teachers because kids can relate to them. You don't relate to young; you relate to good. Blum was good.

HOWARD JONES: Mickey Fisher was teacher, coach, friend, and parent to every kid who played basketball for him at Boys High. He had the respect of everyone in that school. He wasn't a phony.

The first time I saw him was at a Boys High basketball game when I was in the eighth grade. I was on my knees between two guys, watching through the railing of the track that ran above the gym. There was this short guy down on the floor in a red-and-black sweater, coaching the team. I knew who he was. I had heard the older kids who played basketball at the Carlton YMCA talking about him. They said he was fair and had their interests at heart.

The next year, when I came to Boys, I saw Mickey Fisher at work. Each member of the basketball team had to report to him every morning. If you didn't report, you could not practice or play that day. All he wanted was for you to come in and say, "I'm fine. I don't have a problem" or "I'm having trouble in this or that class."

At practice he screamed like a maniac. He was intolerable. He was so frightening, so demanding, you could hate him. But after practice, he would put his arm around you and say, "Son, you know you make me proud of you."

Later on, Mickey got me to do my student teaching at Boys High School, and during that time, Connie Hawkins came along. They called him the Hawk, because of his long hawkish face. He was fourteen years old, undernourished, about six-two. He towered over both of us.

Connie came into the gymnasium, and Mickey called me over. "Howard, I'm telling this young man that he will be an all-American high school and college player if he comes to school. That's how good he is. But he's missed over a hundred days in elementary school." Then Mickey turned to Connie: "Son, if you listen to me and come to school, I'll make something out of you." Connie loved basketball. He came to school every day. He was the best we ever had.

Mickey started building the strong teams in the fifties with the Sihugo Greens, the Vinny Cohens, the Solly Walkers, the Lenny Wilkens. Jefferson, Erasmus, Lincoln had very good teams. But through the fifties and sixties, Boys High dominated basketball. Mickey Fisher did so much for the kids; every one of them graduated. He did so much for the school and the community. People focused on the team. They took pride.

KARL BERNSTEIN: "You're all a bunch of Kings Highway bourgeoisie," Miss Deborah Tannenbaum would tell us. "You hang around in front of Dubrow's getting vicarious thrills out of life." I didn't understand what she was talking about. Miss Tannenbaum was only about five feet tall, but she was dynamite. She taught only the best English classes at Madison, and on such a high level. We read *Portrait of an Artist*, and I became scared to death of going to hell. I hardly ever opened my mouth, I was so afraid of the woman. But I sat down and took the English Regents and got a 96.

I thought Miss Amy Hemsing, who taught Latin at Madison, was

"The afterschool activities meant everything. You made friends, got to know your teachers on a different level. A teacher always had such a great aura for us."

old enough to have been there when Rome burned. On one exam, I forgot everything and got a 50. "This is not the kind of work you do," she said. She ripped up the paper and didn't count the grade.

JUDY BERGER: We were incoming sophomores, waiting outside the room the first day of classes at Lafayette. Our teacher was late. Finally, this very heavy man came along. His sheer size was enough to scare the daylights out of us. We followed him into the room, took our seats, and began filling out the Delaney cards. He took a look at them and shouted in that booming voice: "Sophomores? Sophomores? How dare they give me sophomores? I'm going to see the chairman!" And he stormed out.

That was my introduction to high school and Marvin Feldman. That history class became the first time in school that I felt ill at ease because of my ignorance. Mr. Feldman spouted theories, opinions, dates, and quotes. He appeared to know everything. And of course, later on in life, I learned he really did.

STAN GOLDBERG: Marvin Feldman forced us to think. He would throw questions out, directing them from Stan to Don to Judy and then back to him. He would make provocative statements. Every other teacher told us all the American presidents were great—not Mr. Feldman.

CAROLINE KATZ MOUNT: "Schub-Shostack-and-Shapiro" was a song in one of the Sings that described three literary, intellectual English teachers at Lafayette. Dr. Schub was a Shakespearean scholar, Mr. Shostack wrote the Regents Review and College Prep books, and Joe Shapiro was chairman of the department and also a songwriter. "Round and Round" was his biggest hit. He was born in England and retained that kind of elite Oxfordian manner, but he was also a charming, bon-vivant type. He would get excited about literature and read the dramatic parts in his resonant voice. I thought he sounded like Laurence Olivier. Alice Roth, who also taught English, was a Barnard graduate. She was so composed and witty. She used to say girls who are pretty often rely on their looks and don't bother developing a personality. Those who are not pretty work on their personality, and that's much more important. I didn't know where I fit in. But I knew I wanted to be like her.

DONNA GEFFNER: It was Mrs. Roth who brought Sing to Lafayette. Sing, wonderful Sing! It was all over Brooklyn. Lincoln was doing their Sing, and Midwood was doing theirs, and that made you have a real school spirit in addition to your class spirit, which you had even though you knew the seniors would probably win.

The excitement started in September. It built all through the fall as you wrote the script and cast the show and rehearsed the chorus and solos. And then finally, in December, just before Christmas, the climax—three glorious nights of performance.

Scenes from "Sing, wonderful Sing!"

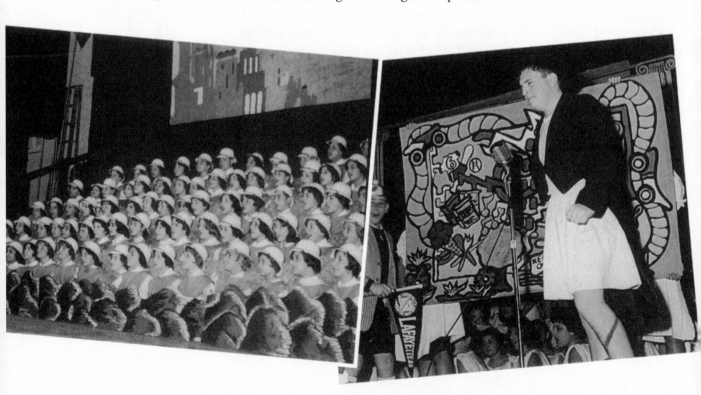

LARRY STRICKLER: The curtain would open, and there would be this massive immobile chorus on risers, a dazzling display. There were as many as three hundred kids in a chorus, all dressed alike, and when they did their animated hand-motions with sequined gloves or shakers or flags, it was quite a spectacle.

DONNA GEFFNER: Sing gave students a chance to really express themselves. Writers, dancers, singers, actors, musicians, artists, costume and set designers, lighting people—everyone got a chance to show off his or her talent. And if you didn't have a special talent and were just part of the chorus, you were important, too. Each class—sophomores, juniors, seniors, and sometimes even freshmen—put on its own show. You'd start with nothing, just a couple of ideas for a theme. Then you'd decide on one and write a whole show based around it with inside jokes, takeoffs on teachers, and clever, satiric lyrics set to familiar melodies. "I'm the klepto in the G.O." (student government), sung to the melody of "Tip-Toe Through the Tulips," was the big hit of the "psychology" theme one year. In my senior year, our theme was "Camelot." Ironically, that was in 1963, and we went on less than a month after President Kennedy was assassinated.

Sing rehearsals got underway by mid-October, when it was starting to get dark early. We'd begin after classes ended and go on into the late afternoons and evenings. The school building would close. The hallways would be darkened, the classrooms empty. It was magical, theaterlike.

MARNIE BERNSTEIN: The bus would be waiting for us after rehearsal. How unusual it was to be coming home from school in the dark. All the way down Bay Parkway, Christmas lights were strung from one side of the street to the other. The store windows were decorated with tinsel and stars. And we'd be riding home, singing at the top of our lungs: "Mr. Sandman, send me a dream, . . ." even though we had just spent the last three or four hours rehearsing.

DONNA GEFFNER: The afterschool activities meant everything. You made friends, got to know your teachers on a different level. A teacher always had such a great aura for us.

KARL BERNSTEIN: Jack Barnett, the acting chairman of music at Madison, a bald, fat, roly-poly man, produced a five-night run of *Patience*, the entire Gilbert and Sullivan operetta, conducting a full orchestra and directing two casts. He also was one of the conductors of the All-City Orchestra, which had kids from all five boroughs. I

THE MUSIC DEPARTMENT
James Madison High School
MAX NEWFIELD, Principal
presents—

PATIENCE
An OPERETTA by GILBERT and SULLIVAN

Directed and conducted by MR. J. A. BARNETT
Chairman Music Dept.

May 18, 19, 20 • 1949
J. M. H. S. AUDITORIUM

made first stand playing the cello at All-City, which meant having to go to Brooklyn Tech at nine o'clock every Saturday morning for a three-hour rehearsal. The conductors were all teachers who gave up their Saturdays to do this. Twice a year we gave concerts at Carnegie Hall.

NORMAN SPIZZ: It was like a microcosm of the big-band days at the Paramount when Lincoln High School held its annual jazz concert. The dance band was three trumpets, three trombones, five saxes, and three rhythm. We played all the numbers: "One O'Clock Jump," "Sing, Sing, Sing," "Tangerine," a lot of Glenn Miller, Freddy Martin. When we had the solos, we stood up and the lights would shine on us. Kids got up and danced in the aisles till the cops came and stopped them, because it was a fire hazard. Our dance band was the best in the city. Playing in it was like being the captain of the football team. We had dance-band sweaters—white with a big *L* on it. Those sweaters could get you a lot.

MARNIE BERNSTEIN: The annual concert at Lafayette was always on a beautiful night in May. The auditorium would be bathed in a pink glow and crowded with parents and brothers and sisters of performers in the orchestra, the marching band, the jazz band, the glee club, and the cantata.

Our junior year, Terry's parents got there late and had to sit up in the balcony. We were in the middle of Tchaikovsky's "Waltz of the Flowers," when out of the corner of my eye I saw something fly by. Everyone turned for a moment. There was Terry's father hanging over the balcony railing and sailing down paper airplanes. That was just the kind of thing you'd expect from him. He was such a zany guy.

While the first violins of the Lafayette orchestra did the melody to "Waltz of the Flowers," Terry and I played the second violin part: "bum-bum, bum-bum." Before us on the podium, Grace Greenwald, ever true to her name, conducted on her tiptoes. Amazingly, the whole collection of instruments—even the big bass fiddles and kettledrums, the tubas and bassoons—followed the wand of this diminutive silver-haired lady who looked like a tiny ballerina atop a music box. How Mrs. Greenwald, with the manner of an angel and the gentlest of voices, got a bunch of kids to make the finale of Beethoven's Fifth really sound like music is something I will never forget.

ANGELO BADALAMENTI: Mrs. Greenwald was "Mama," and Louis Pierro, chairman of the music department, was "Papa." They were short in size but long on talent—first-rate violinists. In every

other way, they were totally different, yet they complemented each other. Mr. Pierro was a formal and elegant man, impeccably dressed, with wavy dark hair and a twirling mustache. If Toscanini had been a school teacher, he would have been Mr. Pierro. He spoke softly, but all he had to do was give us a look, and we got quiet. Mrs. Greenwald, on the other hand, was so warm and soft and sweet and beautiful. I had a terrific crush on her.

NORMAN SPIZZ: Ben Goldman, the music teacher at Lincoln, was a frustrated songwriter and a terrific conductor who really knew his stuff. He was tough. If you didn't do your thing, he threw you out of the band. But if you were serious, he was there for you, got you jobs playing up in the Catskills, at proms, bar mitzvahs.

ANGELO BADALAMENTI: You got fifteen or twenty dollars a night playing at bar mitzvahs and weddings all over Brooklyn, plus all you could eat. At the Italian weddings of that time, there would be literally fifty sandwiches at every table, and they would just keep coming and coming. They used to call them football weddings. Someone would call out, "Pass the provolone," and you'd fling it like Joe Namath across the room. "Ham and cheese." *Boom!* I would bring along my brother's empty trumpet case, and at intermission, when the band would eat, I would stuff the case with sandwiches. Monday mornings I'd be the most popular boy in the Lafayette High School cafeteria. All my friends would sit at this long table and we'd have an encore of the football wedding. Those were known as Angelo's sandwich days.

KARL BERNSTEIN: Barry Greenberg was the star tuba player at Madison and brought the house down with his performance of "Tubby the Tuba," with the whole orchestra behind him. He was a skinny kid with blonde curly hair and bright twinkly eyes, and always into some kind of mischief. But he was such a good musician, he managed to get away with everything. We were hanging out in the instrument room one day when Mr. Rattner came in unexpectedly. Barry didn't have a chance to put out his cigarette, so he threw it into the tuba. Mr. Rattner was in the middle of explaining something when he stopped and sniffed. "Barry," he cried, "your tuba, it's on fire!"

ABE LASS: Neil Sedaka was a fantastic piano player, very talented, and also very charming. I used to come down in the afternoons when the school band was rehearsing and sometimes we'd play duets.

"Lincoln was such a creative force in my life."

— Neil Sedaka

NEIL SEDAKA: I was the accompanist in the pit, rarely a performer. But at one Ballyhoo show in the auditorium, I sang and played the piano to a song I wrote called "Mr. Moon." It was in the new doo-wop style, and it caused a riot. Everybody got up, all the toughies were cheering and dancing.

Mr. Lass called me to his office. There was a second show that afternoon and he said, "Neil, I really think that you should sing something other than 'Mr. Moon.' It incites all the kids a little too much. It's very wild music."

The kids got wind of this and passed around a petition insisting I sing "Mr. Moon" again. And, of course, I did. That made me a bit of a hero—so much so that I could go to the sweet shop where the toughies hung out. These were kids from Coney Island who wore the DA haircuts and leather jackets. There was this guy Alfred Abasso and his girlfriend, Frenchie, who piled her hair on top of her head. They said, "There's Mr. Moon. Let him in. Let him in."

Lincoln was such a creative force in my life. Music teachers like Ben Goldman and Alice Eisen, who led the chorale, inspired so many

Celebrities

13. Most Likely to Succeed—Caroline Katz
14. Most Popular Girl—Barbara Ventura
15. Most Popular Boy—Nick Lampariello
16. Class Poet—Louis Nordstrom
17. Class Scientist—Joel Schiff
18. Prettiest Girl—Sue Benedetto
19. Handsomest Boy—Irv Moskowitz
20. Class Artist—Mark Sherman
21. Person Who Did Most For Sing —Jeff Lass
22. Best Dressed Girl—Elsie Tom
23. Best Dressed Boy—Bob Price
24. Miss Co-op—Amelia Marchica

of us. I went to school with Mort Shuman, who wrote many of the Elvis songs later on, and did *Jacques Brel Is Alive and Well.* When I entered, Lou Gossett was graduating, and he was singing with a group. Neil Diamond lived across the street and went to Lincoln after me. All of us got so much from our teachers.

ANGELO BADALAMENTI: They made us feel special, worried about us, wondered what books we were reading. A teacher at Seth Low Junior High started me playing the French horn. I took it up in school and then went on to private lessons with a man who had played in the John Philip Sousa band. In high school, I played the piano and the French horn in the band and orchestra. On the basis of the French horn, I got a scholarship to Eastman School of Music. It was only because of the school system that I got the opportunities that made my musical career possible.

All through high school, I was busy writing songs. Before graduation, I went to Mrs. Greenwald. "I think I have something that could

be the processional march for our graduating class. May I write it?"

"Absolutely, Angelo. Go for it. Do it."

I developed three themes. A friend of my brother's orchestrated it. And they used it. "Processional March composed by Angelo Badalamenti"—that's how it was listed on the graduation program.

That's what comes back when I think of high school: the creative environment, the quality of the teachers, the way they encouraged us: "Absolutely, Angelo. Go for it."

The Lafayette High School
faculty in the mid 1950s.

Hanging Out and Making It

WE'RE THE GIRLS OF SIGMA RHO
YOU'VE HEARD SO MUCH ABOUT.
WHENEVER WE GO MARCHING,
YOU HEAR THE PEOPLE SHOUT:
"THOSE ARE THE GIRLS OF SIGMA RHO
YOU'VE HEARD SO MUCH ABOUT . . . ."
—Club song

JOYCE SHAPIRO FEIGENBAUM: The key to belonging was being a member of one of the popular clubs. They were like mini-sororities, and getting in depended on superficial things like looks and personality and whom you knew. But if you belonged, you were "in," and you would announce that by wearing your club jacket, with the name across the back, when you walked up and down one of the big thoroughfares like Kings Highway on Friday nights.

BOB ERTEL: The Midwood crowd walked Avenue J from Coney Island Avenue to Seventeenth Street and gathered at Cooky's. After school, if the weather was bad, we'd go down to Arty's Poolroom, which we called Barricini's Basement in front of our mothers. A lot of older guys hung around there, and we enjoyed shooting pool and shooting the breeze with them.

A date was usually the movies: the Midwood on Avenue J, the Kingsway or the Avalon on Kings Highway. We double- and triple-dated all the time. As seniors, we migrated from Avenue J to Kings Highway, where the Madison, Lincoln, and Lafayette kids hung out.

LARRY STRICKLER: In *American Graffiti* they drove their cars; that's California. In Brooklyn, we walked. We walked Kings Highway from Coney Island Avenue to Ocean Avenue. We walked with a lilt, with one hand in our pocket, the other waving "hi." That's where we learned to schmooze. How was popularity measured in the Kings Highway area? By the time it took you to walk from Coney Island Avenue to Ocean Avenue. The shorter the time, the less popular you were. How long did it take me? Five days.

MARTY ADLER: A few blocks before Ocean Avenue, just past the Brighton el, was Dubrow's Cafeteria. That's where you ended up on a Friday night. If you were lucky enough to have a car, you kept it down to three guys so there'd be room in case you picked up some girls. The Madison and Midwood cheerleaders were there, and they were the prettiest. You'd take them to a movie or someone's party. Around midnight you'd drop by Dubrow's again to see if any of the other guys were around. You'd tell stories about what happened that night and hook up for a ball game the next day.

HERBY GREISSMAN: The Famous Cafeteria on Eighty-sixth Street under the West End el was a hangout for kids from Lafayette and New Utrecht. They'd give you a ticket when you went in, and when you ordered something they punched out the price. We would go in, get a ticket, go out, come back in again, and get a second ticket. Then we would take the cheapest thing for ten or fifteen cents, and that's what we used when it came time to pay the bill. But in between, we had the other ticket that we used to run up the tab. The big tab of a dollar-fifty or two dollars, we threw away. I'm sure everyone knew that gimmick. How they stayed in business, in my wildest dreams I can't imagine.

JOYCE SHAPIRO FEIGENBAUM: The kids converged on the tables in the front of the Famous. The old retired men occupied the tables in the back. Everyone stayed for hours on end. For me, it was a place of refuge away from my noisy, crowded apartment, where everybody was always yelling. I did my homework there.

BOB ERTEL: Gragnano's, on McDonald Avenue near Eighteenth Avenue, was a mecca for the New Utrecht and Brooklyn College crowds. It wasn't a cafeteria, but a pizza parlor—one of the first of its kind. There was no such thing then as buying pizza by the slice. Three or four kids would order a pie.

PHIL FAGIN: You could sit over a cup of coffee and a Danish for hours at the Famous Cafeteria on Eastern Parkway and Utica Avenue for a big twenty-five cents. The workers there were kibitzers. "A fly in your soup? It doesn't drink much." Or "Did you teach that fly how to do the backstroke?"

GAIL EISEMAN BERNSTEIN: Friday afternoons we'd rush home from Erasmus to get ourselves ready for our Friday night pilgrimage to Garfield's Cafeteria, on Church and Flatbush Avenues. It took awhile. First, you had to set your hair. I had put a streak in my hair with peroxide and ammonia, and I hung my head out the window so the sun would make it lighter. That was my dip. To get the right height on it, I put the bobby pins vertical to my head. Then I tied two Modess sanitary pads together, rolled the rest of my hair over them, put some gooey stuff on top, and waited for it to dry and harden. It came out a beautiful page-boy fluff. For a while I wore the Italian bob with spit curls—those little half-curls on the forehead, which I plastered with sugar and water to get them to stay. Then I put on makeup. I carefully drew the little line extending out from the corner of the eyes with a Maybelline pencil—doe eyes—and I put on lipstick, either Tattoo Orange or Tattoo Pink. Then I got dressed. We all wore skirts that were puffed up with crinolines. To make my horsehair crinolines stand out, I washed them in water and sugar and layered them one on top of the other over an umbrella. We wore nylon sweater

sets: a short-sleeved sweater underneath and matching cardigan on top. If we wanted to look sexy, we wore the cardigan by itself, buttoned down the back, over one of the pointy bras: ice-cream bras, cone bras, carnival bras. We would tie a little kerchief around the neck or stick a dickey with our initials on it under the sweater. We wore loafers with bobby sox—the heavy wool sox from Davega. We folded them over and held them in place with a big rubber band around the top that cut off the circulation.

When we arrived at Garfield's, we never went inside. We stood on the corner and saw who came around. If someone interesting went in, we went in too. A girl could sit with a single Coke all night. We'd meet a lot of boys, but we never went anyplace after Garfield's. We'd give the boys our phone number and hope they called.

STEWIE STONE: Garfield's rice pudding with hot fruit sauce on top was the greatest delicacy in the world. But the food was secondary. The getting together was what mattered. Going from table to table on Friday night was like going from blanket to blanket on the beach.

Every high school crowd in Brooklyn had its own cafeteria, and every high school crowd in Brooklyn had its own section of the beach marked off by a jetty, a line of rocks, on each side. Ours was Bay 2 in Brighton. The closer to the sign you were, the hipper you were. And you didn't wear a bathing suit, you wore dungarees and a T-shirt.

BOB ERTEL: It was blanket-to-blanket from boardwalk to shore, especially when the tide was up and you had to move back a little farther. But you wouldn't lay down to relax or get a tan. The beach scene was standing on the sand and going into the water to horse around or cool off. It was a big social thing. The girls wore these latex one-piece bathing suits. By today's standards, they were not very revealing, but of course there were a couple of chesty girls who stood out.

MAX WECHSLER: The whole beach scene was one of sweat and suntan oil and saltwater—liquid stuff, sex. It was an environment that stimulated all the senses. There was so much to look at: the way the bathing suits fit, how much they revealed, the changing positions of the bodies on the blankets. The grainy sand always got into your bathing suit when you lay on the rough army blankets, discreetly making out under the sun. The beach was a turn-on.

"The whole beach scene was one of sweat and suntan oil and salt water — liquid stuff, sex."

MARNIE BERNSTEIN: The Lafayette kids stayed on Bay 7, at the end of Ocean Parkway. Portable radios were still pretty rare, but guys would bring down bongo drums, and we'd sit in a big circle and do calypso songs. Joyce and I swam out to the third barrel at the end of the rope. It was way over our heads, and we weren't such terrific swimmers, but somehow we never worried. We'd bob up and down sitting on the rope, look out at the endless horizon, and sing our own harmony to "Blue Moon."

JOYCE SHAPIRO FEIGENBAUM: On the Fourth of July in 1955, we were working out the parts to that song when Billy Barrett passed our blanket. He said to his friends, "These chicks can really sing"—the ultimate compliment—and sat down beside us. That's how we met him.

Billy was a Lenny Bruce–type character—hip, verbal, quick on the uptake. He'd say and do anything outrageous. Once we got caught in a traffic jam. Billy got out and started directing traffic, and everyone listened to him. Another time we were on the Sea Beach express going to the city. The train was crowded. All of a sudden, I look up and there's Billy, hanging from the bar overhead like a monkey. He was a skinny guy with a shock of black straight hair falling into his face, glasses that were forever sliding down his nose, a wide manic grin, and a wild laugh that sounded like a donkey braying. That doesn't exactly add up to a John Garfield. But all the girls were crazy about him.

MARNIE BERNSTEIN: I hadn't seen Billy for about six months when we met at Claire's engagement party. She was the first one in our crowd to get engaged, at the age of sixteen. But she was Syrian, and they all got married very young. I had started college by that time and brought along a boy I was dating, a medical student at Columbia P & S, no less. Billy cut in while we were dancing. "Where'd you get that 'yeshiva bucher' from?" he asked. Then he turned on the charm. "You look sensational, just like Eva Gabor. Wait till I tell Jerry [an old boyfriend]." That was it. I never saw the medical student again.

JOYCE SHAPIRO FEIGENBAUM: Billy and his friends were out of the mainstream. They weren't as serious and upwardly mobile as many of the other boys. They were into progressive jazz instead of rock 'n' roll. They had an irreverent sense of humor, would make fun of things we considered sacred, like religion or the president, shock us with their language. Larry Pino, one of them, was a soda jerk in the little candy store next to the Marboro Theater. He was a romantic who took himself very seriously and liked to swing around lampposts like he was Gene Kelly.

The Syrian-Jewish boys in Bensonhurst belonged to a club called the Silver Knights. Two of them took Stella and me to the Copacabana, where Martha Raye was appearing. It was an expensive date. After, they took us back to their clubroom, which was in a finished basement furnished with a few discarded and sagging couches. Stella and her date settled into one of them. Instead of an overhead light, there were lamps all over the room. My date, who was looking for his reward, was walking around switching all the lamps off. I took off my shoes,

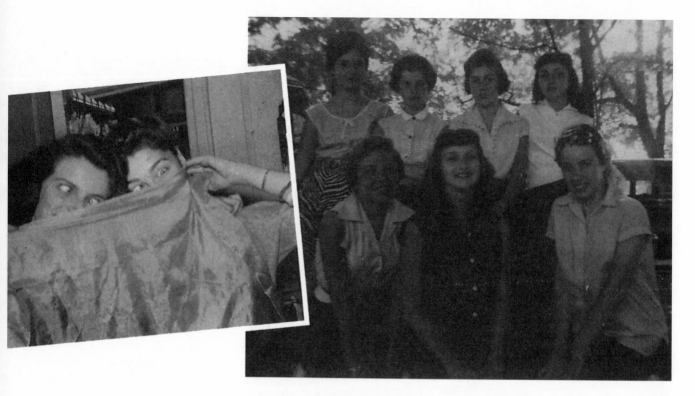

tiptoed behind him, and as soon as he switched a lamp off, I switched it back on.

Those guys were also atypical. They were terrific dancers and could do elaborate mambo and cha-cha breaks. They were also very sexually aggressive—except with women of their own kind, the ones they ended up marrying.

BILL FEIGENBAUM: Girls resisted sexual aggression. They fought hard to protect their virginity. They might do all kinds of things, which wasn't bad either, but not go "all the way." On the other hand, it was more rewarding in those days before sexual liberation. Guys felt more masculine, and I think girls felt more feminine. After, I missed the challenge of conquest.

NORMAN TIPOGRAPH: The spot for conquest was between Oriental and Manhattan Beach. It was called the Desert and was where all the young lovers went.

DORIS MODELL TIPOGRAPH: We took a blanket and some sticks, made a tent, and crawled underneath. It was hot!

NORMAN SPIZZ: When we had access to a car, we went to a little strip of beach off the Belt Parkway, just east of Sheepshead Bay, called Plum Beach. The water was polluted, and it smelled of fish, but it had a nice parking lot that overlooked Jamaica Bay. The big joke was we were going to watch the submarine races.

KARL BERNSTEIN: Our last Boy Scout meeting of the year was a cookout at Plum Beach. No Boy Scout is ever without his flashlight, and at Plum Beach, the kids ran around shining them into the cars.

GAIL EISEMAN BERNSTEIN: We stopped at Plum Beach and turned the headlights on the parked cars. We didn't see much, just steamy windows and people jumping apart.

TOM BOORAS: As kids, we were warned not to play on the docks of the East River near where we lived. But as teenagers, they became our favorite places for necking. At first we sat on boards, but once we got our fathers' cars, we would drive down and park at the end of the dock. It was a deserted area, but every once in a while a night watchman would come around and shine his light and get rid of you.

NORMAN SPIZZ: A lot was supposed to happen at all these lovers' lanes, but the girls of that era were not so willing.

JOYCE SHAPIRO FEIGENBAUM: Our undergarments were enough to inhibit anyone. They were as formidable as a suit of armor. Our bras were Exquisite Form, with the cups stitched around the tip to make our breasts look like they came to a point. When I bought my first bra, I couldn't fill it, so I stuffed it with tissues. There was no pantyhose then; our stockings were held up by a kind of girdle called the two-way-stretch. Under summer dresses, we wore a

braselette—a one-piece foundation that was a combination strapless bra and girdle, with plastic bones running from top to bottom.

When we had parties in a finished basement, they'd turn the lights down low, and we'd dance to some doo-wop music. The guys would try to dry-hump, and the girls in their horsehair crinolines would struggle to avoid body contact. Along with the music, you'd hear the shifting crinolines: *swish, swish, swish.*

BOB ERTEL: The problem was finding a place to have parties and keep other people from crashing. So in my senior year, we formed a group called the Fabulous Fifteen and came up with the idea of naming a Girl of the Week. Her photo was taken, and she was entitled to have a party in her home.

JOE SIGLER: The beauty of Brooklyn was that if you were popular with the girls, you could go out with a girl who lived in the same building as another girl you went out with, and they wouldn't even know one another because it was so immense. You didn't need a car because everything was in the same area. But every guy wanted one.

BILL FEIGENBAUM: In 1958, my father bought me a 1939 LaSalle Cadillac. It had a running board, a pearlized steering wheel, and whitewall tires. I painted it bright red and drove down Ocean Parkway to Coney Island. There were always girls along the way. Once, eight of them piled in.

ELLIOT GUNTY: My brother Morty had a 1955 red Cadillac convertible. It was half a block long, with beautiful red-and-white leather seats and a white top. That June, he got a month's gig in Las Vegas. The night of my prom, a telegram arrived: "Be Careful! Signed: The Owner." The Caddy was mine for the prom and the month.

BOB ERTEL: I went to the 1956 Midwood senior prom with a girl named Sheila. I wore a white dinner jacket, and she wore a pastel-colored organza gown with a puffed-up skirt. She looked terrific. Together with two other couples we rented an "air-conditioned" limousine for a total of thirty-nine dollars for the night and debated over whether we should give the driver a five- or a ten-dollar tip.

After the prom at the Waldorf Astoria, the limo took us to the Latin Quarter, where we saw Johnny Ray. Then we went to Basin Street to see Ella Fitzgerald. We spent every buck we had. One of the gals lived in a big house, and she invited us to come back there for a breakfast party. And then we all went down to Brighton Beach. We probably slept on the beach. But we don't remember it quite that way. We were so strong, so full of energy, it seemed we just went right into the next day without any sleep.

STEWIE STONE: I went with this girl who had a red Buick convertible, and we parked in a deserted part of Canarsie. It was the sexiest—fooling around on the plastic seat covers of that Buick until the cops came and shone the lights on us.

I had the key to my father's dance studio, which had a comfortable couch. But my father would always leave something lying on the couch, and the next day if it had been moved, he'd want to know why I was there and what I was doing. So I had to find other places.

The first time I went with a girl to the Golden Gate Motel in Sheepshead Bay, I was still living at home. Every kid in Brooklyn lived at home. Nobody got their own apartment till they got married. As soon as I got into the motel room, I turned on the television. The

"You didn't need a car because everything was in the same area. But every guy wanted one."

girl was surprised. "What are you doing?" she asked. "Did we come here to watch TV?"

"I told my mother I was over a friend's house watching television," I explained, "and when she asks questions about the programs, I have to know what to tell her."

My mother asked questions, and I was more afraid of my mother than anything else. To this day, whenever I go into a motel room, I turn on the television.

JOEL MARTIN: I was with this girl from Erasmus who lived up the block from me. We were petting on a chaise lounge in the finished basement of her house. Suddenly we hear her mother's footsteps on the stoop. Panic! I can't describe it. Sheer terror! Worse than the scene in *Psycho*. The *clop-clop*ping into the house, her high heels on the linoleum floor overhead. The girl says, "Go, go, go!" Quickly I pull myself together and zip myself up. I hurt myself down there. Doubled up in pain, I go out the side door, run down the alley, up the block, and into my house. My mother, naturally, is awake.

"What's wrong with you?" she asks.

"Stomachache."

"How did you get a stomachache? I know—I warned you not to eat goyisha franks at Ebbets Field."

TOM BOORAS: In those days, kissing a girl with your mouth open was considered a mortal sin. Every Saturday I had to go to confession and admit to it. I would go into a very dark room with two confessional boxes and screens so the priest could not see me. After, the priest gave me absolution and told me what my penance was. Then he said, "OK, Tom, don't forget to be at the 10:15 mass tomorrow." I lived so close to the church, I couldn't be anonymous. Finally my friends and I got smart. We began going down to St. Peter's Church at the foot of Atlantic Avenue. Hispanic people had begun moving into that parish in the mid-fifties, and they had a Spanish-speaking priest. St. Peter's became the busiest place for confessions. All the Irish kids went there.

MARTIN SPITZER: We thought about sex and talked about it, but it was never outward and open, the way it is today. It was all innocent stuff, mostly kissing. We were a fraternity of Lincoln and New Utrecht kids. During the basketball season, we were always at the games. Then we'd be partying in rented finished basements. The cheerleaders would be down and everything—happy, happy occasions.

SHELLY STRICKLER: When rock 'n' roll first came out, people said it was far out and dangerous, that it would get us into trouble. But it was all so mild. What was the worst thing we did? Neck in the balcony?

I didn't like rock 'n' roll right away. I liked Joni James and Patti Page, Perry Como and Eddie Fisher. But we played the songs at parties in finished basements. We danced the Fish at the JCH. It worked itself into our crowds.

NEIL SEDAKA: Carole King went to Madison but hung out with the kids from Lincoln. Pizza was still new then, and one night we went to try it at Andrea's Pizza Parlor, on Brighton Beach Avenue. We were waiting for our order when someone put a nickel in the jukebox, and "Earth Angel" by the Penguins came on. We were mesmerized. The Penguins went "ooooooh," and we went wild. That was our first exposure to pizza and rock 'n' roll.

MURRAY THE K'S
HOLIDAY REVUE
FEATURING
BEN E. KING   LITTLE STEVIE WONDER
JAN and DEAN   THE DRIFTERS
THE SHIRELLES   GENE PITNEY
MIRACLES
THE DOVELLS   THE ANGELS
                    JAY and the AMERICANS
THE TYMES   THE CHIFFONS

ROGER GREEN: "The soul in the hole" was what we called a sunk-in section of the park adjacent to P.S. 44 on Madison Street in Bedford-Stuyvesant. Late summer nights, the local soul singers would gather there, get up on the park benches, and perform. All the kids in the neighborhood thought they could sing doo-wop and would try to outdo each other with songs like "Twinkle, Twinkle Little Star." Little Anthony and the Imperials came by before they were famous. It was early rock 'n' roll, rhythm and blues, a lot of a capella, a lot of call-and-response. Grown-ups from the tenements across the street leaned out the windows to listen. Young people gathered round. They'd

**The old Brooklyn
Paramount, site of the
famous rock 'n' roll shows.**

build up a little pit with loose bricks, stick a potato on a branch, cook it, and eat it while listening to the singing.

NEIL SEDAKA: We lived and breathed music. We sang doo-wop in the school gym and in the lobbies of apartment houses, which had wonderful echoes, on the street corners and outside the candy stores. Our music was an escape from the adult world; it was our own little club, our own little niche.

HOWARD RAPP: We did the fifties-style harmony to songs like "The Closer You Are." At first we were ten kids, then sixteen, then twenty, then thirty. When the people in the buildings complained, we moved on to another corner, and then another one. We also had a group of a lead singer and four backup guys. I was the first tenor. That was how high my voice was.

GAIL EISEMAN BERNSTEIN: We would get up at four in the morning, leave the house at five, walk down to Church Avenue, and take the IRT downtown to Nevins Street. From there, we'd walk to the Fabian Fox or Paramount and stand in line for the 10:00 A.M. rock 'n' roll show. We saw the Platters, the Penguins, Bill Haley and the Comets. Once Eddie Fisher was featured in an Alan Freed show.

We got seats in the front row, threw him mash notes, and screamed as he sang "Oh My Papa" and "Bring Back the Hands of Time."

HOWARD RAPP: The rock 'n' roll shows at the Brooklyn Paramount ran about ten days during the times the kids were off from school, five performances a day of three-hour shows, with one act coming out right after the other. It was kind of a throwback to vaudeville, except it was all music and there was so much audience participation. Kids sang along, danced in the aisles. The lines to get in were enormous, but no one minded.

Alan Freed and, afterward, Murray the K signed groups before they were popular and pushed their records on the air. By the time the show came on, the records were hits and the groups well-known. They picked the Brooklyn Paramount, I guess, because it was so close to Manhattan. What Alan Freed accomplished at the Brooklyn Paramount was great. But he got caught up in all kinds of scandals like payola and having kids out robbing cars during his rock sock hops. His TV show got canceled, and everyone disassociated from him.

In 1963, right after Labor Day, Murray the K had a show at the Brooklyn Fox, right down the block from the Paramount, which by then was part of Long Island University. My uncle Charlie Rapp managed a group of Filipinos called the Rockyfellers: four children, aged seven, nine, thirteen, twenty-two, and the father, who was about four-ten and played the biggest bass fiddle you could believe. They had a number-two record at the time: "Look at Killer Joe Go." Although I was only fourteen, I worked backstage as chaperon and office representative. Whenever I looked out the dressing-room window, I'd see mobs of kids behind barricades waiting for a glimpse of the stars. "Look," they screamed when they saw me, "it's one of the Rockyfellers." I'd go out for something to eat, and kids would be all over me for an autograph. I signed Tony's name, because we were the same age.

Stevie Wonder made his first appearance at that show. He was thirteen years old. From the way he acted backstage, I wondered if he was really blind. He had a way of knowing who different people were that was uncanny. It was like he had an extra sense. In a jam session, he sang a number, "Fingertips," that became his first hit record.

HERBY GREISSMAN: We played records in our clubroom, which was a finished basement on Sixty-fifth Street. We also played cards, smoked cigarettes, made out with girls, and hung out there when we played hooky from school. The monitor in my homeroom class marked me present whenever I played hooky. But one day she played hooky too, and my alibi went down the drain. My father happened to be home when the dean called and said, "Your son's not in school."

I'm in the clubroom playing cards. All of a sudden, one of the fellows runs in from off the street and says, "Herby, your father's coming!" I duck into a back room. My father comes in. "Where's Herby?"

"We haven't seen him, Mr. Greissman," my friends say. "He must be in school."

He leaves without a word. Later that day he asks me where I was.

I said I went to school. He says, "Who are you bullshitting? I was in the clubroom, and I saw three guys playing cards with four hands." That time, he caught me.

Another time when I played hooky and heard he was on the warpath, I ran out of the clubhouse down five blocks to Sixtieth Street. There I met the school bus on the way home. I got on, and when the school bus pulled up in front of my house, I nonchalantly got off. That time, he didn't catch me.

One Saturday, we hung around the candy store with nothing to do. Nobody had money. Everybody was hungry. One of the guys suggests we crash a wedding. It seemed like a good idea. So we got dressed up and went over to the Aperion Manor, on Kings Highway. On Saturday nights in the summertime, they don't start until late, so we got there just in time.

You know a wedding's not like a bar mitzvah, where everyone knows everyone. You got two sides. My friend goes up and kisses the bride, congratulates her. Whoever it was, we said we were from the other side. We ate whatever we liked from the smorgasbord. When they were about to start the ceremony, we gave back the yarmulkes and went home.

I was good at running because someone was always chasing me. Victor Gordon's candy store around the corner had a window opening up to the street so you could buy candy or a paper without going into the store. We drove Victor Gordon crazy. One Saturday night, we're breaking his chops, and he's really pissed. He takes a big soda glass and fills it with water to throw at us. All of a sudden, Casey walks by the window, all dressed up for his Saturday night date. Victor Gordon throws the water, and Casey gets soaked.

The candy store across the street was sold. This woman Molly took it over. She was tough, didn't want to live by the rules. What were the rules? To give us a glass of water during a stickball game. We taught her a lesson. Saturday night she got the delivery of the Sunday papers. We got them and ripped them in half and ran. Or we bought balloons, filled them up with water, went up on the roof of the building across the street, and bombed the store. Or we'd wait for a convertible to go by. Sometimes we'd miss, sometimes we wouldn't. As I said, I was always running.

CLARENCE NORMAN, SR.: I was always running when the gangs came around. There were the Nits, the Robins, the Beavers, the Social Jets. When they came on the block, guys like me disappeared. I lived on the bridge between Bed-Stuy and Williamsburg. But I spent most of my childhood between DeKalb Avenue and down-

Stevie Wonder made his first appearance in 1963 at Murray the K's rock 'n' roll show at the Brooklyn Fox.

town because I knew crossing over to Gates Avenue could be death. These guys had zip guns and knives.

BOB ERTEL: As teenagers, we became aware of gang activities in the neighborhood. One evening we were walking to our bench on Ocean Parkway—every bunch of kids had their bench, where they hung out—when a gang came charging at us. There must have been forty of them and six of us. We thought we were finished, but they pulled up and said, "Aw, it's only the East Fifth Street boys."

TOM BOORAS: Gangs were popular in the downtown area, organized according to territory and neighborhoods. Gowanus had the Gowanus Dukes. The Kane Street Midgets were the kids twelve and under. The Kane Street Stompers were fourteen to thirty years old. They were into knocking over garbage cans or giving cars flat tires—prank things.

HOWARD RAPP: I lived on Taylor Street between Bedford and Wythe. The Hellburners were on one side of Bedford Avenue, and the Phantom Lords were on the other side. My friends and I straddled the line, just wanting to play basketball and hang out at the Williamsburg YMHA. We all got beat up once in a while.

ANNETTE DE LUCIA-CLARK: There were all kinds of gangs in Red Hook: the Mau Mau Chaplins, the Corsair Lords, the Ambassadors, the Saints, the Ft. Greene Chaplains. I was one of the youngest members of the Rebelettes, the female part of the Rebels. It was integrated: Hispanic, black, white, Japanese, Mexican. We wore black-and-hot-pink jackets with our names printed across the back.

   Guys in gangs could be vicious and violent but would rarely go out of their way to start something. It was more a guarding of the turf, something like *West Side Story.*

ALBERT VANN: Compared to the violence today, those gangs were very tame. In some ways, they were a healthy development. They reflected a high degree of organization, had a high regard for the neighborhood. You were only at risk if you didn't live in the neighborhood. Your elders, your seniors, they had no problems. They were well-respected.

ALAN LELCHUK: When I went with my father to the Eastern Parkway Arena to watch the fights, we knew we had to be more prudent on certain streets. There were gangs in Brownsville, but they didn't engage in random violence. They generally stayed on their own turf, except when they had gang fights.

CLARENCE NORMAN, SR.: Every May 30 there was a gang fight in Prospect Park. It was a known thing. We'd have a picnic on the Parade Ground and wait for it to start. We'd watch for a while, and then we'd all have to run.

LUIS COLMENARES: All told there were close to a hundred set for the gang fight at City Park, down just behind the projects area. It was the first time I was ever involved in anything like this. Everyone had chains and knives, bats and sticks. It was the Midgets, the Panthers, and some of the Angels against the Chaplins and Bishops.

We were there on this summer evening to fight these black kids, for what reason I don't know. But they weren't kids. They were men: six feet tall with eighteen-inch arms. They had guns and knives. Suddenly, Johnny Ferris comes out with a shotgun. The black guys stood there stiff. Johnny Ferris starts to scream: "You motherfuckers. Enough of this. I'm going to take all of you out." That was the first time I had ever heard the word *motherfuckers*. I didn't know what it meant, but it struck me that it was some kind of insult.

Then suddenly there was a *"BOOM!"* One of the Chaplins got wounded. Then there was a conference between the leaders of both sides. What started all the trouble was a rumor about a girl. Who started it, we didn't know. What girl, nobody seemed to know. Finally, it got settled and everybody went home.

ANNETTE DE LUCIA-CLARK: For weeks all the gangs were preparing for a gang fight in the Carroll Street Park. Kids were getting grease to put on their faces to protect against bites and scratches. There were the chains and the knives, the belts and the sticks. I was going along as part of the crowd, walking to the site of the fight with my girlfriend. "We must be out of our minds," I told her. "We can't go in there. What happens if we get killed?"

Then I joined the community center in my housing project, and it was a nice change from that kind of scene. We danced the lindy, the mashed potato, the fly, and the twist. We listened to Elvis and the Platters.

Miss Adams, a black counselor, suggested I compete in the Miss Gowanus Community Center Pageant. I was the only white girl who entered. The kids voted, and I won first place. I got a trophy and became eligible to compete in the citywide competition. I knew I could never enter, because one of the requirements was you had to make your own dress, and I had no money for anything.

But Miss Adams and her friend Mr. Johnson told me they would help. Mr. Johnson took money out of his own pocket and helped me buy white material. Their friends helped me sew it, and I actually wound up making a dress. It was, "Oh my God, me, Annette, made a dress?" I couldn't even read and write properly.

I had only had ragged hand-me-downs, dungarees, borrowed clothes—never anything nice like that before. I felt self-conscious and told the people at the community center I was dropping out. The whole thing was too high and mighty for me. But they would not let me. "You'll do fine," they insisted.

So I took part in the pageant and came in fourth runner-up in the city. Of course, the people at the Gowanus Community Center thought I should have finished higher. But for me, it was wonderful. Who would ever think that somebody in a poverty-ridden neighborhood, a gang member, a girl who grew up in an area where drugs and alcohol were on the street corners, could have such an experience? I had never thought I was pretty. But now I not only felt pretty, I believed I was different. I had assumed all of Brooklyn was like Gowanus. But now I saw there were other neighborhoods. I knew that I did not have to be part of a gang. I realized I could make choices.

ALBERT VANN: What kept me out of loopholes that young people can fall into was playing basketball. When we were not in school or working, we played. We played day and night, in the rain, in the cold. Patchen Park on Madison and Park, Kingston Avenue Park were places to show your stuff. In order to keep playing, you had to win.

DISCOVER easily you can read cer's Canterbury Tales when you use

CHAUCER CANTERBURY TALES— AN INTERLINEAR TRANSLATION

$1.50

A line of Middle English coupled with a line of Modern English

It was difficult to win against those guys who were three or four years older, but we always tried.

So many came out of that basketball playing—Sihugo Green; Solly Walker of St. Johns; Frank Thomas, who was my teammate at Franklin K. Lane and is now president of the Ford Foundation; Connie Hawkins, who was a little behind us (we like to think we nurtured him along); Tommy Davis, who played for the Dodgers. Basketball was always preeminent for me. I played varsity basketball—junior high school through college.

"What kept me out of loopholes that young people can fall into was playing basketball."

HERB BERNSTEIN: We played at Wingate Field. When it got dark, we moved cars over and lit the court with headlights. Saturday mornings, I couldn't wait to get up and run over there. I played basketball on court number one, a privilege I got by being good. It was three-man ball, one basket against the fence. Great games, great ball players. There were lots of fights and lots of hassles. If you lost a game, you could sit and wait for four hours to get back on the court. So you wouldn't lose. You played till you dropped. Then you went to get a hamburger and french fries and went back to play some more. The girls used to come down, and we'd show off. It was a big social thing.

STARR FROST GOLDBERG: The boys were on the teams, and the girls were the cheerleaders, or they sat in the stands and watched their boyfriends play ball. Even if we were good at a sport, we would giggle through the game and try not to make ourselves look that good. We were afraid we might beat the boys.

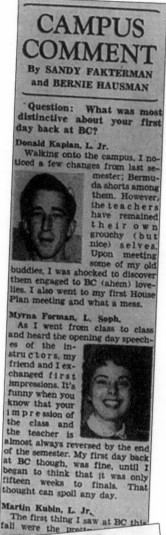

STAN GOLDBERG: When the schoolyard closed, we moved on over to the JCH on Bay Parkway and Seventy-ninth Street. I was selected to play in the all-star basketball game of the Junior League there, and it was a big thrill.

MAX WECHSLER: My local basketball league team had an away game at the JCH. Coming by bus from Williamsburg into Bensonhurst was like a trip into an upscale neighborhood. It had trees, wide boulevards, cleaner streets.

Our coach was a tough guy who always told us to play physical, to bang the players on the other teams around. That was part of the secret of our success, although we had some talented players too. I considered myself one of them.

The game began. My matchup was against a guy who had long arms and curly black hair. I shook hands with him before the game started and said, "Good luck." He didn't answer. But about three minutes into the game, I could tell this guy was letting his basketball ability do his talking. He scored off me every time he got the ball— a couple of driving lay-ups, a jump shot, a set shot.

During a time-out, the coach yelled at me, "You're letting that guy eat you up alive. Smack him around a little. Maybe that'll slow him down."

I kneed him, elbowed him, pushed him. Nothing helped. He was like a machine out there. Like I said, I thought I was a fairly good basketball player. But he was in another league. My physical play fouled me out of the game early in the second half. When the game finally ended, he wound up scoring forty-five points off me and the two other guys who followed in my place. I found out later his name was Sandy Koufax.

That was part of growing up. You thought you were a hot-shot ball player, and then you came up against a Sandy Koufax. It was a testing ground, finding out what you were made of, how well you could take failure, where you should set your sights.

BOB ERTEL: Up and down our street in Borough Park, they graduated from high school and went to work. But at Midwood, people were taking the College Boards, discussing different colleges, applying to places like Princeton, Yale, Michigan—major-league stuff. Mrs. Bradshaw, the goddess of college admissions, took great care of the ones who had the best potential for the better schools. Out of the Fabulous Fifteen, our social group, twelve went to out-of-town schools, two went to CCNY Engineering, and I went to Brooklyn.

JIM SLEEPER: To go to college most anywhere else, you really had to have money. But the large concentration of socialist immigrants in New York believed you should be able to get a college education without having to pay for it. There was a very unusual coming together of certain forces in New York City in the thirties, forties, and fifties. The values of immigrant socialists combined with FDR's political clout to make this a city with incredible resources and tremendous vitality. That really stamped Brooklyn. A unique set of public colleges was created, among them, Brooklyn College.

DONNA GEFFNER: All you needed was the grades: a 92 average for girls, an 88 average for guys—and we never thought to question the inequity of those criteria. For those of us from European backgrounds, this was a great opportunity. A registration fee of twenty-five dollars and a complete college education.

ALAN LELCHUK: Brooklyn College continued for me what I had with Jefferson and with the Dodgers—a strong sense of community, of excellence, of loyalty and fondness. You were going to college. Your father and mother had never gone, and you were bettering them.

Since my average in Jefferson wasn't high enough, I spent my first year at Brooklyn in night school. As it turned out, that was the best thing that happened to me in college. I joined up with the night-school magazine, *Nocturne*, where I met people in their thirties, veterans from World War II and the Korean War. It was a real literary brigade. Here were these mature guys with this seventeen-year-old kid on their hands who couldn't write his name. If I didn't know something, they didn't say shut up. They molded me. They gave me my first books to read, my indoctrination into literature. I began writing stories on the train. By the second year, I had earned good enough grades to matriculate into day school, but I remained with the *Nocturne*.

There was a real sense of excellence among the faculty. They were teachers, not celebrities going on television. I studied the classics. My Greek teacher was Vera Lachman, a Jewish lady who had escaped from Germany. She was very serious, very spare. I wrote plays in those days. She would take me to the lily pond in one of the sunken gardens that flanked the library. We would sit there and discuss the plays. It was exactly the educational experience one should get, being alone with a teacher in an isolated environment and talking about something that you were passionate about.

SOLOMON AIDELSON: I came to this country at the age of twenty-two, a Holocaust survivor. Nobody wanted to hear about the Holocaust at that time. No one wanted to touch the wounds. I had come from a very religious family and was ordained as a rabbi at a very young age, but I had no formal schooling since the first grade. What I wanted desperately was a secular education.

When I learned the Ford Foundation had given two million dollars to Brooklyn College to evaluate people who are self-taught, I applied, was accepted, and became a student at a regular college for the first time in my eventful life. It was a difficult and worrisome period, but it was also wonderful. In Eastern Europe, I had belonged to a sub-culture that had no relations with the main culture aside from buying and selling. Even in Brooklyn, I had been in all-Jewish surroundings. Now, I was in a different atmosphere.

Teaching during the day and going to school at night, I had very little time for leisure. But in the summers, when I didn't have to teach, I took the time to notice the campus. I looked to the right and to the left, and it was a very beautiful sight.

KARL BERNSTEIN: During my time, Brooklyn College was just four pink-brick Georgian buildings and a campus green we were not allowed to walk on. The library, La Guardia Hall, with its clock tower, dominated the whole scene. On either side of the library were sunken gardens: one had a lily pond, the other had a rose garden. Whitman, the performing arts center, opened in my senior year. Before that, all the way back to Flatbush Avenue was open campus. Behind the college, where Avenue H and Nostrand Avenue meet, there used to be experimental gardens with all kinds of plants and flowers and a little pond where biology majors worked on plant genetics. Walking around the campus, you felt like you were in an all-American out-of-town college, not in Brooklyn, New York.

Students Find Room Missing

Speech 19.1E was supposed to meet Tues. in 350W. That's what the schedule of clases said and that's where Speech 19.1E set out for, bright and alert.

Only one thing was wrong. The architect forgot to put a 350W in Whitman Hall. Such oversights happen all the time. so Speech 19.1E, undaunted, looked upstairs and downstairs in the big new building. They finally ended up on the roof. Only no 350W.

Somebody had the inspiration to call the speech department. "Yes," a voice said, "A mistake was made." The correct room was 023W.

Down to the catacombs of Whitman Hall trekked Epeech 19.1E to find 023W. It was a real challenge. But, alas, there was no 023W. Speechless, now, Speech 19.1E walked around in a state of traumatic shock.

A kindly student came around and cleared the matter up. It was all very simple. 023W was really inside 024W (not to be confused with 350W which doesn't exist at all). Spech 19.1E convened slightly late.

SHELLY STRICKLER: I missed out on a whole different acculturation not going away to college. I got on a different bus and went the other way with the same people I knew all my life. But my parents couldn't afford anything else, and I have to admit I got a first-class education. You went to public school, to high school, and then on to Brooklyn College. And you would be successful.

MIRIAM KITTRELL: My father said, "What are you crazy? What is this mishegoss? You have to go to college? Be a bookkeeper. Get married." But he couldn't stop me. I went to Brooklyn College. I worked in the lab, and I thrived.

ANGELO BADALAMENTI: We had our dreams, we worked at them, and we always talked about making it. Artie would tell me, "Angelo, you're gonna make it, I know you're gonna make it." I'd tell him, "Artie, you're gonna make it." We had this need to be successful, to step out of this lower-middle thing. What we had was not bad, but it wasn't enough. We knew there was a bigger, a greater world out there.

That World Is Gone

STEWIE STONE: You thought things would never change. You'd hang out on the corner, go to the movies with your friends, grow up, get married, go over to your parents for dinner. You thought Brooklyn would always be Brooklyn.

IRVING RUDD: One night in the early fifties, Walter O'Malley was in his chauffeur-driven Buick headed home after a night game at Ebbets Field. Around the area of what is now the Meadowbrook Parkway, he got stuck in a traffic jam and noticed that a tremendous amount of traffic was headed west. "What's all that?" he asked the chauffeur.

"It's the people coming home from the trots, Mr. O'Malley."

O'Malley's ears perked. A counterattraction. Bingo! Smack! Click! O'Malley was a shrewd man. He already saw the demographics. Why were these thousands of people going to Roosevelt Field instead of Ebbets Field?

MAX WECHSLER: In August 1955, when the Dodgers were in first place blowing away all their opposition, stories appeared in the newspapers that the team had scheduled eight games for 1956 in Jersey City. That could have been another country. Fans protested on cardboard signs: "Leave us not go to Joisey." But people thought O'Malley was bluffing, throwing down the glove, making his move to pressure city officials to give him a new stadium in Brooklyn. They might play a couple of games in Jersey City, but the Dodgers leave Brooklyn? Unthinkable.

The Dodgers had gotten their name from the fans who once dodged the crisscrossing trolleys that converged on Ebbets Field. But trolleys were becoming rare in Brooklyn. More and more people were driving to the games, yet there was very little parking near the stadium, and auto vandalism was increasing. O'Malley had seen studies that predicted the area would soon be unsuitable for night games. And the ballpark, built in 1913, was in need of repair.

Robert Moses offered O'Malley a site for a new stadium by the Brooklyn-Battery tunnel. "It's a good site for *you*," O'Malley told Moses. "Everyone will have to pay a toll. But with a cemetery on one side and the river on the other, it's worse than Ebbets Field." He was offered a site in Flushing Meadows. "I might as well move to the West Coast," O'Malley said. "It won't be the Brooklyn Dodgers in Queens."

DORIS MODELL TIPOGRAPH: My father chaired the committee to "Keep the Dodgers in Brooklyn." Thousands of people took part in the protest parade he arranged. "If the Dodgers leave, that's the end of Brooklyn," he said.

PRECEDING PAGE
Henry Modell, the ultimate
Brooklyn Dodgers fan, in a
bittersweet moment. (Note
the *X* crossing out the *B* on
Henry's Dodgers cap.)

LUIS COLMENARES: Just before I started high school, the city told us we had to get out of our apartment. This guy came to the house. He was bald and wore eyeglasses. He had this large attaché case. He gave my mother some papers to sign. She refused. My mother and the other tenants were brought to the court building. Several times they went back and forth. The tenants were there. A bunch of lawyers was there. People asked questions. "Be quiet," they were told. "We're trying to conduct a hearing."

We were paying $27.50 a month for a seven-room apartment with two bathrooms. Concord Village was being built on the site of what had been a neighborhood lumberyard. They offered us a two-bedroom apartment there. Who could afford that?

We thought, Who the hell is doing this? We'd like to kill him. They said, "We're going to build these beautiful buildings, and you'll have first call on them." We got information about buying an apartment. I thought, Who the hell buys an apartment? You buy a house, not an apartment. But my mother had signed these papers and thought she would buy. Then she found it would cost $250 a month. She almost had a heart attack. Finally, to keep things simple, we left, moved up to Canada.

Blocks of beautiful old houses were bulldozed. One of them was where Walt Whitman set the type for *Leaves of Grass* back in 1855. Nobody cared about that or about all the people that got pushed out. A thriving ethnic neighborhood in Brooklyn Heights just got destroyed. In its place is Cadman Plaza Co-ops.

MATT KENNEDY: Our Coney Island neighborhood was a series of one-family houses. Many had Belgian brick fronts—that's a finer form of brick that was brought over in the ships as ballast; it lasts forever. When urban development began, these homes were condemned and the families forced out. They knocked down all the one-family houses and put up twenty-six-story buildings with balconies overlooking the ocean: low-income here, middle-income there, low-income here. Urban development and planning wiped out a very strong Coney Island neighborhood. All the mama-and-papa stores on Mermaid Avenue were killed off. There's no more shopping in the neighborhood. You don't go out after dark.

MURRAY HANDWERKER: The closing of Steeplechase was a big blow to Coney Island. Two square blocks closed up. Fred Trump wanted the land to build high-rise, middle-income housing. He wanted to change the zoning from amusement to residential. I felt it was

important to have amusement zoning in a beachfront, boardwalk area. I fought him, and I beat him.

Robert Moses hated Coney Island. He wanted to wipe out the private amusement area. He tried to get the Cyclone torn down. He didn't want the Aquarium. When it was built, he had that overpass constructed connecting it to the subway to keep the people visiting the Aquarium from mingling with the crowds. I fought Moses also. I fought him all the way because I felt Coney Island had a place in New York.

When I think back on the old days in Coney Island, I think mostly of the people: Pat Auletta, Louis Gargiulo, the managers and workers at Nathan's. It was a joy. When the bureaucracy of the city of New York began bothering us, I lost enthusiasm. It was no longer a joy. That's when I stopped.

People complain to me that Nathan's frankfurters are not the same as the ones in Coney Island. I give them two reasons: one, the salt air; two, the three-quarter-inch U.S. Steel griddles we had. The thin griddles they use today don't hold the heat.

JUDY BERGER: The city took down twenty or thirty houses adjacent to Washington Cemetery on Twentieth Avenue that had belonged to lower-middle-class, predominantly Italian people who took great

It was hard to imagine the Dodgers not being Brooklyn.

pride in their neighborhood. The last high school to be built in Brooklyn, Franklin Delano Roosevelt, opened on that site in 1965. Black kids from out of the neighborhood were bused into the school. The day the building opened, "Niggers go home" was scrawled on the front. The ten-block walk the kids had to take from the F station on the subway became a gauntlet. They were frequently beaten up. But in the school, the student government leaders were black kids from out of the neighborhood.

JOAN MAYNARD: In the forties and fifties, Bedford-Stuyvesant was a stable, integrated neighborhood. But out on Long Island, white people were not buying fast enough into the new housing tracts. So the real estate interests shook things up. There was a conspiracy to destroy integrated, solvent neighborhoods to make money. Bed-Stuy went, and it went very fast.

WILLIAM THOMPSON: The speculating was a conscious and deliberate thing, no question about it. Starting in the 1950s, there was redlining and sophisticated blockbusting. The people who came in via blockbusting busted the houses up, rented out rooms, created illegal rooming houses.

JOAN MAYNARD: When a house became empty, it was rented to a family with a lot of social problems. People living nearby wanted to move out. The real estate interests moved in and bought these houses for cheap prices.

WILLIAM THOMPSON: The shutout was very subtle. Nobody said where you could and couldn't live, but where a bank might give a black person a mortgage on Hancock Street, it would never give him a mortgage in Bay Ridge. Blacks could only move out in concentric circles: to Crown Heights, then to East Flatbush, Flatbush. The ring has gotten bigger and bigger in Brooklyn, but the leaps have not been made. White people could move wherever they wanted to, and as redlining and blockbusting started to happen, they got out of the neighborhoods. That is what made them change.

JOAN MAYNARD: Many of the homeowners were older people who had struggled all their lives and tried so hard to keep the block up, but they could not get mortgages to make improvements on their homes. The banks decided who would get and who would not get. I saw this happening.

Farewell to the old Ebbets Field Jan. 1958

EBBETS FIELD
APARTMENTS
A PROJECT OF
THE KRATTER CORP.

"You thought things would
never change."

JIM SLEEPER: Bankers actually drew a red line on a map around
the areas where they would not make mortgage loans. It was not a
formal document, more a consensus of bankers looking over a map
and saying, "That neighborhood's going bad. Let's not make any loans
from here to here." If people in a certain neighborhood cannot get
home improvement loans or can't get a mortgage loan to buy a house,
then property values go way down. And people are panicked into
selling and getting out. It is a death sentence to a neighborhood that
has nothing to do with the creditworthiness of individual applicants.
Redlining became a self-fulfilling prophecy.

HOWARD JONES: Coming out of an integrated experience, I
always felt that as long as people lived together, knew each other,

The Brooklyn waterfront used to be like a company town.

things would be all right. Redlining changed all that. It stopped the mingling.

PHIL FAGIN: By 1963, most of the Jews and Italians had moved out of Brownsville. My father observed a few youngsters breaking into an apartment. They started to throw bricks at him. My father said it was time to go.

STEWIE STONE: The landlord started neglecting our building. My parents were living with exposed wires. We moved.

JOE SIGLER: After I got married, we lived in the same building on Ocean Avenue that my father and I had moved into when I was fourteen. Back then it had a doorman, nice furniture in the lobby. But over the years, the doorman went, the furniture went. Still, it was OK. My wife would walk the carriage in the park. In 1967, we moved to Rome. When we returned a year later, things had changed a lot. One of the buildings started taking in welfare people, and the next thing you knew there was a fire, and undesirable people started hanging out. My uncle Peter got mugged in the elevator. It wasn't what we wanted.

FRANK BARBARO: Red Hook, Carroll Gardens, South Brooklyn—I can remember when those waterfront areas used to be like a company town. Most of the longshoremen left their houses and walked five minutes to the pier. There were times when they weren't working.

They waited for the ship to come in. When it did, they worked twenty-four, thirty-six, forty-eight hours at a clip. It used to take three hundred to four hundred longshoremen a whole week to unload and load cargo on a single ship. Then they got that big paycheck. They paid off the loan shark, paid off the bookie, got Mama's wedding ring and the trumpet back from the hock shop, and paid off the clothing store for the new Easter outfits. It was a brutal life.

By the late fifties, people who had good jobs—bosses, superintendents—began moving out of the waterfront communities to the suburbs. By the sixties, most of the Italians had left. Today, fifty men unload and load maybe three times as much cargo in one day as three hundred to four hundred men did in one week years ago.

I go back to the old neighborhoods, and it's an eerie feeling. I remember the social halls, the pool halls, the music. At every party, there was somebody with a mandolin or a harmonica. I remember the vibrancy, the pulsating feeling of life and humanity. That world is gone.

JIM SLEEPER: The people in the first wave, those who left Brooklyn in the late forties and early fifties, were not fleeing crime and deteriorating neighborhoods. Suburbia was marketed. VA and FHA mortgages combined with the great interstate highway system made it attractive and possible to own a suburban home. People wanted to get out of their cramped, immigrant neighborhoods. They didn't want to live in the apartment above their parents. Theirs was a move to greener pastures, not flight from blockbusting.

The people in the second wave, those who left Brooklyn in the late fifties and into the sixties, moved out of anger and fear. The brokers and speculators had channeled in tenants in ways that made the neighborhoods undesirable. The first blacks that came in many cases were homeowners. But when the banks refused to lend them the money to build up their homes, the decline accelerated. Whereas earlier, white people moved from one neighborhood to another they thought was better—say, Brownsville to Flatbush—now there was a feeling that the whole borough was in peril. If they had the wherewithal, they went out to the Levittowns and less-expensive suburbs as best they could, or out to Queens when it was being developed in the postwar years. The minority newcomers were left stranded, high and dry. And obviously the departure of jobs—the breweries, the Navy Yard, the Dodgers—accelerated the decline. Chronic unemployment and all the things that go along with it came to be. The softened real-estate market triggered a cycle of deeper decay.

JOAN MAYNARD: The first drug that I heard about was marijuana. People called it Mary Jane. I knew a musician who used it. It was a scandal. Some entertainers were paid off in heroin. Then the mob brought it into the black community. The attitude they had was clearly expressed in the movie *The Godfather*: "They're not people anyway."

ALBERT VANN: Drugs broke up so-called gangs and led to the destruction of the strength of fundamental relationships in our community. They were the prime cause of the destabilization of the black family.

ROGER GREEN: The "soul in the hole," that gathering spot for local soul singers in the park on Madison Street, had originally been a source of release, a diversion, a coming together. But by the mid-sixties, the music had changed. Now it was expressing protest. Poets began coming through, and their poetry was very political. The "soul in the hole" became a reflection of the political and social changes that were occurring. There was more anger.

BOB LIFF: By the mid-sixties, the Brooklyn College campus was filled with a lot of civil-rights activity and protests against the Vietnam War. When a Navy recruiter set up a table in Boylan Hall, the campus leftists, many of them members of SDS, demanded another table. The college administration, which still bore the scars of former president Harry Gideons—the great red-baiter of the fifties—refused. There was an attempted sit-in. The administration called the cops, who started dragging people out. There was tremendous chaos. Most of the campus shut down. It made the first story on Huntley-Brinkley two nights in a row—which was how you measured things in those days.

   Brooklyn College was still largely Jewish then, although not the Brooklyn College that belonged to memory. It had a significant black student population and some brainy Asian kids. We pushed for open admissions. We sent ten busloads down to the March on Washington.

ROGER GREEN: There were people who were on the periphery of the civil-rights movement, who had a sense that here up North things weren't all that bad. But the assassination of Martin Luther King, Jr., in the spring of 1968 devastated them. It challenged them. The question of violence versus nonviolence became a serious debate.

ALBERT VANN: In 1967, I became acting principal at I.S. 271, in Ocean Hill–Brownsville. It was a transition time for the community. We began asking, What is taught? Who teaches? There was no African-

American history in the schools, and very few black teachers. The curriculum did not reflect us in any way. Our parents were not involved in the schools. We started the battle for community control of our schools, for decentralization.

HOWARD JONES: Ocean Hill–Brownsville was the first showcase of a community-run school. They would pick their own principal, pick their own faculty. In the fall of 1968, the teachers' union responded with a strike. To the people in the community, the majority of the people striking were white, and they were stopping them from starting a community school, which they needed to address their identity as blacks.

ABE LASS: That strike was over who was going to run the schools. It was a terrible period. There was great pressure to open the schools and conduct classes. By law, only the principal can do that. And I felt if anyone else would open the school, it would be over my dead body.

EVERETT KERNER: Ocean Hill–Brownsville created great animosity between those who thought the schools should be opened and

The Brooklyn-Queens Expressway plunged right through the heart of neighborhoods.

those who disagreed. Both staff and supervisors were out on the picket line. After it was all over, there were people in the same school who never spoke to one another again.

ABE LASS: Being on the picket line for almost two months, I had time to think of where the school system was going, and whether that's where I wanted to go. I took a long look down the pike, as they say, and saw nothing good was happening. When you put the responsibility for running a school system in the hands of people who are not teachers or administrators, I don't see anything good or promising on the horizon. Nobody has been able to demonstrate decentralization makes for better education. It makes for more jobs, more horse-trading, more corruption, more bad educational decisions—also more bickering and politicized situations in the lower schools—and it's passed along to the high schools. Nowhere else in the country does it exist. Once you give money and power to community groups, it's impossible to take it away without a revolution in the streets.

I decided then I was going to retire. I was only in my early sixties. It was almost unheard of at that time. But I didn't want any more of it. I had had it. This wasn't what teaching was about.

JIM SLEEPER: Ocean Hill–Brownsville broke the spine of the city's civic culture. People who had given their lives to the liberal vision found themselves deprecated and cursed. The political system was extending civil rights to people at the same time the economic

system was pulling the economic rug out from under them. They were enraged, and they had a lot of scores to settle. On the other side, you had Jewish people, Italians, and others who had struggled up from their own ghettos and had managed to become something. The tragedy was miscommunication and shouting back and forth. Brooklyn has never really truly recovered.

HOWARD JONES: Ocean Hill–Brownsville was the downer, the watershed. That was the flood. Nothing got better after that. People could no longer live together. The melting pot that I grew up in was gone.

ABE LASS: The teachers won the strike but lost the war. Right after the strike they started busing kids. In '71, we got about a hundred or so from Ocean Hill–Brownsville, where the strike had started. From there it's all downhill.

RALPH GASARCH: I was teaching at Lincoln then and saw the impact of change. It wasn't just busing, it was the skip-zoning that brought in kids from out of the neighborhoods and the accompanying tensions. Open-enrollment busing brings children to a school their parents opt for. With skip-zoning, parents have no say. Many students had to travel long distances because the school they were assigned to was so far away, and they became a disruptive element.

JUDY BERGER: In 1968, black kids rampaged through FDR. We had mounted police. The staff felt the principal was applying a double standard by allowing the black kids to hang out and not the whites. I felt the times they are a-changing. The liberalism I had as a high school student was starting to be chipped away. It was hard to maintain my youthful optimism. The high hopes and expectations had not materialized.

ALBERT VANN: I put what happened in perspective. I understand what happened, why it happened. I know changing society is not done without upheaval and confrontation.

CLARENCE NORMAN, SR.: The Hasidic community was already in place in Crown Heights by the early sixties, as blacks were coming in. We live side-by-side, next door to each other, in a truly integrated community. However, the integration is parallel. It only becomes interactive when there's a crisis. There have been serious problems between the black and the Hasidim in Crown Heights, and the media certainly has not helped. But there's vitality here, a lot of good middle-class black folk who plan to stay, a thriving Jewish community.

In 1967, with Crown Heights undergoing a transition, with a lot of whites moving out and blacks gradually moving in, our church purchased the Park Manor Catering Hall. Any Jewish person who came out of Brooklyn probably remembers it as the Twin Cantors, at 450 Eastern Parkway. The main banquet hall became our sanctuary. The upstairs banquet hall became our Sunday school. The bridal room became our chapel. Our church is *the* Baptist church in Crown Heights, with a membership of two thousand.

So many of the Jewish catering halls and synagogues have become churches. I look at what happened as a progression. Certain religious groups use a building. They move on. Others come in.

HELEN FRIED GOLDSTEIN: B'nai Israel of Bay Ridge was a distinguished synagogue, the only Conservative synagogue in the area for many years. Sometime in the 1960s, it was sold to a Protestant church. Not long after, I went inside. Against all reason, I expected to see my grandfather, tall and elegant, up on the *bima* before the Ark, as I had seen him so many times in the past. I expected to see his picture still hanging in the vestibule, for he had been a leading lay figure in the Conservative movement and this synagogue. It was heart-wrenching, because as far as I'm concerned that place belongs to my grandfather.

**Brooklyn seen from above:
"the whole density and
intensity and diversity."**

But then I entered the sanctuary and took a seat in one of the pews. I looked up at the Tiffany-like stained-glass windows, the sunlight spilling through the biblical scenes, and I imagined a little girl sitting there today, distracted by the brilliant colored light just as I used to be. It was all right. After all, it could have become an OTB parlor.

CHARLES HYNES: The sad part about Flatbush is that many of the Jews, Irish, and Italians who gave it great stability ran away as soon as they saw the first black face. People believed property values would drop, and they would not be able to sell their homes. That did not prove to be the case. My block is filled with people of color and all the others.

JIM SLEEPER: There's no question that some of the new immigrants are laying the same foundations in Brooklyn that other immigrants did generations before. Brooklyn had always been and remains an incubator, pumping out athletes, political leaders, impresarios, entertainers.

ROBERT MERRILL: Why did Brooklyn produce so many famous people? It was fighting life for space. The fact that we survived all this made us strong. As we grew older, we appreciated the finer things even more than the guy who lived in a quieter, less-crowded environment.

ALAN LELCHUK: Brooklyn occupied a place in the national mythology. People made jokes about it, but it was a universe unto itself. Now and then, Texas and Manhattan came in. But if the rest of the country had dropped out, that was all right. Brooklyn had enough fighting against itself, playing against itself, communing against itself.

MEL ALLEN: It was the poor working people of Brooklyn against the rich people of Manhattan. It was Brooklyn against the world. It was one of the five boroughs, but Brooklyn seemed to be a separate city. Maybe it was. Maybe it is.

FRANK BARBARO: When I first came to Bensonhurst, there was a wealth of Jewish organizational life: a Mr. & Mrs. club, a Hadassah club, a Deborah club. The temples were alive and used. The JCH was a hub of activity, supported by a lot of wealthy professional and business people. The Italian community was held together with CYOs,

How the city looked from the Brooklyn side in pre–World Trade Center days.

religious groups, people making novenas. Every church was overflowing. That was Bensonhurst.

Now synagogues are half-empty, maybe worse. The temples on Seventy-second and Bay Parkway and on Seventy-fifth Street have shut down. The kids moved to other neighborhoods; mama and papa stayed, mama died, or they decided to go to Florida. The cohesiveness of a group that interacted and interfaced and produced a dynamism is lost.

But Bensonhurst has held. Some of the Jews remain, and there are a lot of second-generation and recently arrived Italians who have built a very tightly knit community. The Italians are getting organization-minded; they're approaching the stage the Jews were in. We're in a hiatus, but we're getting there again.

And the old ethnic neighborhoods are being filled with recently arrived immigrants: Asians, Pakistanis, people from the Caribbean, Hispanics, Russian Jews. There may not be much interrelationship yet. But when these people are economically liberated, they will start their organizations and begin to interrelate with the other people.

ELI WALLACH: Some of the sections are coming back, even better than ever. There's a new cachet to Brooklyn.

NEIL SEDAKA: I go back. I ride on the Cyclone and still thrill to the first drop. I have a frank and french fries at Nathan's. I drive through the old neighborhood. I have to do it; it draws me. I'll never forget where I came from.

ABE LASS: So many have this terrible, terrible yen to come home again, to recapture the first fine careless rapture. In the mid-seventies, a Lincoln reunion in Los Angeles attracted people from all over the country, people who went back to the beginning of the school. What was it that brought people from all over to share memories of a school? What did the word *Lincoln* do to all these people?

JIM SLEEPER: There are dreams, mournful dreams. A sociologist calls this grieving for a lost home. I am convinced that countless people who left Brooklyn have felt that. The borough is haunted by ghosts for me—not because of past relatives, but simply at the thought of people who lived there and left, and also because the whole density and intensity and diversity just seizes me by the throat. Going to Lundy's, going to swim at the St. George Hotel, taking a trolley down to Coney Island and smelling the salt air even before you got there, the sense that the borough was like a vast empire with beaches and hills and woods in Prospect Park, with tenements and rows and rows of infrastructure. My greatest dream is to be able to get into a time machine and make it 1952 and just roam free across the borough.

MARNIE BERNSTEIN: In 1993, I was invited to speak at the sixth-grade graduation of P.S. 226, a school I had graduated from in

"So many have this terrible, terrible yen to come home again." A serene stretch of Shore Road along the bay.

1952. Driving down the Bensonhurst streets that hazy June morning, I felt I could so easily slip right back into the time of my childhood. Every house and driveway and yard and tree looked unchanged.

In the school auditorium, there was the same familiar sense of expectancy. Parents, serious and seemingly respectful of the event they were about to witness, filled all the available seats. Then the music teacher began to play "Pomp and Circumstance" on the old Knabe grand piano. Silently, I sang the still-remembered words—"Land of hope and glory, mother of the free . . ."—as the processional of sixth-grade graduates began. Two lines down the aisle of the old auditorium—one boys, one girls—in that same formal step, the toe of the back foot hesitating for a moment at the heel of the one in front before completing the step.

Another generation of children. Many new immigrants: Russians, Asians, Latinos; many more African Americans; also children with physical handicaps—invisible in my day. But in all the important ways, they are us, hopeful, repeating the same ritual in their navy skirts and pants, their white shirts and red ties, their fresh, sweet faces full of eagerness and optimism. Brooklyn as it was for me continues to be.

KARL BERNSTEIN: I search the borough for my past. I drive past an abandoned building on Atlantic Avenue in East New York. Once it was the Borden Dairy Plant; now, all that remains are two beautiful mosaics of Heidi and the cows on a yellow-brick wall. I walk up a ramp to the boardwalk in Coney Island past a wall that was once part of a bathhouse. It still is adorned with bas reliefs of mermaids and seahorses, and seashells. I pass the old Namm-Loeser store on Fulton Street and make out the name Frederick Loeser and Company, carved in stone above the plate glass window; that dates back to the time before Namm and Loeser merged. I ride down Surf Avenue and wonder why the red, yellow, and blue trolley poles are still standing so many years after the wires were cut down. Or why they never took up the trolley tracks that cross Rockaway Parkway at the subway terminal and run smack into a fruit stand, or dismantled the signal tower for the Norton's Point trolley at the Stillwell Avenue subway station or the trolley shelters at the Brooklyn end of the Williamsburg Bridge.

I pause at the old movie theaters, most of them converted to different use. The Claridge, on Avenue P, is a kosher catering hall. The Avalon, on Kings Highway, is a Pathmark drugstore. The Triangle, on Quentin Road across from Joyce Kilmer Square, is a furniture store, although it still has the marquee. The Jewel, which used to show foreign films when they first became popular, is a porno theater. The Vogue is a nursing home. The Midwood is a commercial building. But the funny thing is, in my mind's eye, I see them as they were.

I dream about home, and it's always the house in Brooklyn. I'm coming home on a cold day, and as I turn the corner from Kings Highway onto East Seventh Street, I brace myself for the cold wind I know will hit me in the face. I put my head down and pull my collar up and push through the wind till I pass the apartment house. Then it's OK, only a little bit farther to my house. Whenever I turned that corner, I knew I was home.

My grandmother had bought our two-family semi-attached house during the boom days of the twenties, brand-new. She wanted to buy a different house down the block, because it had a beautiful tree in front. To her dying day, she complained that they bought the house out from under her. But my father planted a silver maple for her. He tied it to keep it straight, and ultimately the rope got caught up in the tree. In the winter we could see it about ten feet off the ground.

Sometimes I go back and look at the house. The people who bought it have put in new windows. They opened up the roof with skylights. They took down walls. You wouldn't recognize it. But I do. I see it all just like it was. And best of all, the tree is still there.

P.S.

PAT COOPER: *President Roosevelt came down to Red Hook and made a speech, because they were starting work on the Brooklyn-Battery Tunnel. The teachers from P.S. 142 took all the kids to hear him.*

"My fellow Americans," he said, "we are going to give you this tunnel. It will cost thirty-five cents each way, but once this tunnel is paid, you will have it for nothing."

"He's a liar," I said to my friend. I was always a smart little kid.

"Once it's paid," the president repeated, "you will have it for nothing, and you will be closer to Manhattan."

"Who the hell wants to be closer to Manhattan?" I said.

Acknowledgments

Our special thanks to Judy and Joel Berger for reading an evolving manuscript and providing insightful feedback; to Gail and Karl Bernstein for a wealth of recall, photos, and artifacts; and to Doris Modell Tipograph and Norman Tipograph for a treasure trove of Modell and personal memorabilia.

We also thank for their interest and assistance Anthony Cucchiara, archivist and head of Special Collections, Brooklyn College Library; Lori Duggan Gold and the Brooklyn Botanic Garden; Frederic Frommer; Miriam Ginsberg; Roger Harris; Pearl Jackson; Charles Jones, director of public relations, New York City Technical College; Caroline Katz Mount; David Korman and St. Ann's Center for Restoration and the Arts; Clara Lamers of the Brooklyn Historical Society; John Manbeck, archivist and head of the Kingsborough Historical Society, Kingsborough Community College; Howard Rapp; Cathy Ryan of St. Francis College; Fiorenza Sigler; Gordon Silverman and the Jewish Community House of Bensonhurst; Roz Starr; Nat Weinstein; Gary Wojtas, director of public relations at the Brooklyn campus of Long Island University; and our agent, Don Congdon.

We are grateful to our aesthetically attuned editor, John Radziewicz, for once again being enthusiastically supportive and unfailingly correct in judgment; to Trina Stahl, who handled the impossibly complex job of designing this book, succeeded so admirably, and got an education about Brooklyn in the process; and to the staff at Harcourt—Dan Janeck, Christa Malone, Marcella Forster, Ginger Boyer, Steven Cooley, Maggie DeMaegd, and Candace Hodges—for their help and input.

Finally, our thanks to everyone who shared with us memories, perceptions, and photos. This is your life.

Picture Credits

Judy Berger: Pages xvi (top), 8 (middle), 21 (right), 37 (right), 83 (second from right), 108, 122, 140 (top), 143, 145 (bottom), 173 (left), 176, 181 (top), 182 (top), 183, 192 (bottom); Karl Bernstein: Pages iii (left and second from left), vii (top and bottom left, top right), xiii (top right), xvi–xvii (middle), xviii (top), 20 (left), 30 (inset), 31, 45 (top), 46 (bottom), 53, 57, 76 (bottom), 80, 83 (left), 94 (inset), 98, 104 (inset), 114 (middle), 126 (top and middle), 127 (left inset), 128 (bottom), 132, 150 (bottom), 165, 180, 182 (inset), 186, 191, 203 (top), 205 (top), 216, 218, 220, 238–39; Sam Bernstein: Pages xiii (bottom right), xiv (second from top), xv (top and bottom), 3 (inset), 8 (top and bottom), 76 (middle), 130, 145 (top); Bettmann Archive: Pages 3, 87, 146, 215; Frances Blum: Pages viii–ix (bottom), xiv (bottom), xvii (second from top), 2, 6 (middle), 32, 34, 73 (top), 77 (right), 110, 133, 154 (top, third from top); Tom Booras: Pages 56, 159, 198, 205 (bottom left), 214; Brooklyn Academy of Music: Pages 17 (middle), 64; Brooklyn Botanic Garden: Page 5 (both); Brooklyn College Library (courtesy of the Special Collections Department): Pages 9, 88, 97, 160, 167, 219 (both), 221 (both), 228, 231, 232, 237; Brooklyn Historical Society: Pages 35, 91, 94, 106, 210, 234; Jack Eagle: Page 65; Gail Eiseman Bernstein: Pages iii (far right), viii–ix (third from top), xvi (third from top), xviii–xix (second and fourth from top), 17 (second and fourth from left), 24, 44 (both), 46 (top), 48, 49, 51, 52, 54, 58, 66, 68, 70 (middle), 100 (bottom), 123, 124 (top), 158 (inset), 178 (bottom), 206 (top), 207 (left); Fagin Family Collection: Pages x (right), 18, 50 (bottom), 70 (top and bottom), 75 (both), 77 (left), 95, 112, 142; Bill Feigenbaum: Pages ix (second from top), 90; Frommer Collection: Pages iii (middle), vii (bottom right), viii (third from top), xiii (top and bottom left), xiv (third from top), xv (second from top), xviii (second from top), xix (top three), 6 (top), 15, 17 (left and right), 27, 28 (all), 32 (inset), 39 (top), 41 (top), 47, 60 (top), 64 (inset), 79, 100 (top), 118, 124 (bottom), 126 (bottom), 146 (inset), 154 (second from top), 162 (top), 173 (second from left, far right), 192 (top and middle), 193 (both), 196 (inset), 200 (middle), 202, 203 (middle and bottom), 204 (both), 205 (bottom right), 207 (inset), 211 (both), 215 (inset); Michael Gershman:

Index